About the author

Joel Kovel is Distinguished Professor of Social Studies at Bard College. He has written ten books, including the first edition of *The Enemy of Nature* (2002) and *Overcoming Zionism* (2007). He has edited *Capitalism Nature Socialism*, a journal of radical ecology, since 2003 and has been active in green politics, running for the US Senate in 1998, and seeking the Green Party's presidential nomination in 2000.

JOEL KOVEL

The enemy of nature

The end of capitalism or the end of the world?

Zed Books
LONDON | NEW YORK

Fernwood Publishing
HALIFAX | WINNIPEG

The Enemy of Nature: The End of Capitalism or the End of the World?
was originally published in 2002. This updated and expanded edition
was first published in 2007.

Published in Canada by Fernwood Publishing, 32 Oceanvista Lane,
Site 2A, Box 5, Black Point, NS B0J 1B0 <www.fernwoodpublishing.ca>

Published in the rest of the world by Zed Books Ltd, 7 Cynthia Street,
London N1 9JF, UK and Room 400, 175 Fifth Avenue, New York,
NY 10010, USA <www.zedbooks.co.uk>

Copyright © Joel Kovel, 2007

Second impression, 2008

The right of Joel Kovel to be identified as the author of this work has
been asserted by him in accordance with the Copyright, Designs and
Patents Act, 1988.

Cover designed by Andrew Corbett
Set in OurTypeArnhem and Futura Bold by Ewan Smith, London
index: <ed.emery@thefreeuniversity.net>
Printed and bound in the EU by Biddles Ltd, King's Lynn
www.biddles.co.uk

Distributed in the USA exclusively by Palgrave Macmillan, a division
of St Martin's Press, LLC, 175 Fifth Avenue, New York, NY 10010.

Library and Archives Canada Cataloguing in Publication
Kovel, Joel, 1936-
    The enemy of nature : the end of capitalism or the end of the
world? / Joel Kovel. -- 2nd ed.
Includes bibliographical references and index.
ISBN 978-1-55266-255-7
    1. Environmental economics. 2. Capitalism--Environmental aspects.
3. Marxian economics. 4. Environmental policy. I. Title.
HC79.E5K68 2007 333.7 C2007-904129-9

ISBN 978 1 84277 870 8 hb (Zed Books)
ISBN 978 1 84277 871 5 pb (Zed Books)
ISBN 978 1 55266 255 7 pb (Fernwood Publishing)

Contents

For everything that lives is Holy
William Blake

All that is holy is profaned
Karl Marx

To my grandchildren:
Rowan, Liam, Tolan, Owen,
and Josephine

Preface to the second edition

I began writing this new Preface in New York City on January 6, 2007, a date which used to be considered the "dead of winter." The thermometer registered 72°F, the streets were full of nervously smiling people, many in shorts, the ice-skating rink where I went for a midday break was a puddle, the Weather Channel was essentially giggling with the story. Wow!, opined the *New York Times* and helpfully pointed out that never before had the city gone so long without snow. But it never mentioned the words "global warming" or that this sort of thing may augur a day within the lifetimes of many now living when this great city, like all others on the coasts, will be substantially under water. Why spoil the fun?[1]

I wrote *The Enemy of Nature* according to the principle that the truth – a sufficiently generous and expansive truth, it may be added – can make us free. If truth gives clarity and definition to our world, if it weans us from dependency on alienating forces that sap our will and delude our mind, and if it can bring us together with others in a common empowering project – a project that gives us hope that we can become the makers of our own history – why, then, then it makes us free even if what it reveals is terrible to behold. Better this than the unrevealed terror in the dark, unenvisioned, without opening to hope, better than what inertly weighs on us under the aegis of the capitalist order.

The Enemy of Nature was written in service of such an ideal. It tries to give expression to an emerging and still incomplete realization that our all-conquering capitalist system of production, the greatest and proudest of all the modalities of transforming nature which the human species has yet devised, the defining influence in modern culture and the organizer of the modern state, is at heart the enemy of nature and therefore humanity's executioner as well.

If our institutions could grasp such an idea, then there would not have been an ecological crisis in the first place and this book would not have to be written. It follows that *The Enemy of Nature* was born in struggle and for struggle, and that it is for the long haul, as long as it takes.

Thus, this second edition. The first, although ignored from above, has had a good, vigorous life from below, a kind of *samizdat* existence comprised of word-of-mouth networks, little pockets of the alienated and disaffected where the book has taken hold, circuits of distribution on the internet, study groups, a course here and there, a few foreign editions.

A second edition is needed, however, to bring the argument up to date. *The Enemy of Nature* can never be a finished work; it must always be in a state of coming together, of becoming more integral – for a book, like all products of human labor, is also a kind of ecosystem. Each of the numberless presentations of this material I have made on five continents over the past five years has been a moment of re-vision, a reworking of this or that in light of changing contexts and the unending unfolding of the crisis. Each of these instances has been enriched by the voices of others; and so all these voices collectively enter into this second version.

While I have no intention of rewriting the central ideas of a text which, in essence, appears more firmly grounded than ever, keeping faithful to the basic logic demands continual modification. This will be seen chiefly at the beginning and end, the former to bring the reader up to date as to the development of the crisis, and the latter to bear witness to the maturation of the notion of ecosocialism. In between, the critique of capital, the philosophy of nature, the rendering of Marxism in ecological form, the notion of the gendered bifurcation of nature, and those other features that comprise the work's inner structure will remain largely as before, with a few improvements/updates added here and there. I intend to turn shortly to these themes in an extended study that has been germinating for some time.

The Enemy of Nature argues that, however capital may restructure and reform itself to secure accumulation, it is incapable of mending the ecological crisis it provokes. I wish I were wrong on this score, but the events of the five years since the first edition was published have done nothing to disabuse me of the notion. The environmental news service I use to keep abreast of developments each day gamely posts a notice calling upon the viewer to "Don't miss the link to today's good news."[2] The findings are a puerile mish-mash of local clean-up efforts, greenwashings of one kind or another, the hucksterings of green capitalists, various techno-fixes, and the noises made by governmental agencies. Yes, there are definite victories along the way, all local and partial, and almost all the result of grassroots effort to bring to bay one corporate intrusion or another. But the large-scale news is virtually all bad, and recounts the steady, albeit fitful and non-linear, disintegration of the planetary ecology. Watch China slide toward ruin and pull the world along with it; watch the coral reefs decay, the polar bears drown, the Indian farmers kill themselves by drinking pesticides, the honeybees fail to come back to their hives, our bodily fluids fill up with unholy effluents as the cancers break out all over despite medical miracles without end, the Niger River delta burn as it destroys the lungs of little children . . . and of course do not miss the inexorability of global warming.

The past year has seen an accelerating awareness, a growing anger and realization of the bankruptcy of capital to contend with the crisis it has spawned. How can it, when to overcome the crisis would mean its own liquidation? There is now a widespread assumption, which was much more limited five years ago, that the problem is not this corporation or that, or "industrialization," technology, or just plain bad luck, but all-devouring capital. This is a salubrious truth, a truth that sharpens the mind and can be worked with and built upon. The human intelligence can be daunted, but it cannot be erased. As the ecological crisis grinds on irrespective of capital's propaganda system and its massive apparatus for fixing the environment, so does capital's legitimacy begin to fray. With this, the possibility of new thinking emerges and begins to flower. On one side, a predictable inevitability, that the system will collapse; on the other, no more than a

ix

hope, grounded however in reality, that a new form of society may emerge no longer dependent upon accumulation and its progressive breakdown of ecosystems. Hence the mandate for this second edition of *The Enemy of Nature*, for the paramount goal of this work will always be to hasten the disintegration of capital's system-logic and to help bring forth a way of being worthy of our human nature.

I will not repeat detailed acknowledgments, as I cannot. How can the numberless people who contributed to hopeful dialogue over the past five years be enumerated or listed? But certain names demand recognition and gratitude for their help in this period: Abby Rockefeller, Doug Tompkins, Jorge Bergstein, Delia Marx, Michael Lowy, Muge Sokmen, Derek Wall, Karen Charman and Dave Channon, Eddie Yuen, the departed and greatly missed Walt Sheasby, Sam Fassbinder, John Clark, Rod Kueneman, Gretchen Zdorowski, Terisa Turner and Leigh Brownhill, Ian Angus, Petter Naess, Sean Sweeney, and the comrades at Zed Books, especially Ellen McKinlay and Julian Hosie, who have kept the faith in dark times.

Notes

1 January 2007 went on record as the warmest January ever measured. The next month, in line with the principle that global warming means irregular weather as much as it does warmer weather, the temperature plunged some twenty degrees over a huge area of eastern and central North America, as massive snowfalls arrived and continued regularly until April 15. The winter ended up colder on the whole than normal – as have the last few (worse luck to have so many of the world's opinion makers not sharing in the main surge of warming). Indeed, Easter 2007 was colder than Christmas 2006 by a considerable amount.

2 www.EnvironmentalHealth News.org

Preface to the first edition

Growing numbers of people are beginning to realize that capitalism is the uncontrollable force driving our ecological crisis, only to become frozen in their tracks by the awesome implications of the insight. Considering that the very possibility of a future revolves about this notion, I decided to take it up in a comprehensive way, to see whether it is true, and if so, how it came about, and most importantly, what we can do about it.

Here is something of how this project began. Summers in the Catskill Mountains of New York State, where I live, are usually quite pleasant. But in 1988, a fierce drought blasted the region from mid-June until well into August. As the weeks went by and the vegetation baked and the wells went dry, I began to ponder something I had recently read, to the effect that rising concentrations of gases emitted by industrial activity would trap solar radiation in the atmosphere and lead to ever-growing climatic destabilization. Though the idea had seemed remote at first, the ruin of my garden brought it alarmingly close to home. Was the drought a fluke of the weather, or, as I was coming to think, was it a tolling bell, calling us to task for a civilization gone wrong? The seared vegetation now appeared a harbinger of something quite dreadful, and a call to act. And so I set out on the path that led to this book. Thirteen years later, after much writing, teaching and organizing, after working with the Greens and running for the US Senate in 1998 and seeking their Presidential nomination in 2000, and after several drafts and false starts, *The Enemy of Nature* is ready to be placed before the public.

It would have been understandable to shrug off the drought as just another piece of odd weather (and indeed nothing that severe has recurred since). But I had for some time become disposed to take a worst-case attitude with respect to anything having to do with the powers-that-be; and since industrial activity was close to the heart of the system, so were its effects on climate drawn into the zone of my suspicion. US imperialism had got me going in this, initially in the context of Vietnam and later in Central America, where an agonizing struggle to defend the Nicaraguan revolution against Uncle Sam was coming to a bad end as the drought struck. The defeat had been bitter and undoubtedly contributed to my irritability, but it provided important lessons as well, chiefly as to the implacability displayed by the system once one looked below its claims of democracy and respect for human rights.

Here, far from the pieties, one encounters the effects of capital's ruthless pressure to expand. Imperialism was such a pattern, manifest politically and across nations. But this selfsame ever-expanding capital was also the superintendent and regulator of the industrial system whose exhalations were trapping solar energy. What had proven true about capital in relation to empire could be applied, therefore, to the realm of nature as well, bringing the human victims and the destabilizations of ecology under the same sign. Climate change was, in effect, another kind of imperialism. Nor was it the only noxious ecological effect of capital's relentless growth. There was also the sowing of the biosphere with organochlorines and other toxins subtle as well as crude, the wasting of the soil as a result of the "green revolution," the prodigious species losses, the disintegration of Amazonia, and much more still – the spiralling, interpenetrating tentacles of a great crisis in the relationship between humanity and nature.

From this standpoint there appears a greater "ecological crisis," of which the particular insults to ecosystems are elements. This has further implications. For human beings are part of nature, however ill-at-ease we may be with the role. There is therefore a human ecology as well as an ecology of forests and lakes. It follows that the larger ecological crisis would be generated by, and extend deeply into, an ecologically pathological society. Regarding the matter from this angle provided a more generous view. No longer trapped in a narrow economic determinism, one could see capital as much more than a simple material arrangement, but as something cancerous lodged in the human spirit, produced by, and producer of, the capitalist economy. It takes shape as a queer beast altogether, more a whole way of being than anything else. And if it is a whole way of being that needs changing, then the essential question of "what is to be done?" takes on new dimensions, and ecological politics is about much more than managing the external environment. It has to be thought of, rather, in frankly revolutionary terms. But since the revolution is against the capital that is nature's enemy, the struggle for an ecologically just and rational society is the logical successor to the socialist movements that agitated the last century and a half before sputtering to an ignominious end. Could we be facing a "next-epoch" socialism – and could the fatal flaws of the first-epoch version be overcome if socialism became ecological?

There is a big problem with these ideas, namely, that very few people take them seriously. I have been acutely aware from the beginning of this project that the above conclusions place me at a great distance from so-called mainstream opinion. How could it be otherwise in a time of capitalist triumph, when by definition reasonable folk are led to think that just a bit of tinkering with "market mechanisms" will see us through our ecological difficulties? And as for socialism, why should anyone with an up-to-date mind bother thinking about such a quaint issue, much less trying to overcome its false starts?

These difficulties extend over to the fragmented and divided left side of opinion, whether this be the "red" left that inherits the old socialist passion for the working class, or the "green" left that stands for an emerging awareness of the ecological crisis. Socialism, though quite ready to entertain the idea that capital is nature's enemy, is less sure about being nature's friend. Most socialists, though they stand for a cleaner environment, decline to take the ecological dimension seriously. They tend to support an strategy where the workers' state will clean up pollution, but are unwilling to follow the radical changes that an ecological point of view implies as to the character of human needs, the fate of industry, and the question of nature's intrinsic value. Meanwhile,

xiii

Greens, however dedicated they may be to rethinking the latter questions, resist placing capital at the center of the problem. Green politics tend to be populist or anarchist rather than socialist, hence Greens are quite content to envision an ecologically sane future in which a suitably regulated capitalism, brought down to size and mixed with other forms, continues to regulate social production. Such was essentially the stance of Ralph Nader, whom I challenged in the 2000 presidential primary, with neither intention nor hope of winning, but only to keep the message alive that the root of the problem lies in capital itself.

We live at a time when those who think in terms of alternatives to the dominant order court exclusion from polite intellectual society. During my youth, and for generations before, a consensus existed that capitalism was embattled and that its survival was an open question. For the last twenty years or so, however, with the rise of neoliberalism and the collapse of the Soviets, the system has acquired an aura of inevitability and even immortality. It has been quite remarkable to see how readily the intellectual classes have gone along, sheeplike, with these absurd conclusions, disregarding the well-established lessons that nothing lasts forever, that all empires fall, and that a twenty-year ascendancy is scarcely a blink in the flux of time. But the same mentality that went into the recently deceased dot-com mania applies to those who see capitalism as a gift from the gods, destined for immortality. One would think that a moment of doubt would be introduced into the official scenario by the screamingly obvious fact that a society predicated on endless expansion must inevitably collapse its natural base. However, thanks to a superbly effective propaganda apparatus and the intellectual defects wrought by power, such has not so far been the case.

Change, if it comes, will have to come from outside the ruling consensus. And there is hopeful evidence that just such an awakening may be taking place. Cracks have been appearing in the globalized edifice, through which a new era of protest is emerging. When the World Trade Organization is forced to hold its meeting in Qatar in order to avoid distruption, or fence itself in inside the walled city of Quebec, or when the President-select, George W. Bush, is forced by protestors at his inauguration to slink fugitive-like along Pennsylvania Avenue in a sealed limousine, then it may fairly be said that a new spirit is in the air, and that the generation now maturing, thrown through no fault of their own into a world defined by the ecological crisis, are also beginning to rise up and take history into their own hands. *The Enemy of Nature* is written for them, and for all those who recognize the need to break with the given in order to win a future.

An attitude of rejection conditioned me to see the 1988 drought as a harbinger of an ecologically ruined society. But that was not the only attitude I brought to the task. I was also working at the time on my *History and Spirit*, having been stirred by the faith of the Sandinistas, and especially their radical priests, to realize that a refusal is worthless unless coupled with affirmation, and that it takes a notion of the whole of things to gather courage to reach beyond the given. There is a wonderful saying from 1968, which should guide us in the troubled time ahead: to be realistic, one demands the impossible. So let us rise up and do so.

Many people helped me on the long journey to this book, too many, I fear, to all be included here, especially if one takes into account, as we should, the many hundreds I met during the politi-cal campaigns that provide much of its background. But there is no difficulty in identifying its chief intellectual influence. Soon after I decided to confront the ecological crisis, I decided also to link up with James O'Connor, founder of the journal, *Capitalism Nature Socialism*, and originator of the school of ecological Marx-ism that made the most sense to me. It proved one of the most felicitous moments of my career and led to a collaboration which is still active. As my mentor in matters political-economic and toughest critic, but mostly as a dear friend, Jim's presence is every-where in this volume (though the truism must be underscored, that its errors are mine alone). I have been indebted throughout to the *CNS* community for giving me an intellectual home and forum, and for countless instances of comradely help. This begins

Preface

with Barbara Laurence, and includes the New York editorial group – Paul Bartlett, Paul Cooney, Maarten DeKadt, Salvatore Engel-Di Mauro, Costas Panayotakis, Patty Parmalee, José Tapia and Edward Yuen – along with Daniel Faber and Victor Wallis, of the Boston group, and Alan Rudy.

A number of people have taken the trouble to give portions of the manuscript a close reading during various stages in its gestation – Susan Davis, Andy Fisher, DeeDee Halleck, Jonathan Kahn, Cambiz Khosravi, Andrew Nash, Walt Sheasby, and Michelle Syverson – and to them all I am grateful. I am further grateful to Michelle Syverson for the active support she has given this project during its later stages.

Among those who have helped in one way or another at different points of the work, I thank Roy Morrison, John Clark, Doug Henwood, Harriet Fraad, Ariel Salleh, Brian Drolet, Leo Panitch, Bertell Ollman, Fiona Salmon, Finley Schaef, Don Boring, Starlene Rankin, Ed Herman, Joan Martinez-Alier, and Nadja Milner-Larson. Mildred Marmur provided, as ever, a guide to that real world which is often too much for me. And to Robert Molteno and the people at Zed, thanks for the help and the opportunity to join the honorable list of works they have shepherded into existence.

Last and as ever, not least, except in the ages of its younger members, I thank the family that sustains me. This begins with my DeeDee, and extends to those grandchildren who represent the children of the future for whom the battle must be fought: Rowan, Liam, Tolan, Owen, and Josephine.

1 | Introduction

In 1970, growing fears for the integrity of the planet gave rise to a new awareness and a new politics. On April 22, the first "Earth Day" was announced, since to become an annual event of re-dedication to the preservation and enhancement of the environment. The movement affected ordinary people and, remarkably, certain members of the elites, who, organized into a group called the Club of Rome, even dared to announce a theme never before entertained by persons of power. This appeared as the title of their 1972 manifesto, *The Limits to Growth*.[1]

Thirty years later, Earth Day 2000 featured a colloquy between Leonardo de Caprio and President Bill Clinton, with much fine talk about saving nature. The anniversary also provided a convenient vantage point for surveying the results of three decades of "limiting growth." At the dawn of a new millennium, one could observe the following:

- The human population had increased from 3.7 billion to 6 billion (62 percent).
- Oil consumption had increased from 46 million barrels a day to 73 million.
- Natural gas extraction had increased from 34 trillion cubic feet per year to 95 trillion.
- Coal extraction had gone from 2.2 billion metric tonnes to 3.8 billion.
- The global motor vehicle population had almost tripled, from 246 million to 730 million.
- Air traffic had increased by a factor of six.
- The rate at which trees are consumed to make paper had doubled, to 200 million metric tons per year.
- Human carbon emissions had increased from 3.9 million metric tons annually to an estimated 6.4 million – this

despite the additional impetus to cut back caused by an awareness of global warming, which was not perceived to be a factor in 1970.

- As for this warming, average temperature increased by 1°F – a disarmingly small number that, being unevenly distributed, translates into chaotic weather events (seven of the ten most destructive storms in recorded history having occurred in the last decade), and an unpredictable and uncontrollable cascade of ecological trauma – including now the melting of the North Pole during the summer of 2000, for the first time in 50 million years, and signs of the disappearance of the "snows of Kilimanjaro" the year following; since then this melting has become a fixture.
- Species were vanishing at a rate that has not occurred in 65 million years.
- Fish were being taken at twice the rate as in 1970.
- Forty percent of agricultural soils had been degraded.
- Half of the forests had disappeared.
- Half of the wetlands had been filled or drained.
- One-half of US coastal waters were unfit for fishing or swimming.
- Despite concerted effort to bring to bay the emissions of ozone-depleting substances, the Antarctic ozone hole was the largest ever in 2000, some three times the size of the continental United States; meanwhile, 2,000 tons of such substances as cause it continue to be emitted every day.[2]
- 7.3 billion tons of pollutants were released in the United States during 1999.[3]

We can add some other, more immediately human costs:

- Third World debt increased by a factor of eight between 1970 and 2000.
- The gap between rich and poor nations, according to the United Nations, went from a factor of 3:1 in 1820, to 35:1 in 1950; 44:1 in 1973 – at the beginning of the environmentally

sensitive era – to 72:1 in 1990, roughly two-thirds of the way
through it.
- By 2000 1.2 million women under the age of eighteen were
  entering the global sex trade each year.
- 100 million children were homeless and slept on the streets.

These figures were mostly gathered around the year 2000, and
served to frame the first edition of *The Enemy of Nature* by calling
attention to a remarkable yet greatly underappreciated fact: that
the era of environmental awareness, beginning roughly in 1970,
has also been the era of greatest environmental breakdown. No
sooner, then, did the awareness of a profound threat to humanity's relationship to nature surface than it became overwhelmed
by a greater force outside this awareness.

Each of the above observations has had its specific causes – the
production of a certain gas, the dynamics of the auto market
or of the habitat of a threatened species, etc. – but there must
also be a larger issue to account for the rapid acceleration of
the set of all such perturbations – and, necessarily tied to this,
the appearance of increasingly chaotic interactions between the
members of this set. There is, therefore, some greater force at
work, setting the numberless manifestations of the crisis into
motion and whirling them about like broken twigs in the winds
of a hurricane.

It is this larger force that the present work investigates, under
an obligation imposed by the colossal failure of the reigning environmental awareness. I say "obligation," because of the gravity
of the present crisis. If we take this crisis seriously enough – and
what, in the whole history of the human race, has had more
momentous and dire implications? – then we are obliged to radically rethink our entire approach. Happily, many more people,
including experts of one kind or another, are now recognizing the
scope of the crisis and what is at stake. Unhappily, they mostly
remain blind to the essential dynamics; thus, the great range of
recommendations are puerile rehashes of what has already failed:
exhortations to live more frugally, to recognize and respect our

3

embeddedness in nature, to recycle, to find and approve better technologies, to vote into power environmentally responsible politicians, and so forth. None of these recommendations is without merit; they all need to find their place in a comprehensive approach. But what makes that approach comprehensive needs to begin with recognition of the "greater force" whose impulse drives the crisis onward.

Now the reader already knows the name of this force from *The Enemy of Nature*'s subtitle: that we face a choice between "the end of capitalism" or "the end of the world." So there seems to be no suspense: as a mystery story, *The Enemy* breaks the basic rule by giving away the killer's name on the dustjacket. But the crime remains unspecified and the revelation superficial, chosen, I must confess, to catch the reader's attention and tug at that rising yet indefinite awareness that, yes, this damned capitalist system is wrecking nature. The real work lies ahead – to make that awareness definite, to clarify what capital is and what nature is, to understand capital's enmity to nature, to understand it as not just an economic system but in relation to the entire human project, to see its antecedents and consequences, and, most importantly, to fathom what can be done about it.

There is certainly no time to waste. The five years since *The Enemy of Nature* appeared have done nothing to dispel its basic indictment. Thus, the World Wildlife Fund's annual "Living Planet" report on the health of the environment for 2006 indicates that the "ecological footprint," a complexly-derived term that signifies the degree to which human society consumes and degrades nature, has risen some 20 percent since 2001, the year that *The Enemy of Nature* went to press.[4]

This has to be understood in context of the only other global parameter that tracks along the same path, namely, the accumulation of capital, which is what the euphemism of "growth" signifies. I do not mean that capital exactly parallels the breakdown of our natural firmament. It really cannot, because capital in its essence is not directly part of nature at all. It is rather a kind of idea in the mind of a natural creature (us) which takes the

4

external form of money and causes that creature to seek more of what capital signifies. As we shall show, it is this seeking, through economy and society, that degrades nature. Thus capital, money-in-action, becomes both a kind of intoxicating god, and also what we call below, a "force field" polarizing our relation to nature in such a way that spells disaster. From being the creature of nature we have become capital's puppet.

A hint of this can be glimpsed in a recent report which outlines the ascendancy of capital over the economic process itself. As of 2005, when the calculations were last made, the money-in-action (stocks, bonds, and other financial assets) flitting about the globe comprised the whopping figure of $140 trillion. As a report in the *Wall Street Journal* put it, this is more than three times the amount of goods and services created that year.[5] It is the motion of this money-wealth that spurs economic activity; thus capital flows induce the flow of nature's transforming. And the more rapid, i.e. reckless, the flow, the more devastating to nature. This of course is not the *WSJ*'s conclusion, but one we develop below. The article merely notes that by 2005, cross-border flows hit $6 trillion, more than twice the figure for 2002, the year *The Enemy of Nature* was published. This is the face of globalization, with capital racing across the planet and sucking nature and humanity into its maw. Moreover, "[g]lobal financial flows are likely to accelerate in the coming years. 'The growth in trade in financial assets is proceeding about 50% faster than the growth in trade' in goods and services, says Kenneth Rogoff, an economist at Harvard." In other words, there is a whirlwind to be reaped.

To account for this and point the way toward its transformation, *The Enemy of Nature* is divided into three parts. In the first, "The Culprit," we indict capital as what will be called the "efficient cause" of the ecological crisis. But first, this crisis itself needs to be defined, and that is what the next chapter sets out to do, chiefly by introducing certain ecological notions through which the scale of the crisis can be addressed, and by raising the question of causality. The third chapter, "Capital," lays out the main terms of the indictment, beginning with a case study of the Bhopal disaster, and proceeding to a discussion of what capital is, and how it afflicts ecosystems intensively, by degrading the conditions of its production, and extensively, through ruthless expansion. The next chapter, "Capitalism," follows upon this by considering the specific form of society built around and for the production of capital. The modes of capital's expansion are explored, along with the qualities of its social relations and the character of its ruling class, and, decisively, the question of its adaptability. For if capitalism cannot alter its fundamental ecological course, then the case for radical transformation is established.

All of which is, needless to say, a grand challenge. The ecological crisis is intellectually difficult and horrific to contemplate, while its outcome must always remain beyond the realm of positive proof. Furthermore, the line of reasoning pursued here entails extremely difficult and unfamiliar political choices. Even though people may accept it in a cursory way, its awful dimensions make resistance to the practical implications inevitable. The argument developed here would be, for many, akin to learning that a trusted and admired guardian – one, moreover, who retains a great deal of power over life – is in reality a cold-blooded killer who has to be put down if one is to survive. Not an easy conclusion to draw, and not an easy path to take, however essential it may be. But that is my problem, and if I believed in prayer, I would pray that my powers are adequate to the task.

In the middle section, "The Domination of Nature," we leave the direct prosecution of the case to establish its wider ground. This is necessary for a number of reasons, chiefly, to avoid a narrow economistic interpretation. In the first of these chapters, the fifth overall, I set out to ground the argument more deeply in the philosophy of nature and human nature. This is entailed in the shift from a merely *environmental* approach to one that is genuinely *ecological*, for which purpose it is necessary to talk in terms of human ecosystems and in the human fittedness for ecosystems, i.e. human nature. If the goal of our effort is to build a free society in harmony with nature, then we need to appreciate how capital violates both nature at large and human nature – and we need to understand as well how we can restore a more integral relationship with nature. These ideas are pursued further in Chapter 6, which takes them up in a historical framework and in relation to other varieties of ecophilosophy. We see here that capital stands at the end of a whole set of estrangements from nature, and integrates them into itself. Far from being a merely economic arrangement, then, capital is the culmination of an ancient lesion between humanity and nature. We will argue that domination according to *gender* stands at the origin of this and shadows everything that follows with what will be called the *gendered bifurcation of nature*. This means that we need to regard capital as a whole way of being, and not merely a set of economic institutions. It is, therefore, this way of being that has to be radically transformed if the ecological crisis is to be overcome – even though its transforming must necessarily pass through a bringing down of the "economic capital" and its enforcer, the capitalist state. We conclude the chapter with some philosophical reflections, including a compact statement of the role played by the elusive notion of the "dialectic."

Then, in Part III: "Paths to Ecosocialism," we turn to the question of "What is to be done?" Now the argument becomes political, and, because we are so far removed these days from transforming society, to a blend of utopian and critical thinking. An important distinction between this and the first edition is that these alternatives are emphasized in the light of what to do about the carbon economy that results in the greenhouse effect, and therefore, provides the most salient dynamic of global warming. This entails critically confronting the important contribution of former Vice-President Al Gore, and his *An Inconvenient Truth*. We begin with a survey of existing ecopolitics in Chapter 8, to see what has been done to mend our relation to nature, and to assay its potential for uprooting capital. One aspect of this critique is entirely conventional, if generally underappreciated. We emphasize that capital stems from the separation of our productive

7

power from the possibilities of their realization. It is, at heart, the imprisonment of labor and the stunting of human capacities – capacities that need full and free development in an ecological society. Therefore, all existing ecopolitics have to be judged by the standard of how they succeed in freeing labor, which is to say, of our transformative power. The chapter ranges widely, from the relatively well-established pathways to those relegated to the margins, and it generally finds the existing strategies wanting. It concludes with a discussion of an insufficiently appreciated danger, that ecological movements may become reactionary or even fascistic.

Having surveyed what is, we turn in the last two chapters to what could be. In Chapter 9, "Prefiguration," the general question of what it takes to break loose from capital is addressed. This requires an excursion into the Marxist notion of "use-value," as that particular point of the economic system open to ecological transformation; and another excursion into the tangled history of socialism, as the record of those efforts that tried – and essentially failed – to liberate labor in the past century. Finally, the chapter turns to the crucial matter of ecological or, as we will call it, ecocentric, production as such, using for this purpose a synthesis with ecofeminism, a doctrine that connects the liberation of gender to that of nature. We conclude with the observation that the key points of activity are "prefigurative," in that they contain within themselves the germ of transformation; and "interstitial," in that they are widely dispersed in capitalist society. In the final chapter, "Ecosocialism," we attempt a mapping from the present scattered and enfeebled condition of resistance to the transformation of capitalism itself. The term "ecosocialism" refers to a society that is recognizably socialist, in that the producers have been reunited with the means of production in a robust efflorescence of democracy; and also recognizably ecological, in that the "limits to growth" are finally respected, and nature is recognized as having intrinsic value, and thereby allowed to resume its inherently formative path. This imagining of ecosocialism does not represent a kind of god-like aspiration to tightly predict the future, but is an effort to show that we can, and had better begin to think in terms of fundamental alternatives to death-dealing capital. To this effect, a number of pertinent questions are addressed, and the whole effort is rounded off with a brief and speculative reflection.

Some last points before taking up the argument. I expect some criticism for not giving sufficent weight to the population question in what follows. At no point, for example, does over-population appear among the chief candidates for the mantle of prime or efficient cause of the ecological crisis. This is not because I discount the problem of population, which is most grave, but because I do see it as having a secondary dynamic – not secondary in importance, but in the sense of being determined by other features of the system.[6] I remain a deeply committed adversary to the recurrent neo-Malthusianism which holds that if only the lower classes would stop their wanton breeding, all will be well; and I hold that human beings have ample power to regulate population so long as they, and specifically women, have power over the terms of their social existence. To me, giving people that power is the main point, for which purpose we need a world where there are no more lower classes, and where all people are in control of their lives. If people would voluntarily limit their childbearing to one per family, the global population would decline to about one billion in the next century – needless to say, a very problematic option, yet indicative of the possibilities.

The Enemy of Nature need make no apologies for moving within the Marxist tradition, and for adhering to fundamental tenets of socialism. Primary among these, and as we will see, theoretically foundational for this work, is the necessity of emancipating labor, or as Marx put it in both the *Communist Manifesto* and Volume I of *Capital* (in the section on the fetishism of commodities), developing a "free association" of producers. But its approach is not that of traditional Marxism. What Marx bequeathed was a method and point of view that require fidelity to the particular forms of a given historical epoch, and the transforming of their own vision as history evolves. Since Marxism emerged a century before the ecological crisis matured, we would expect its received form to be both incomplete and flawed when grappling with a society, such as ours, in advanced ecosystemic decay. Marxism needs, therefore, to become more fully ecological in realizing its potential to speak for nature as well as humanity. In practice, this means replacing *capitalist* with *ecocentrically-socialist* production through a restoration of use-values open to nature's intrinsic value.

I expect that many will find the views of *The Enemy of Nature* too one-sided. It will be said that there is a hatred of capitalism here which leads to the minimization of all its splendid achievements, including the "open society," and its prodigious recuperative powers. Well, it is true that I hate capitalism and would want others to do so as well. Indeed, I hope that this animus has granted me the will to pursue a difficult truth to a transformative end. In any case, if the views expressed here seem harsh and unbalanced, I can only say that there are no end of opportunities to hear hosannas to the greatness of Lord Capital and obtain, as they say, a more nuanced view. Nor is hatred of capital the same, I hasten to add, as hating capitalists, though there are many of these who should be treated as common criminals, and all should be dispossessed of that instrument which corrupts their soul and destroys the natural ground of civilization. This latter group includes myself, along with millions of others who have been tossed by life into the capitalist pot (in my case, for example, by pension funds in the form of tradeable securities; in all cases by holding a bank account or using a credit card). One of the system's marvels is how it makes all feel complicit in its machinations – or rather, tries to and usually succeeds. But it needn't succeed; and one way of preventing it from doing so is to realize that in fighting for an ecologically sane society beyond capital, we are not just struggling to survive, but, more fundamentally, to build a better world and a better life upon it for all creatures.

Part I | The culprit

2 | The ecological crisis

The contours of ecocatastrophe

Some time around the turn of the millennium, the crisis through which we are passing reached a stage in which the numbers of refugees fleeing environmental breakdown surpassed those displaced by war. According to the Red Cross's *World Disasters Report* for 1999 – the worst year on record for "natural disasters" – some 25 million people (58 percent of the total refugee population) were displaced the previous year as they fled from drought, floods, deforestation, and degraded land.

The Red Cross is sophisticated and knows that there is scarcely such a thing as a natural disaster. As its president, Astrid Heiberg, said of this occurrence, the situation inherently brings together "society" and "nature":

> "Everyone is aware of the environmental problems of global warming and deforestation on one hand and the social problems of increasing poverty and growing shanty towns on the other, but when these two factors collide, you have a new scale of catastrophe." [Moreover,] Dr Heiberg predicts that "combination of human-driven climate change and rapidly changing social and economic conditions will set off a chain reaction of devastation leading to super-disasters."
>
> ... Current trends are putting millions more into the path of potential disaster. One billion people are living in the world's unplanned shanty towns [most driven there by a set of factors which include breakdowns in nature], and 40 of the 50 fastest growing cities are located in earthquake zones. Another 10m live under constant threat of floods.[1]

A grim watershed, indeed, that catastrophic effects from environmental sources would grow to exceed those stemming from human aggression. But as the president of the Red Cross indicates, the distinction has more to do with bookkeeping than with basic mechanisms. Surely there is not natural catastrophe in one column and human aggression in another, as in the neat calculations of accountants. Human aggression has always had a lot to do with disruptions in the natural ground of society – consider all the conflicts driven by disease, crop failure or drought – while disruption of nature is virtually always related to human activity, which is all-too-often marked by "aggression." Is not war an assault on nature as well as human beings? In truth, the "environment" itself is marked virtually everywhere by human hands, and what we call nature has a history – which, however, is plainly entering a new phase.

But if nature has a history, then it is not "out there," disconnected from humanity. It is not, in other words, an "environment" surrounding human habitation and useful to us. It is part of us, or to put it better yet (since there is not a nature-part and a non-nature-part to us), an aspect of our being, absolutely essential even if not the whole of it. Certainly the portion of nature we call our body needs to be viewed this way. The millions of refugees from catastrophe are also inhabited by catastrophe in the deformation of their bodily being, or, to put it in familiar terms, their ill health. No one should be so foolish as to ignore the massive eruptions of diseases, for example, the AIDS pandemic, as a major contribution to the present crisis. And if all this is so, then it is misleading to call the crisis one of the environment.

Society and nature are not independent bodies bouncing off each other, like billiard balls. Therefore, the crisis is not about an "environment" outside us, but the evolution, accelerating with sickening velocity, of an ancient lesion in humanity's *relation* to nature. To think in terms of such a relation is *ecological* thinking, which requires that we see the world as an interconnected whole. From this standpoint we are part of that whole, to which we connect as a natural creature whose relation to nature requires that nature be transformed. In other words, our "human nature" is to be both part of the whole of nature and also distinguished

14

from it by what we do to it. This boundary is called *production*; it is the species-specific activity that defines us, and its outcome is the economy, the polity, our culture, religion, and the way we inhabit our bodies. Thus human life is complicated, restless, and full of conflict, as every intelligent person knows.

We do not have an environmental crisis, then, but an *ecological crisis*, in the course of which our bodies, our selves, and the whole of external nature are undergoing severe perturbations. Since production is the key to human nature (a theme we develop in more depth in Chapters 5 and 6), the ecological crisis is also about what can be called the *conditions of production*. These include energy resources, technologies, and also the bodies who have to get to work each day. Thus, a question such as that of "peak oil," which concerns the obviously important matter of just how long the economy can keep using non-renewable fuels,[2] will enter into the ecological crisis. But so will patterns of disease no matter how influenced by extrinsic factors.[3] And so will patterns induced by warfare, or terrorism, each instance of which is a consciously designed, intentional process – "mayhem," we might call it – to tear things apart that should be connected, like limbs from bodies, or societies from their food supplies. Eventually this will tear apart – disintegrate – the planetary ecology. War entails terror by state-devised means, and terror means widespread fear and demoralization. Therefore wars are not only to kill and sow mayhem but also to work with certain feelings. Extending this line of reasoning, subjectivity is part of the ecological crisis.

As the ecological crisis involves the interactions between nature and humanity, it can be represented in two kinds of accounts, depending upon which end we are regarding. From the side of the relationship that entails nature, we see a multitude of ensembles of the natural world, internally related and interconnected throughout the great whole that is the universe. We call these *ecosystems*, and understand them to be units of the crisis viewed objectively, sites where it is unfolding – the atmosphere for global warming, the seas related to this variously as sinks of energy (generating currents like the Gulf Stream), habitations for fish, locations of coral reefs, etc. As for these reefs, one of the great wonders of the world, another ecosystemic crisis comes into view as we learn that increasing concentrations of CO_2 cause a tiny yet momentous acidification of the oceans; this inhibits the calcification necessary for formation of shells and coral reef, this in turn radiates outward to affect all creatures who interact with them, and ultimately, then, to all other ecosystems. It is the essential nature of ecosystems for each to be bounded and internally related, on the one hand, and connected to all other ecosystems, on the other. Thus nature, which we read at this end, may be defined as the integral of all ecosystems.

Viewed from the other end, that of humanity, we see the same processes as refracted through the human, social world. Humans are insignificant in the great scale of things, and nature will roll on as did the "great shroud of the sea" after we disappear like the drowned sailors of the *Pequod*. Yet humanity has made this crisis happen through its folly, and our survival is at stake in its resolution, along with that of countless innocent creatures. What is objective from the standpoint of nature are, in human terms, narratives constructed as we stumble about our stage.

Some of these cluster into catastrophic spectacles, monstrously born. They belong to history and mark the evolution of the crisis. Since the appearance of the first edition of this work we have seen what the president of the Red Cross warned as the advent of a "chain reaction of devastation leading to super-disasters."

Endless terroristic war A hurried note, called "November 2001," was appended to the Preface of the first edition of *The Enemy of Nature* to register the fact of 9/11, which had occurred just after the book went to press. It was observed that as "the ecological crisis is like a nightmare in which the demons released in the progressive domination of nature on a world come back to haunt the master [so therefore does] something of the same hold for terrorism," the violent reaction of those who have lost dignity as a result of imperial penetration of their societies. The passage continued: "the dialectics of terror and ecological disintegration are joined in the regime of oil ... the chief material dynamic of the ecological crisis, and ... the organizing principle for imperial domination of those lands where the conflict is being fought out."

We know only too well how the conflict has played itself out over the past five years, though, needless to say, not how it will end.[4] Notwithstanding, the invasion of Iraq has revealed the following:

1. That the modern imperial state, here Anglo-American, is a machine for the waging of endless war.
2. That this war is not against other states but against societies; thus it becomes increasingly the performance of a Hobbesian jungle of each against all. The condition of modern Baghdad simply beggars the imagination.
3. That in this process liberal democracy becomes increasingly overtaken by recrudescent fundamentalisms; the liberal state tosses aside the gains since the Enlightenment, descends into barbarisms such as the abandonment of Habeas Corpus, a principle that has stood for 800 years, and formalizes systems of torture.
4. That the impetus for the war is the perception by the imperial center of the end of the petroleum era, that reckless expansive period driven over the past two hundred years by the assumption that nature offers an endless gift of energy to its human master.

This is the first instance when a world power has acted on the perception, not that its resources are inadequate (as Germany and Japan did in the 1930s), but that the *world's* resources are no longer capable of sustaining the regime of growth. In other words, the invasion of Iraq, though legitimated by the incitement of terror, has been the first war primarily conditioned by global ecological crisis.[5]

Many hope that this malignancy will pass once the Bush administration leaves Washington in 2008. However, there are simply too many structural factors at work to expect a significant respite. On the other hand, "Bush the Lesser" has presided over so disastrous a sojourn in office as to perhaps decisively usher in the decline of United States imperial power – a development whose incalculable implications will play themselves out in the period ahead.

When the waters came The stone age did not end when the world ran out of stone, and the oil age will not end when the world runs out of oil. The waters will end it first ... the waters or lack of waters, the floods and droughts, and, most of all, the rising seas. In the first edition of *The Enemy of Nature* I could write that "reputable scientists have disagreed that global warming is even taking place, or that it is related to the inputs of carbon dioxide or methane, or that it is permanent, or that it is a bad thing." Five years on, no honest person can make such a statement. There is essentially no dissent among the scientific community that it is happening, that the great share of the problem is due to carbon emissions, that it is here to stay and can at best be mitigated, and that it is a very bad thing – although honest disagreement will still occur about exactly how things will unfold. Meanwhile the corporate sector and its politicians and PR specialists still do their best to cast doubt on the phenomenon; they'd be fired if they didn't, considering how enormous are the stakes. But at least there is a growing awareness that we are up against something unprecedented and that the future hinges on how it is approached. Thus, global warming has become the defining issue of the ecological crisis as a whole.

There are now a number of excellent studies of global warming and what is to be done about this, and there is no need to review the immense amount of knowledge that has been built up over the last few years.[6] I would only mention the chief new finding, that the process is subject to various non-linear and chaotic developments whose overall import is to enhance the likelihood of a rapid, perhaps precipitous, deterioration in the fairly near future. As for the first pattern, we have the prospects, first, that the melting of tundra ice can release huge amounts of trapped methane, CH_4, an even more aggressive greenhouse gas than CO_2; and, second, that the melting of North Polar ice, now a fixture, eliminates most of the albedo effect whereby solar energy is reflected from ice. With the same ambient radiation now being absorbed by dark water, the whole process begins to exponentially run out of control, introducing new and chaotic factors.[7]

We have already seen enough dreadful harbingers, for example, the thousands of heat-related deaths in Europe during the summer of 2003. But no calamity so epitomizes the fate awaiting humanity as a result of the ecological crisis as Hurricane Katrina, which largely destroyed the city of New Orleans on August 28, 2005 in a flood of biblical proportions. As this is being written some seventeen months later, the city is still in shock, with large numbers of its citizens still displaced, the educational system a shambles even by the standards of American ghettoes, and a rash of murders and a pandemic of severe mental disturbance signifying the breakdown of civil society.[8]

Katrina is definitely in the category of super-disaster, and, if there is any truth to the scenario of global warming, will be only the first of a series, to be succeeded by still more violent events. Each disaster is of course unique and to a degree unpredictable. But they also manifest an anatomy in which distinct lines of development intersect chaotically, the aggregate defining a set of uncontrollable disintegrations of ecosystems – until the system as a whole comes to rest in a quasi-stable and ecologically retrograde development. In the case of Katrina, this played out as follows:

1. The power of the hurricane was due to global warming that had heated the waters of the Gulf of Mexico to unprecedented levels. A Category 1 storm in the Atlantic stalled across the Florida peninsula, wandered into the Gulf, and, agitated by extremely warm water, grew into a Category 5 monster before the world's horror-struck eyes.

2. The storm blasted a city that had been left vulnerable by generations of neglect and bureaucratic incompetence. Most

strikingly, the levees necessary for defending the city against marauding waters were in a shocking state of neglect due to inept planning. In addition, wetlands protection had lapsed dreadfully in the Mississippi Delta – all this being part of the tendency, highly developed in the United States – to neglect infrastructure when it does not contribute immediately to the generation of wealth.

3. Associated with this, government – local, state and federal alike – showed a striking inability to cope with the situation. Cronyism, corruption, patronage scandals, and indifference marked all levels, though conditioned by peculiarities inherent to each, from the underfunding and demoralization of the largely black urban communities, to the phenomenal cynicism and corruption of the Bush administration, epitomized by the head of FEMA ("You're doing a heckuva job, Brownie") Michael Brown, and his boss Michael Chertoff, head of Homeland Security; this was demonstrated, finally, in the behavior of the President himself, who headed for San Diego as soon as he heard of the catastrophe in New Orleans. This is the extension of a political culture that has always been suspicious of "government," that is, of public bodies that might stand against the march of private profiteering.

4. The unavailability of agents to help out in emergencies of this sort, for example, the National Guard. Where were they? In Iraq, of course, carrying water for imperialism. Their absence was determined by the underlying forces that drive the Iraq war, just as much as the ferocity of the storm was determined by the underlying forces that drive global warming.[9] These forces converge in the system of ruthless profiteering called capitalism.

5. Of special significance to this city have been the corroding effects of racism and poverty. These conditioned every aspect of neglect, and inhibited the emergence of such solidarity as could have met the blows of the storm with some efficacy. Scarcely an independent variable in this mess, the racist wounds nonetheless require particular attention, inasmuch as racism tends to produce a kind of invisibility. In any case, if humans are part of nature, then society is the human ecosystem *par excellence*; and

a racist society burdened with the poverty that follows racism in every way, is a sick, or, as we will discuss further, a *disintegrating* ecosystem, one that cannot adapt to changing circumstances and heal imposed wounds.

6. Finally, and also absolutely characteristic for the kind of society we are examining, the calamities visited upon New Orleans by an inflamed nature and a corrupted urban environment become in turn *opportunities* for the business community to step in and, in the classical capitalist way, make a lot of money out of destruction. What Katrina did became also a kind of urban clearing, and in turn an ethnic cleansing, as the poor and black folk who contribute little to the march of profits (both as producers and consumers) were swept aside like so much flotsam by the aftermath of the storm. The ground on which they lived is now being prepared for "luxury condominiums" and the like.[10] Meanwhile, the under-races are scattered in their misery, and the racist core of the society festers away.

Ecological collapse

The reader may have observed that, thanks to perpetual warfare, internal corruption, and the blowbacks from the ecological crisis engendered by its capitalism, the United States, richest and most powerful of all the nations ever upon this earth, has been sliding downhill quite a bit. This is of course what tends to happen to empires, except that no empire has ever had to contend before with a global ecological crisis set forth by its ruling system of production. When Rome fell, Europe slipped into a dismal decline, but the rise of Islam and the great societies of Persia, India, and China smoothly took over the pace. Now the entire planet, like a single foundering boat, is being overwhelmed. China is not standing in the wings waiting to replace the United States. China and the United States are locked together as producer (with ultra-cheap labor) and consumer (groaning with debt), and above all, as twinned eco-destabilizers thanks to their embrace of ruthless accumulation. And each is undergoing internal corruption and decay as a result.

From this standpoint, the crisis is dragging the metropolis down to the level of the despised periphery. The Gulf Coast represents a part of the United States in the same category as, say, the unfortunate nation of Somalia. Both have become places where a kind of disintegration of society has been accompanied by the emergence of what the pundits call a "failed state," with chaotic results. To be sure, there is still a long way between the two cases, as anybody who has visited Africa will attest. But it is the direction that counts, and the fact that what has brought this calamity to bear upon the United States is a process that stems from its very bowels and most definitely has a great deal of momentum remaining, so long as the basic terms of industrial capitalist society remain in place. Under the sign of progressive ecological breakdown, New Orleans, then, may be regarded as Mogadishu, USA, and a harbinger of generalized state failure under the impact of the ecological crisis.[11]

The unhappy nations of Africa, upon whom so many disasters have rained down in the past several centuries, were not always that way. When Europe first found them and began its invasions, African peoples were needless to say not trouble-free, simply because it is impossible for human beings to be so. But they had dignity and social cohesion, and many observers placed them on a developmental par with the Northerners. How they fell so far is not for us to detail here. But whatever its intricacies, their descent obeyed the great law of ecological transformation, that societies, which live in interaction with nature, can disintegrate when the fabric of their existence is disturbed – in Africa's case, chiefly by the inroads of empire, the slave trade, and so on. Think of any particular society as an intricate, and developing, ecosystem; and think of the planetary ecology as a whole comprising all societies interrelating with each other and with their natural firmament – i.e. the "Ecosphere" – in the same way. Now imagine the systemic invasion of an agent whose function it is to break the filaments of connection that give ecosystems their form. Imagine metaphorically that this "fabric" is like a wool sweater attacked by clothes moths. One does not at first observe any singular mass impact (though such most certainly occurs in societies, especially in the shape of war). What happens instead is a kind of random snipping way of the strands that hold the sweater together and give it its form. For a while nothing is noticed. Then the observer spots a little hole here and there; and then more holes, and the joining together of little holes into big ones. The holes grow in scope and scale, and with it the connections that give the sweater its form and function break down – disintegrate. Eventually, the sweater as a whole disintegrates, falling apart in the hand. It is thrown into the dump, and as "waste" rejoins the great cycle of nature.

So do individuals when they die; and so do societies – whether imperialized African societies or, in this case, the imperium itself. All tend to disintegrate when set upon by agents that disintegrate the fabric of their form. For Africa, as for indigenous America, these agents were, and have been, those of the empire. The empire itself, meanwhile, succumbs from its own internal decay process, along with the reflux of its effects on the periphery.

Viewed from nature's end of things, this crisis appears as an incapacity to mend itself, or as we can say, to buffer the ecosystemic breakdown brought about by its human child. Put more formally, the current stage of history can be characterized as *structured by forces that systematically degrade and finally exceed the buffering capacity of nature with respect to human production, thereby setting into motion an unpredictable yet interacting and expanding set of ecosystemic breakdowns.* The ecological crisis is what is meant by this phase. In it we observe the desynchronization of life-cycles and the disjointing of species and individuals, resulting in the fragmentation of ecosystems human as well as non-human, along with vast changes in species composition, as well as the more formal environmental aspect of things.[12] Humanity is not just the perpetrator of the crisis; it is its victim as well. And among the signs of our victimization is the incapacity to contend with the crisis, or even to become conscious of it.

The outcome of the ecological crisis is doubly impossible to predict, first of all because it depends on the interaction, both non-linear and chaotic, of innumerably vast ecosystemic processes. If we cannot predict the weather for more than a few days at a time, how can the integrity of the ecosphere as a whole be predicted over the next decades? The second reason is more important, for it is a function of how humans respond to growing awareness of the crisis, and this remains to be decided. Will states, in order to stave off their internal rot and failure, resort to ever more authoritarian and fascist means?[13] Will people awaken, rise to the challenge, restructure their production, which means, build a new kind of society, and create the new world with ecologically rational technology? This, as they say, is the rub, and the focus of the concluding section of the book.

Notwithstanding, things have gone on in such a manner since *The Enemy of Nature* was first published as to warrant a few predictions. Let me say, then, that from where I sit, it seems out of the question that the crisis can leave us unscathed. I see, then, within the lifetime of many alive today (certainly my own grandchildren), a period of a great "die-down," resulting from the combined effects of massive habitat alteration (especially by rising seas) on the one hand, and on the other, from the tremendous disruption in production owing to processes such as deforestation, soil and water loss, new pandemics, and the like.

I shudder to put a number to this, but it will be such as to render population *per se* as a relatively moot point, except as relative to the resource levels left intact by the impending breakup. I do not, however, think of this great collapse as the extinction of the human species – unless the breakup is accompanied by wars in which nuclear weapons are used and the end-time of "nuclear winter" supervenes. Short of this (quite possible) eventuality I think humanity will go on, even under the thermal conditions of breakaway global warming. We are, when all is said, simply too resourceful and adaptable a species, and with too great a knowledge base, to give up altogether. Eventually, yes, we will disappear, since everything must pass. But though I along with the reader will probably not live to see it, what we call the ecological crisis will some day, perhaps, say, by the end of the century, be ushering in a new phase of our most interesting history.

The shape this takes will entail the replacement of Lord Capital by a more ecologically rational way of production.[14] Of that I am quite certain, as I should think, would be anybody who looks closely enough at the enmity toward nature embedded within our mighty economy. All of which it to say that it is time to take just such a look, so as to prepare the way for a future.

3 | Capital

A case study

There is a substance called methyl isocyanate (MIC), which does not exist in nature but was introduced into the ecosphere by industry in the last century. A simple but very potent molecule (CH_3NCO), MIC is widely used in the manufacture of pesticides and herbicides because of its reactivity and deadly effects on living organisms. According to the website of the US Environmental Protection Agency:

> MIC ... is an ester of isocyanic acid (HNCO). The parent isocyanic acid is a weak acid and exists in equilibrium with cyanic (HCNO) acid [the differences between the two HNCOs being in the spatial configuration of the atoms]. MIC's boiling point is yet to be clearly established. It is a highly volatile and inflammable gas; its vapors are denser than air; it is stable under dry and neutral conditions at room temperature but can violently react in the presence of acids, alkali, and the like. The carbon center in the isocyanate group is electron deficient (electrophilic) and therefore will react with electron-rich (nucleophiles), e.g.: water, alcohol, phenol, alkali, and the like.

Being denser than air, MIC vapor does not dissipate but settles on whatever is nearby. If exposed to water-bearing bodily tissues, it reacts violently, leading to changes that cannot be contained by the normal protective devices of the affected organism. The amount of energy released by the ensuing reaction swiftly exceeds the heat-buffering capabilities of the body. As a result, many molecules of service to the organism are degraded and/or thrown into disarray, while others that are toxic are formed. Put simply, the body suffers severe burns, especially of exposed tissues rich in water, such as lungs and eyes. Chest pain, breathlessness and severe asthma result immediately. If the exposure is high, blindness, severe bacterial and eosinophilic pneumonia, or laryngeal edema and cardiac arrest follow.

What has been said so far would explain at the physiological level why a person who inhaled MIC, say, as she slept, could become deathly ill. Within this framework, we can say that MIC "causes" the illness and death. Needless to say, such an explanation would tell us nothing about another set of questions, namely, why was the sleeper in such proximity to MIC, and more, what is methyl isocyanate doing in the environment in the first place, at so close a distance that it interacted with bodies? To repeat, MIC does not exist in nature; and were it by chance to issue from some natural source like a volcano, its fabulous reactivity would ensure it a very transient existence. How, then, does MIC happen to be present so that bodies are affected by its violent chemical proclivities? In other words, MIC can cause the illness, but not itself. There needs be a cause at a higher level of generality that brings MIC into existence and deploys it in certain ways. This property of being able to set other causes into motion is what we mean by the "efficiency" of a cause.

What "causes" MIC is the fact of being *produced*, through the conscious alteration of nature to serve human ends, in this case, industrial ones relevant to the development of agriculture. Industry, however, does far more than produce large amounts of strange substances; it also alters the human ecology, putting some people in its way, and serving others. Chemical science will be necessary to understand how MIC affects living tissue. Industrial production, however, understands science and nature in order to bring substances like MIC into the world, and to gather them for its uses, in this case, the manufacture of pesticides for the purposes of modern agriculture. To understand the full event, then, and not just the pathological effects on the organism, requires a grasp of the history and social relations of production, of its industrial turn, of the peculiarities of pesticide manufacture – and in this instance, of the reasons why so deadly a substance escaped sequestration and found its way into human bodies. And if the poisoning took place in many lungs all at once, why they all happened to be there together to receive MIC's deadly embrace.

The reader will have doubtless gathered by now that I am referring to a very specific ecocatastrophic event: the release, on December 4, 1984, of 46.3 tons of methyl isocyanate from the factory run by the Union Carbide corporation, an American transnational with a pesticide-manufacturing facility in Bhopal, India. The gas escaped around midnight, and so it found the inhabitants of Bhopal, great numbers of whom lived close to the factory, sleeping. It is impossible to convey in words the suffering this caused. But some results can be enumerated: an estimated 8,000 people died on the spot and as many afterward, with over 500,000 injured, some 50,000 to 70,000 of those injuries permanent.[1] People were still dying, fifteen years later, at a rate of between ten and fifteen a month, and today, more than twenty years on, the dying and disability continue, and the ruins of the factory still deface the city and leach toxic materials into the environment.[2]

The worst industrial accident in history, Bhopal has become synonymous for the hazards posed to human beings by the industrial process, and an emblem for the ecological crisis itself. To understand the cause of Bhopal may give a window on the cause of the crisis, not in the sense that this is to be composed of horrendous accidents such as this, but because in Bhopal's magnitude all the elements of the crisis as a whole are concentrated. To comprehend Bhopal, however, we need to expand our thinking from the physiological dimension to include the role played by human agency, along with its ideological implications. Understanding this event, where not one but thousands of lives were mutilated, involves the judgment of competing claims and differing views of reality. Methyl isocyanate, as the active cause of bodily damage, is a mute killer without motive or interest in the outcome of its chemistry. When, however, we attempt to understand the causes of the accident at Bhopal, we need to think beyond the molecular level. For example, the element of *money* now enters the picture. It is not just the vast amounts at stake as a result of the disaster – some $3 billion in damages originally asked by the Indian government, with $470 million finally agreed to by Carbide (plus $50 million in legal fees, and $20 million offered for construction of a local hospital)[3] – but money's full power in human existence: in short, a whole social order is entailed, of power, and meaning, and the relationships between the actors of society. And now, too, we look for a kind of causation that would best comprehend these specifically human–ecological issues. But let us be concrete, and consider what happened at Bhopal that deadly night in 1984. Essentially, the questions come down to this: what was MIC doing in Bhopal in the first place? Why was it released in such a manner? Why were the people so exposed, and why so shabbily treated? And as for the responsible agents, what were the driving forces acting on them?

To the first question the answer is that Union Carbide put it there for its purposes, that is, the corporation caused the factory to be built where and when it pleased. In a literal sense, this is an absurd statement. Union Carbide is not a person who can put anything anywhere; and the actual people who immediately caused the MIC plant to arise in Bhopal were a great mass of laborers, architects, suppliers, etc., most of whom had no direct relation to the company but were hired by subcontractors. Yet we cannot claim that these workers built the factory except as the necessary but partial final human instrument, just as the tools in their hands were necessary but partial technological instruments. Therefore the answer to the question of what caused a factory, or any other social product, to be built would be: that which effectively organizes the social labor that went into it. And, since labor is the human faculty of making events happen, said cause, which organizes all the others, becomes efficient.

In a different kind of society, where workers controlled their productive life activity, or where, as in aboriginal society, the whole community did the same, we would be entitled to end our account of what caused the factory to arise with citation of the people who actually constructed it. But in our kind of

Capital

society that statement would be false, since under the regime of capital workers do not self-determine their activity. For an understanding, therefore, of the social organization of a vast number of individual activities we would have to turn to that which commands and controls them all in production, and in this case such an agent would have to be the Union Carbide corporation, despite the fact that it is headquartered thousands of miles away and served to express the interests of individuals who need never have set foot inside India, much less Bhopal.

We may say, then, that the workers, etc., were the instrumental causes of the factory at Bhopal, while the Union Carbide corporation was the efficient cause. That is, Carbide was the agent capable of organizing and fruitfully combining all the factors required for the production of the factory, and, once it had been built, for the manufacture, distribution, and sale of the products, including MIC as an intermediary product. In any complex phenomenon, many causal processes are at work. But insofar as the phenomenon functions as a whole, we may identify an overarching, integrating kind of cause that sets the instrumental causes into motion, regulates them, and directs them toward an end – and the alteration of which would be necessary to change the phenonemon as a whole. Such is what is meant by the efficient cause.[4]

Each cause is specific for the level of effect it sets into motion. Methyl isocyanate is the efficient cause of the bodily devastation which ensues upon its inhalation, just as Union Carbide was of the factory at Bhopal. But what drives Carbide? And what of the incident of December 1984 and its social sequelae? What caused that, and how does this relate to the question of an "efficient cause"? Here is where conflicting views of reality enter most forcefully, because so much is at stake. Carbide has not denied that Bhopal is the site of its factory or that MIC is its product – in fact it is quite proud of the fact and the role it has played in the so-called "Green Revolution," which has augmented food production in nations of the South. As the company laid out in its website, "Ironically, the plant at Bhopal had its origin in a humane goal: supplying pesticides to protect Indian agricultural production," and more generally, to enhance the "'Indianization' of industry in that country" through its "willingness to offer expertise, readiness to comply with Indian laws, and acceptance of a gradual approach to developing Indian consumer markets. Union Carbide's investment had gained us widespread good will – or so we thought." Insisting on the integrity of its safety standards and quality controls ("a deeply ingrained commitment ... [with] stringent internal standards dating back to the 1930s"), the company is deeply distressed by having been "recast ... as an archetypal multinational villain, exploiting India's people and resources," a "caricature [no doubt] designed to gain access to Union Carbide's financial resources." As for the tragic incident, with respect to which "from the first day, we had been moved by compassion and sympathy," the company had done its own investigation proving that the cause of the disaster "was undeniably sabotage. The evidence showed that an employee at the Bhopal plant had deliberately introduced water into a methyl isocyanate storage tank. The result was the cloud of poisonous gas." Alas, this truth has not caught on, apparently due to the Indian government's "apparent indifference to the plight of the Bhopal victims."

It is a coherent explanation: the disaster at Bhopal was not Union Carbide's fault, but that of a disgruntled employee, compounded by the callousness and fecklessness of the Indian government. In this universe of meaning, configured by the ever-present specter of legal action and major financial consequences (remember the $50 million spent by the corporation to defend itself), causality equals *blame*, to be determined legally. A similar discourse prevails throughout the ecological crisis, which tends to get reduced to a series of individual acts for which blame – and financial allocations on the basis of blame – become the relevant criteria.

The discourse of blame, or fault, or legal responsibility, is essential when it comes to parcelling out a degree of justice and restitution for victims. Nor, in this instance, is it difficult to ascertain, given the fact that patient investigation has disclosed a mountain of evidence relevant to understanding the fatal night. Let me summarize, to indicate the particular dissection of this one horrific eco-disaster, and to point a way toward a wider understanding.

- Carbide never named the saboteur, nor submitted its claims to a court of law under judicial rules of evidence. It rather deduced his agency from an analysis of the structure of its plant and let the matter rest at that.[5]
- The company failed to notify the authorities of the large amounts of MIC stored at the plant. More, they had designed the plant in a way that made accidents more or less inevitable, as by using carbon steel valves that corroded when exposed to acid.
- Prior to 1978, Carbide produced its pesticide, Sevin, without directly using MIC. It switched to the use of the deadly intermediate in order to produce more cheaply, and began manufacturing it in Bhopal in 1980. In fact, the German corporation Bayer made Sevin without MIC, in a safer but more expensive way.
- Local authorities urged the plant to be built in another part of Bhopal, in an industrial zone out of range of the population. Carbide refused, saying this was too expensive.
- The plant was losing money, because the demand for pesticides was down, and hence chronically overproduced MIC, which Carbide couldn't unload.
- This led to an effort to cut costs, beginning in 1982. To quote Kurzman, "such cuts ... meant less stringent quality control and thus looser safety rules. A pipe leaked? Don't replace it, employees said they were told. Just patch it up. MIC workers needed more training? They could do with less (including using instruction manuals in English, which few could read). Promotions were halted, seriously affecting employee morale and driving some of the most skilled to seek work elsewhere."[6] By late 1984, only six operators, rather than the original twelve,

were working with MIC. The numbers of supervisory personnel also had been halved; while there was no maintenance supervisor on the night shift. Thus, indicator readings were checked every two hours rather than hourly, as required.

- In late 1981, inhalation accidents began appearing at the plant. Experts from the US appeared and warned of a "runaway reaction" inside an MIC storage tank. This followed other warnings from 1979 and 1980. Warnings from the Indian authorities went unheeded. In October 1982, a leak of MIC caused five workers to be hospitalized.

- The local authorities had no instruments to monitor air pollution near the plant.

- When the workers at the plant, through their union, protested the safety hazards, they were ignored. One worker who went on a fifteen-day hunger strike was fired.

- Although workers originally wore safety equipment, the growing slackness caused this to be jettisoned. More than 70 percent of workers were docked pay for refusing to deviate from the prescribed safety routines. All the while, pressure to keep making MIC as swiftly and cheaply as possible was sustained.

- The night of the accident, a leaking carbon-steel valve was discovered, which allowed water to slip into the MIC tanks. This was not repaired, as it would have taken too much time; in other words, would have been expensive.

- In addition, the alarm on the tank had not worked for four years, and there was only one manual backup system instead of the four-stage system used in the US. The flare tower that burned escaping gas had been out of service for more than five months, as was the vent gas scrubber. The refrigeration system installed to inhibit the volatilization of MIC was also idle, to save power costs. Nor was the steam boiler designed to help clean the pipes in active operation, for the same reason. Virtually every relevant safety instrument, from shutdown devices, to monitoring tools, to temperature gauges, was either in short supply, or malfunctioning, or designed improperly.

The maintenance temperature of the MIC was kept at 20°C, though the manual called for a temperature of 4.5° (this lower figure, needless to say, being much cooler than the average temperature of Bhopal, hence more expensive to maintain). In addition, "Carbide's Bhopal plant was designed in such a way that, after the deadly gas leak began, the main safety system – water sprays intended to 'knock down' such a leak – could not spray water high enough to reach the escaping stream of gas. In sum, the plant's safety systems had been designed negligently. Internal documents show that the company knew this prior to the disaster, but did nothing about it."[7]

• Finally, the tank that exploded had been malfunctioning for a week. Instead of dealing with it, the plant authorities used other tanks, and let this one sit, and, in effect, stew. One outcome of "stewing," as any cook knows, is the build-up of pressure and temperature, both of which can trigger further reactions in suitable substances.

So there is no question as to who was to *blame* for the horror at Bhopal. Despite the crocodile tears and bleating protestations, Union Carbide stands revealed as precisely the "archetypal multi-national villain" it tries to deny being. Indeed, the only question remaining at this level is why the firm was not held fully accountable for its criminal negligence. However, the issue of blame, while necessary, is by no means sufficient to grasp the meaning of Bhopal, nor does it clear up the question of causation.

MIC can be held to be the efficient cause of bodily harm, as its molecular bonds provide the destabilizing force to tear up the delicate balance of a living ecosystem. Just so is Carbide the efficient cause of the building of the factory at Bhopal. However, when it comes down to this incident, we see that Carbide is itself subjected to other forces, and that the notion of efficient causation requires that these forces be given their due. There is no mystery here: at virtually every point listed above we find that Carbide did this or that to *lower its costs*; further, that the "this and that" had the effect of summating the risks that the monstrously

34

dangerous MIC (itself chosen as a product in order to lower costs) would escape; and that, further, Carbide's blameworthiness consisted precisely in the callous and self-serving way it was prepared to put Bhopal in harm's way in order to lower costs. Its evasion of legal responsibility needs to be understood within the universe of meanings that cluster about this prime necessity, from particular legal and public relations maneuvers to the whole international setup that makes an ancient and proud country like India so unable to stand up for the rights of its own people.

The efficient cause here, then, would have to comprise not just the particular greed of this corporation, but the system imposing upon it the never-ending pressure to cut costs – or, from the other side – to *make profits*. Carbide says it was in India to make pesticides. But it makes pesticides in order to make money. Being a quintessential capitalist corporation of the modern type, Union Carbide has to make money – and has to keep making it faster and faster – in order to survive in the world configured by its master, capital.

An "accident" is merely the statistically unpredictable end of a chain of circumstances. Therefore, accidents are continuous with a range of less spectacular but equivalently disruptive destabilizations. Where a sufficient number of "cost-cuttings-in-the-name-of profit" occur, there is an accident waiting to happen. At times, this may be facilitated or triggered by human error – possibly itself a product of the same complex (an under-trained, demoralized, alienated staff, for example). However, the "human factor" fades as an independent cause to the extent people are shaped and distorted by the profit complex. If we take Carbide's own explanation to be true for present purposes, as phony as it actually is: suppose it was more than mere error that destroyed the plant, but a saboteur who maliciously set the gas loose that night. What shaped him, then? Was it inscrutable evil or the product of a chain of determinants within the force field of profit-seeking? Was he one of the workers who had been "disciplined" for refusing to cut corners, or fired for going on strike, or was he simply brutalized by a concatenation of causal factors descending upon him from a hellish human ecology? Was he psychotic – and if so, was this some kind of genetic programming, or did it, too, descend from the mass of alienations that comprised his life world, alienations in whose composition the dominant social system will be found to occupy a place at the end of every line?

It is not that other factors are missing from the network of causal processes that summate to cause an accident, or, beyond that, the ecological crisis itself. To the contrary, they must be present, inasmuch as complex events are overdetermined. But they are present as scattered individualities, while through and around them, a great force field shapes and combines them into the effective events that move the world. The more globally and in terms of the whole we regard these things, the less we think in terms of individual blame or look for the "accidents" that disrupt what is otherwise to be construed as a rational process. Now we inquire whether the process is rational in the first place, and whether or not in this light, "accidents are waiting to happen." We also come to ask the larger question of whether the *normal* and non-accidental functioning of the system is in itself ecodestructive – in which case it is the system that continually generates insults to ecologies of one kind or another and has to be transformed. An attention limited to the particular contours of the individual event loses track of that larger pattern, of the merits of pesticides themselves, and more generally, the "Green Revolution" of which they comprise an essential part,[8] along with the never-ending ordeal to which the nations of the South, like India, are subjected in the world system.

Then there was the payoff. On the very day that the Indian government backed away and agreed not to prosecute Carbide any further, as if by a miracle the company's stock went up by $2 a share on the New York stock exchange. This seemingly small figure takes its significance from the fact that the settlement of $470 million cost Carbide's shareholders only $0.43 a share. Therefore those who held Carbide stocks were, so to speak, richer by $1.57 a share after the company "suffered" the consequences of causing a nightmare to descend upon the people of Bhopal.

But why did the price of Carbide stock go up? The answer is brutally revealing: because the company proved – in this first large-scale industrial accident case affecting a transnational corporation operating in the so-called Third World, or South – that it *could get away with murder*, now and in the future. Wall Street knew then that business could go forward, and that the orderly extraction of profits from the South had become more secure.

Wall Street (to be more exact, "finance capital") is the command and control center of the system. The little numbers that flicker by on its tapes are common reductions of the potential for capital expansion as deployed over the manifold energic points of the dominant order. In this way, the individual factories and the managerial decisions affecting them are made in the light of a larger and more comprehensive entity, a gigantic force field that polarizes every event within its range of influence, even as it continually seeks to expand that range. This is how the rules of the game are played out. It also follows that the individual motives of Carbide's executives are meaningless except as public relations material. Ward Morehouse has written in regard to this event: "Had [Carbide's management] been genuinely forthcoming and made truly disinterested offers of help on a scale appropriate to the magnitude of the disaster, they would almost certainly have been confronted with suits by shareholders seeking to hold the management accountable for mishandling company funds."[9]

Thus, it was capital that constrained Carbide. But there is another side, which makes this an "if pigs had wings they would fly" type of argument. People who are genuinely forthcoming and disinterestly helpful do not become managers of large capitalist firms. The tender-hearted are pushed off the ladder on which one ascends to such positions of power. For capital shapes as well as selects the kinds of people who create these events.

The story of Bhopal and its corporate miscreant continues. Carbide got out of the pesticide business, but on February 7, 2001, merged with the Dow Chemical company, which does make pesticides – it made Agent Orange for use during the Vietnam War. The new chemical colossus operated in 168 countries and pulled in more than $24 billion in revenue. The president and chief executive of Dow stated that the merger should save at least $500 million annually, though regrettably 2,000 jobs would be lost as well. None of the men at individual fault for Bhopal has ever been brought to justice, nor, I think, will be in their lifetime.

The mystery of growth revealed

The "giant force field" is a metaphor for capital, that ubiquitous, all-powerful, and greatly misunderstood dynamo that drives our society. The established view sees capital as a rational factor of investment, a way of using money to fruitfully bring together the various features of economic activity. For Karl Marx, capital was a "werewolf" and a "vampire," ravenously consuming labor and mutilating the laborer. Both notions are true; and the second one, applied to nature as well as labor, accounts for the ecological crisis in all essential features. From the standpoint of the ecological crisis, corporations like Union Carbide are the soldiers of capital, and institutions at a higher level in the system, such as stock markets, the International Monetary Fund (IMF), the Federal Reserve Bank, and the Department of the Treasury, etc., its general staff. Once these relationships are appreciated, Bhopal is seen in clearer perspective – as an individual accident, the repetition of which might be avoided if industry is careful enough, and, more essentially, as the manifestation of anti-ecological tendencies inherent to capital, which will have their day one way or another so long as capital comes to organize social production. These latter are threefold:

1. Capital tends to degrade the conditions of its own production.
2. Capital must expand without end in order to exist.
3. Capital leads to a chaotic world-system increasingly polarized between rich and poor, which cannot adequately address the ecological crisis.

The combination makes an ever-growing ecological crisis an iron necessity so long as capital rules, no matter what measures are taken to tidy up one corner or another.

We need to examine why we talk of capital as though it has a life of its own, which rapidly surpasses its rational function and consumes ecosystems in order to grow cancerously. Capital is not in itself a living organism, needless to say. It is, rather, a kind of relationship like that set up by a cancer-causing virus that invades living human beings, forces them to violate ecological integrity, sets up self-replicating structures, and polarizes the giant force field. It is humanity living as capital, people who become capital's *personifications*, that destroys ecosystems.

The Faustian bargain that gave rise to this way of being arose through the discovery that fabulous wealth could be achieved by making money first of all, and things through the making of money. Everyone knows that capitalist production is for profit and not use – and if they don't know this at first, they can learn it right away from watching Wall Street discipline corporations that fail to measure up to standards of profitability. Capitalists celebrate the restless dynamism that these standards enforce, with its drive for innovation, efficiency and new markets. They fail to recognize – because a kind of failure of recognition is built into their being – that what looks like resourcefulness and resilience from one side becomes on the other an addiction and a treadmill to oblivion.

Commodities appeared at the dawn of economic activity, and commodity production became generalized with the advent of capital. The germ of capital is inserted into each commodity, and can only be released through consumption, and, with this, the conversion of what is desirable into money. To employ a formalism employed by Marx, which we shall find helpful to express our ideas as we proceed, every commodity is a conjunction of a "use-value" and an "exchange-value."[10] Use-value signifies the commodity's place in the ever-developing manifold of human needs and wants; while exchange-value represents its "commodity-being," that is, its generalized equivalence, an abstraction that can be expressed only in quantitative terms and as money. Broadly speaking, capital represents that regime in which exchange-value predominates over use-value in the production of commodities – and the problem with capital is that, once installed, the process becomes self-perpetuating and expanding.

If production be for profit, that is, for the expansion of the money-value invested in it, then prices must be kept as high as possible and costs as low as possible. As prices will tend to be held down by the competition endemic to the system, in practice, cutting costs becomes a paramount concern of capitalists. But costs of what? Clearly, of what enters into the production of commodities. Much of this can be expressed in terms of other commodities, for example, fuel, machinery, building materials, etc., and, crucially, the labor-power sold by workers for wages, which is the heart of the capitalist system. However, if the same analysis is done upon the latter, at some point we arrive at entities that are not produced as commodities, yet are treated as such in the great market that defines capitalism. These are the abovementioned "conditions of production," and they include publicly produced facilities, i.e. *infrastructure*, the *workers* themselves, and, last but certainly not least, *nature* – even if this nature already contains, as it almost always does, the hand of prior human activity.

The process is a manifestation of the ascendancy of exchange-value over use-value, and entails a twofold degradation. In the first place, we have the commodification of nature, which includes human beings, and their bodies. However, nature, as we shall examine further in Part II, simply does not work this way. No matter what capital's ideologues say, the actual laws of nature never include monetization; they exist, rather, in the context of ecosystems whose internal relations are violated by conversion to the money-form. The essential argument for environmental economics within the capitalist system is that by privatizing nature people learn to care for it as their property. However, the problem is that, being made property, nature is *a priori* severed from its ecosystemic ways of being. Thus the ceaseless rendering into commodities, with its monetization and exchange, breaks down the specificity and intricacy of ecosystems. To this is added the devaluation, or basic lack of caring, which attends what is left over and unprofitable. Here arise the so-called "externalities" that become the repositories of pollution. To the extent the capital relation, with its unrelenting competitive drive to realize profit, prevails, it is a certainty that the conditions of production at some point or other will be degraded, which is to say, natural ecosystems will be destabilized and broken apart. As James O'Connor has demonstrated in his pioneering studies of this phenomenon, this degradation will have a contradictory effect on profitability itself (the "Second Contradiction of Capital"), either directly, as by so fouling the natural ground of production that it breaks down, or indirectly, in the case that regulatory measures, being forced to pay for the healthcare of workers, etc, re-internalizes the costs that had been expelled into the environment.[11] In a case like Bhopal, numerous insults of this kind interacted and became the matrix of a ghastly "accident." For Bhopal, degradation was concentrated in one setting; while the ecological crisis as a whole may be regarded as its occurrence in a less concentrated but vastly more extended field, so that the disaster is now played out more slowly and on a planetary scale.

It will surely be rejoined to this that a great many countervailing techniques are continually introduced to blunt or even profit from the degradation of conditions of production, for example, pollution control devices, commodification of pollutants, etc. To some degree these are bound to be effective. Indeed, if the overall system were in equilibrium, then the effects of the Second Contradiction could be contained, and we would not be able to extrapolate from it to the ecological crisis. But this brings us to the second great problem with capital, namely, that equilibrium and confinement of any sort is anathema to it.

Accumulation

In this respect, Marx wrote in his *Grundrisse*:

> However, as representative of the general form of wealth – money – capital is the endless and limitless drive to go beyond its limiting barrier. Every boundary is and has to be a barrier for it. Else it

would cease to be capital – money as self-reproductive. If ever it perceived a certain boundary not as a barrier, but became comfortable within it as a boundary, it would have declined from exchange value to use value, from the general form of wealth to the specific, substantial mode of the same. Capital as such creates a specific surplus value because it cannot create an infinite one all at once; but it is the constant movement to create more of the same. The quantitative boundary of the surplus value appears to it as a mere natural barrier, as a necessity which it constantly tries to violate and beyond which it constantly seeks to go.[12]

The depth of Marx's insight should be appreciated: capital is quantitative in its core, and imposes the regime of quantity upon the world: this is a "necessity" for capital. But capital is equivalently *intolerant* of necessity; it constantly seeks to go beyond the limits that it itself has imposed, and so can neither rest nor find equilibrium: it is irremediably self-contradictory. Every quantitative increase becomes a new boundary, which is immediately transformed into a new barrier. The boundary/barrier ensemble then becomes the site of new value and the potential for new capital formation, which then becomes another boundary/barrier, and so forth and on into infinity – at least in the logical schemata of capital. Small wonder that the society formed on the basis of producing for the sake of capital before all else is restlessly dynamic, that it introduces new forms of wealth, and continually makes the past forms obsolete, that it is obsessed with change and acquisition – and that it is a disaster for ecologies.

Since each boundary/barrier is a site for commodity formation, this becomes the prescription for the "generalized commodity production" that is one of capital's hallmarks. Needless to say, the process does not occur neatly, as though capitalists sat around and selected their spots for new commodities. To some degree, of course, they do – imagine network executives trying to develop new sitcoms, or the auto manufacturers a new line of SUVs. But the more interesting examples are those where the unplanned and more or less spontaneous actions of the system create novel conjunctures, which are then seized upon as new places for profitable activity. The prospect dear to capitalists, of making businesses out of trading pollution credits, or the pharmaceutical industry's search for new antibiotics to meet the new diseases set forward by ecological destabilization itself, are examples of this kind. The constant creation of anxieties and needs by the restless movement of the system is constantly funnelled into the circuits of new commodity activity. Does capitalism create an isolated, anxiety-ridden self whose survival requires being placed upon a market? Well, then, capital will also step in to create commodities to service this tensely narcissistic state of being – articles of fashion and image, with technologies to service these and a cultural apparatus to go along – in the case of fashion, say, a whole range of magazines, cosmetics, sexual aids, photographic studios, advertising agencies, public relations firms, psychotherapies, and so on.

Capital's regime of profitability is one of permanent instability and restlessness. Even in the ruling class, no one "rules" without perpetually proving himself, and the CEO who does not increase the rate of profit will be swiftly tossed aside. Nor can anyone rest content with the given, but must constantly try to expand it. Growth is simply equated with survival as a capitalist, for anyone who fails to grow will simply disappear, his assets acquired by another. No matter how much one has, one never really has anything; everything must be proved to exist anew the next day. Hence that well-known trait of the bourgeoisie: no matter how rich they become, they always need to become richer: notice the behavior of Wal-Mart or Microsoft. All of the fabulous "growth" of the last decades has not by one iota reduced the drive to accumulate still more, nor can it ever so long as capital reigns. The sense of having and possessing dominates all others precisely because its reality can never be secured. Strictly speaking, individuals can step off this wheel – make their fortune and retire to raise polo ponies or cabbages, or become an environmental guru. But they cease thereby being personifications of capital; and others immediately step forward to take their role.

Money – the form of capitalist value – abstracts and dissolves all relationships, replacing them with the cash nexus. This sets going the ruthless competitiveness inherent to capital, since if money is the only true bond, then there are no true bonds at all, and universal envy, suspicion, and mistrust reign. The "system works," for the competition so induced becomes the motor forcing eternal growth as the price of survival. And because money can effortlessly expand even as its material substrate is bound by the laws of nature, the great pools of capital emerging from the ceaseless transactions provide the benchmark of growth, and, as they gather, press yet further for expansion. The pressure of capitalist growth is therefore *exponential*, that is, it becomes proportional to the total magnitude of the accumulated capital pressing for discharge. As Marx put it in another passage from the same work:

> The barrier appears as an accident which has to be conquered. This is apparent on even the most superficial inspection. If capital increases from 100 to 1,000, then 1,000 is now the point of departure, from which the increase has to begin; the tenfold multiplication; profit and interest themselves become capital in turn. *What appeared as surplus value now appears as simple presupposition, etc*, as included in *its simple composition.*[13]

If we unpack this highly compressed passage (the *Grundrisse* was written as a notebook for Marx's own study, and not for an outside reader), Marx is saying that in the regime of capital any original profit is only a starting point. If the same process is carried forward through a second cycle, the same expansionary force will be observed, operating, however, from the higher level. If 10 of some monetary unit goes to 100 the first time around, there will be a tendency for it to go to 1,000 the second time around. Therefore capitalist production is not only expansionary (since money has to be thrown into circulation for it to become capital, and a surplus value needs to be gained), but exponentially so. As Marx commented in *Capital*:

The repetition or renewal of the act of selling in order to buy (i.e., C–M–C')[14] finds its measure and its goal ... in a final purpose which lies outside it, namely consumption, the satisfaction of definite needs. But in buying in order to sell (i.e. M–C–M'), on the contrary, the end and the beginning are the same, money or exchange-value, and this very fact makes the movement an endless one.

For more money is just money with a larger number written upon it, and so:

At the end of the movement, money emerges once again as the starting point. Therefore the final result of each separate cycle, in which a purchase and consequent sale are completed, forms of itself the starting point for a new cycle. The simple circulation of commodities – selling in order to buy – is a means to a goal which lies outside circulation, namely the appropriation of use-values, the satisfaction of needs. As against this, the circulation of money as capital is an end in itself, for the valorization of value only takes place within this constantly renewed movement. The movement of capital is therefore limitless.[15]

Capital's disregard for boundaries except as barriers to be surpassed arises from this fundamental property. Every boundary in the real world is useless to capital unless it can be monetized and placed into an M–C–M' circuit, at the end of which another circuit must begin. Any delay or retardation in the flow is registered as a mortal threat. If a boundary, or a feedback process, or an ecological warning signal, is produced by one investment cycle, this becomes the starting point for another. It is even a bit misleading to talk of boundaries as merely barriers. That they are, inasmuch as capital needs to keep in motion and so must refuse all boundedness. But the barrier-boundary is also the point of investment, commodification and exchange. Therefore capital needs and seeks barrier-boundaries as sites of growth. It is like the oyster's building of a pearl about a grain of sand, but where the life-activity of mollusks and other creatures who

Capital

45

live in ecosystems is defined by exquisite internal regulation, capital's growing is like a reckless addiction, which tends to possess individuals in direct proportion to their position in the capitalist command structure. Of course, a degree of prudent calculation is *de rigueur* as well (see next chapter). But this is not internal to the process of accumulation; it is rather applied from without, as a way of enabling the passion. Thus all reforms are installed to permit growth to proceed unchecked.

In case anyone should doubt this enthrallment, consider the following, drawn from the early part of 1997, a moment of heady expansion for the world-system. This news was greeted as though a sign of the Second Coming. In a major article in the *Wall Street Journal* of March 13, 1997, the author, G. Pascal Zachary, sampled the opinion of experts from the highest levels of the economic system, and found them unanimous in declaring permanent victory for capital on a global scale (the only exception was the doubting George Soros, who thought the boom only "may last a century"). "The positive side is spectacular," said Harvard economist Jeffrey Sachs; while Domingo Cavallo, architect of Argentina's neoliberal restructuring (soon to collapse and nearly destroy its economy) added, "We've entered a golden age." The phrase, "golden age," also expressed the sentiments of the new UN General Secretary Kofi Annan;[16] while Joseph Stiglitz, at the time the World Bank's chief economist – though soon to resign, and widely considered these days a voice of reason among economists – added that with a "reproducible" world growth rate of 4 percent predicted over the next twenty years, "economic growth will reach historic levels that will, in turn, open up a new frontier for industrialized countries."

In the same newspaper of April 28, Renato Ruggiero, then director of the World Trade Organization, gave his perspective to the good news. World trade is what has brought us this blessing, increasing by a factor of fifteen in the last four decades (and up to twenty at this writing, a decade later). Simple algebra gives a clearer notion of the wonder of 4 percent growth over two decades, by translating it into a *doubling* of the production of goods and services. Around 2020, then, roughly two of every-thing produced in 2000 will be produced: twice as many cars, twice as many jet planes, twice as much insecticide, twice as much material wealth in China and India. All this, according to the WTO leader, because of trade (the "open economies" grew annually by an average of 4.5 percent between 1970 and 1989; the "closed" ones, only by 0.7 percent – and now there are scarcely any closed economies remaining), and open markets for capital; and it makes the US multinational corporations "almost giddy." Boeing, for example, looked forward to $1.1 trillion being spent to double the size of the jet fleet in the next twenty years, three-quarters of this coming from abroad. Four times as many escalators were being built in China as in the US; meanwhile the world was experiencing such an expansion of consumerism that, to take but one example, Citicorp, starting from scratch in 1990, had 7 million credit card holders in Asia and 2 million in Latin America by 1997. "The potential exists for positive surprises that would drive growth even faster, such as massive sales of govern-ment assets. 'On privatization, we've just scratched the surface,' said Shaukat Aziz, Citicorp's chief planning officer."

Recall: in 1970, only three decades in the span of time, but an eternity so far as capital is concerned, the notion of "limits to growth" seized the world elites, or at least the significant fraction of them who put forth the report of the same name under the authorship of the "Club of Rome." In little more than a genera-tion, then, the notion of containing "growth," which is to say, reining in capital, had been effectively driven from the collective mind of the ruling class.

Fatal carbon trading

With respect to global warming, arguably the supreme in-stance of the ecological crisis, we now find a gathering realization of just how deadly the prospects are, and correspondingly, a flurry of concern from ruling quarters. But the chaotic world-system keeps the response lagging far behind the pace of events, while the system-logic of capital makes even those proposals that see

Capital

47

the light of day guaranteed to fail. This is, unfortunately, as it has to be, since global warming is an objective reminder that it is either the end of capitalism or the end of the world. For it is "growth" itself, that is, the capital-driven expansion of economic product, that effectively drives this process with its dire and growing implications.[17] Thus during the stewardship of Al Gore as Vice-President, from 1992 to 2001, annual emissions of carbon in the US steadily rose by 13 percent, from 1,388 to 1,569 million metric tons, for the elementary reason that these were years of strong economic growth. By contrast, during the stagnant years of 1970 to 1982, carbon emissions levels were flat. Roughly 1,160 million metric tons marked the beginning as well as the end of this period, which witnessed the turning point of capital into its neoliberal mode of maximized exploitation.[18] Capital got what it wanted, and the planet got intractable global warming. Now that is a truly inconvenient truth.

Set aside for the moment the efforts by key corporations to obfuscate or delay the inevitable findings.[19] Or the crude efforts by the greatest offender, the United States under Bush the Lesser, to drag its heels, or those of China and India, seized by the tigers of accumulation, to stand outside the agreements. Look only at what is considered the *ultima Thule* of climate regulation, the Kyoto Protocols, passed later in 1997 in the wake of the foolishness described above about the sanctity of growth; and ponder the fact that it is the purpose of this regime to turn over the control of global warming to none other than the capitalist class.

Fantastically complex in design and virtually impossible to implement, Kyoto proceeds on a two-tiered front: to create new markets for trading credits to pollute among the industrial powers, and to create schemes – the "Clean Development Mechanisms" – in the South that would offset carbon emissions by building projects, like tree farms, whose goal is the sequestration of carbon. This immense superstructure, with its ramifications all over the world, rests on two guiding assumptions: *give the corporate sector and the capitalist state the leading role in containing global warming; and do so by making the control of atmospheric carbon the site of new markets and new nodes of accumulation.* These are two sides of the same coin: *to keep capital in control of a process that would otherwise by its inherent logic bring it down; and in so doing, make money out of reducing emissions.*

The defects of this mammoth blunder are myriad. The scheme is inherently incoherent, for it entails innumerable points that simply cannot be measured or compared. This is essentially because it tries to evade the point of a rational policy, which would be to keep the carbon in the ground in the first place – in other words, one that would put limits on capital. In so doing, Kyoto offers opportunities for swindling of all kinds. It is intrinsically disruptive of the periphery and the South as a whole, and of course all the people within it, especially the women who stand to be displaced by the various crackpot schemes for sequestration. Already this latest version of imperial extension has forced substantial numbers of peasants into the teeming metropolises that blight the world, providing a great many unwilling recruits for the sex industries.

Finally, and most revealing, the scheme will fail precisely insofar as it succeeds – for the money that is to be made as a bribe to get corporate cooperation, will of course not be placed in anybody's mattress. It will enter the great circuits of capital and because it cannot sit still lest it become what Marx called a mere hoard, press for discharge through the route of investment. The wealth that will be created through such measures enters hands that know only how to use it to make more money. Will it be the development of new golf courses? Will it be the expansion of air travel? (In the fall of 2006, the UK heard both the necessity of bringing carbon emissions down and the necessity of tripling the already obscene amount of air traffic by 2025.) Who knows? Nor is that the point, since there is no immediate connection between capital accumulation and ecological breakdown. The mediation is given rather through the never-ending pressure for "growth" at all costs, that is, growth which is cancerous and intrinsically ecodestructive through means we have begun to outline, and which inevitably drags greater swathes of the global ecology into its maw.[20]

Global warming really puts capital in the dock, therefore, and it is here that those committed to the survival of a worthwhile life and not to accumulation must take their stand. It is the point where those with eyes to see can tell that unless the entire system built on ceaseless expansion of economic product is transformed – and with it, the fatal addiction to hydrocarbon energy deposited eons ago in the earth – we have no decent chances of survival. A major complication, however, is that the perception of this necessity must be carried out within the precincts of capitalist society itself – the form of social existence built for the accumulation of capital. That is indeed quite a rub.

4 | Capitalism

Capital's responsibility for the ecological crisis can be shown empirically, by tracking down ecosystemic breakdowns to the actions of corporations and/or governmental agencies under the influence of capital's force field. Or it can be deduced from the combined tendencies to degrade conditions of production (the Second Contradiction), on the one hand, and, on the other, the cancerous imperative to expand. Though the Second Contradiction may be offset in individual circumstances by recycling, pollution control, the trading of credits and the like, the imperative to expand continually erodes the edges of ecologies along an ever-lengthening perimeter, overwhelming or displacing recuperative efforts, and accelerating a cascade of destabilization. On occasion, the force of capital expansion can be seen directly – as when President George W. Bush abruptly reversed his pledge to trim emissions of CO_2 in March 2001, the day after the stock market went into free-fall and in the context of a gathering crisis of accumulation. More broadly, it operates through a host of intermediaries embedded within the gigantic machine for accumulation that is capitalist society.

We need to take a closer look at how this society works on the ground. Too much is at stake to close the argument with a demonstration of abstract laws. Capital is no automatic mechanism, and the laws it obeys, being mediated by consciousness, are no more than tendencies. When we say "capital does this" or that, we mean that certain human actions are carried out according to the logic of capital. It behooves us to learn, then, as much as we can about just what these actions are and how they can be changed.

Capital originates with the exploitation of labor, and takes shape as this is subjected to the peculiar forces of money. Its nucleus is the abstraction of human transformative power into

51

labor-power for sale on the market. The nascent capitalist economy was fostered by the feudal state, then took over that state (often through revolution), centering it about capital accumulation. With this, the capitalist mode of production was installed as such – after which capital began to convert society into its image and created the conditions for the ecological crisis. The giant corporations we rightly identify as ecological destroyers are not the whole of capital, but only its prime economic instruments. Capital acts through the corporations, therefore, but also across society and within the human spirit.

Broadly speaking, this has taken place in three dimensions – existentially, temporally, and institutionally. In other words, people increasingly live their lives under the terms of capital; as they do so, the temporal pace of their life accelerates; finally, they live in a world where institutions are in place to secure this across an ever-expanding terrain: the world of *globalization*. In this way a society, and a whole way of being, are created that are hostile to the integrity of ecosystems.

The penetration of life-worlds

The capitalist world is a colossal apparatus of production, distribution, and sales, perfused with commodities. The average Wal-Mart stocks 100,000 separate items (with 600,000 available through its website) and as a drive through America bitterly confirms, Wal-Marts – some 2,500 as of early 2000, with 100 million shoppers a week – spring up everywhere along the roadsides like gigantic toadstools, destroying the integrity of towns and feeding on their decay.[1] By 2006, this creature was spreading across the globe, and plans were announced for building some 300 Wal-Marts in China. There is much more to this than the peddling of mere objects. As capital penetrates society, and as a condition for capital to penetrate society, the entire structure of life is altered.

Each creature inhabits a "life-world," that portion of the universe which is dwelt-in, or experienced.[2] The life-world is, so to speak, what an ecosystem looks like from the standpoint of individual beings within it. The use-values that represent the utility of commodities are inserted into life-worlds, the point of insertion being registered subjectively as a want or desire, and objectively as a set of needs. As capital penetrates life-worlds, it alters them in ways that foster its accumulation, chiefly by introducing a sense of dissatisfaction or lack – so that it can truly be said that happiness is forbidden under capitalism, being replaced by sensation and craving. In this way, children develop such a craving for caffeine-laced, sugar-loaded, or artificially sweetened soft drinks that it may be said that they positively *need* them (in that their behavior disintegrates without such intake); or grown-ups develop a similar need for giant sports-utility vehicles, or find gas-driven leaf-blowers indispensable for the conduct of life; or are shaped to take life passively from the TV screen, or see the shopping malls and their endless parking lots as the "natural" setting of society.

Note a twofold alteration. The commodities so introduced, say, the SUVs, are both ecodestructive and profitable; and the people who use and desire them are, because of their changed needs, themselves changed in an "anti-ecological" direction, that is, they see capitalist life as ordained by nature, and become complicit in the ecological crisis and unable to take action against it. In human ecology, "nature" is first of all a word signifying many things and relationships. Nature is what is past and there before us, it surrounds us, immense, dumb, and uncaring, an awesome or debased Other, infinitely malleable. Capital – nature's actual enemy – plays upon these meanings with virtuosic skill. Its ideologues tell us that capitalism is true to human nature, ignoring how people are indoctrinated to play their assigned roles in accumulation. At the same time, nature is to be completely overcome, consumed as resources, endlessly reworked even in its finest structures, like nanotubes and the DNA awaiting the sorcerers' biotechnology. Bodies are cyborgs, bionic, continuously remade. Everything is to be torn up so that accumulation can proceed. Hence capital's relentlessly forward-looking attitude, and its iron lock on the logic of modernity.

I first became aware of this before I had any coherent realization of what capital meant, as a medical student on a tropical
medicine elective taken in 1961 in the country of Suriname,
freshly broken from Dutch colonialism yet very much still in
the Western orbit.[3] The experience entailed a range of exposures,
to the capital city, Paramaribo, to smaller outlying towns, and,
finally, into the great equatorial rain forest for a three-week trip
by dugout canoe escorted by native guides. I had the chance
to see at first-hand the tribal way of life in an as-yet relatively
preserved rain forest ecosystem, and also something of Third
World urbanization. The reader will not be surprised to learn
of my preference for the former and repulsion from the latter. I
had become subject to an old Western desire: what Melville or
Humboldt must have felt when they encountered lands such as
these. I travelled enthralled by the natural grandeur, and equally
by the vibrant, dignified cultures I encountered along the river
bank, the villages bright and clean, and brilliantly decorated with
indigenous art. All of life was ceremonial, suffused with music
and dance, festive and, so it seemed, whole. One could have called
the riverine village an integral human ecosystem were the term
in circulation in 1961. By comparison, the dusty and dreary town,
under sway of the aluminum company, with barracks for homes,
and the White Man's culture at every turn, was as alienating a
spot as I had ever seen. It was appalling in itself, and especially
appalling was the evident attraction of this dependent culture to
the youth of the villages along the river. Though by our terms they
had little, there was no sign of malnutrition or poverty as such
in the village, yet the youth would leave as soon as they could.
The lure of cash for work, the lure of Coca-Cola, the lure of the
city beyond the small town – essentially, the lure of capital – all
this proved compelling.

My stay was too brief, and my powers of observation too weak,
for more than speculation as to what had destabilized the indigenous people of Suriname in 1961. Typically, however, what
breaks up the life-world of tribal society is some encroachment
upon the land. With the productive foundation of society inter-

rupted, a complex and disintegrative chain of events is set in motion. As old ways no longer make sense, a kind of desire is set loose; and as this is now relatively shapeless and boundless, the virus of capital, with its promise of limitless wealth and godlike transformation, is able to take hold. This is generally accompanied by the mass-cultural invasion that encodes capital's logos in the form of commodities. Once "Coca-Cola, the real thing," replaces traditional reality, the internal colonization that perfects the takeover of peripheral societies is well under way.

Expanding capitalism, like the expanding Catholicism of an earlier conquest, does not so much impose its ways *tout court* as meet the colonized life-worlds halfway. The actual result, then, is generally syncretic, with a considerable persistence of indigenous forms. *Aficionados* of the postmodern are generally pleased with this, which they see as an affirmation of "resistance," "diversity," and the like. But they can be no more pleased than capital, which celebrates diversity as a source of new use-values.

The McDonald's corporation, with some 26,996 outlets in 119 countries as of the year 2000, offers a particularly robust example of capital's global penetration.[4] Since 1955, McDonald's has been a pioneer in the industrialization of eating through conversion of the ritualized event of the meal into "fast food." One impulse to this is the overproduction wrought by capital's endless desire to use technology to squeeze more surplus value from its workers. With an excess of food, its price drops and new ways must be found to increase mass consumption if the value embedded in the commodity is to be realized. Hence fast food and the indoctrination into industrialized eating. As old ways fail to make sense under the assault of capitalist culture, new and syncretic desires, needs, and commodities are inserted. Rather than simply push beefburgers to its growing clientele in Asia and Latin America, McDonald's offers them Vegetable McNuggets in India, Teriyaki Burgers in Japan, McHuevos in Uruguay, etc. What looks superficially like the persistence of cultural codes, is also, and more profoundly, a kind of Trojan Horse, allowing capital a colonizing access to tradition, fraying the indigenous cultural forms, and weakening resistance to the culture of beef. Every trick of the trade is pressed into action – clowns, children's games, playgrounds, an advertising budget second to none. Capital gets its commodities, and the people get an alien community to further break up life-worlds and invent new desires and needs.

Capital's invasion takes place across an ecosystemic manifold encompassing both culture and nature, with points of commodity formation arising everywhere. From this standpoint it is artificial to distinguish the symbolic and material aspects of events – though certain material effects of McDonaldization deserve mention. For example, since McDonald's first planted its flag in Hong Kong, twenty-five of its top fifty outlets around the world were located there in 2000, the average weight of a local teenager had risen 13 percent, and the age of girls at menarche had dropped to twelve, compared to seventeen in mainland China. Hong Kong now had the second highest childhood cholesterol levels in the world, after Finland. Meanwhile, in the twenty-eight years since McDonald's entered Japan, its 2,000 outlets (as of 1997) controlled 60 percent of the hamburger market and the per capita fat intake tripled.[5] These effects parallel those in America and across the world, which has seen an unprecedented increase in both obesity and hunger, to the point where the numbers of overweight and starving people are roughly equivalent.[6] This is, to repeat, the *normal* working of the system, highly praised and emulated, and not the result of accidents like Bhopal. Such figures do not enter the ordinary "environmental" appraisals, but they are as much part of the ecological crisis as pollution with dioxin (whose bodily accumulation, it may be added, is proportional to how much fat is in the diet).

A similar process is played out in the sphere of gender. As ecosystems are broken up and rearranged under capitalism, a fraction of women in metropolitan regions attain considerable autonomy and opportunity, while conditions for the world's majority sharply deteriorate. This is evident in the high percentage of women in sweatshops around the world (where fine motor skills and patriarchally imposed docility are valued); the burgeoning sex trade industries, where numberless women have now, in the era of free trade, become actual slaves (as have innumerable others in the sweatshops); as well as the general rise of rape and spousal abuse as concomitants of a disintegrating social order, so far gone that a recent UNICEF report indicates that nearly half the world's women come under attack by those closest to them.[7] This was not at all the case in precapitalist societies.

As capital penetrates, its disintegrating effects on ecologies are shown most dramatically at the boundaries. That is why instruments like the North American Free Trade Agreement (NAFTA) have been such disasters for the towns along the US–Mexican border. The environmental pollution has been well documented,[8] but that affecting human ecosystems, especially those incorporating gender, are less well known, and can be illustrated by an example from one of the largest cities along the border.

The city of Juárez, Mexico, across from El Paso, seems simply tossed over the desert. There shouldn't be concentrations of people in these places, and wouldn't, were they not so close to the largest markets on earth. But the people arrive, wave after wave from the South, living in shanty-towns, or *colonias*, and looking to make a living in the *maquiladoras*, or assembly factories set up to take advantage of the opportunities provided by NAFTA. Many of the workers are young, seventeen and under, and most are women – some 60 percent of the 170,000 *maquiladora* workers in Juárez earn $20–25 for a six-day week where the cost of living is at least 90 percent that of the United States, and the turnover rate is over 100 percent a year.

A fair guess says 2 million people inhabit Juárez, great numbers subsisting in cardboard or corrugated metal shacks, on the 1,100 miles of dirt road within the city, with hijacked electricity, water bought from trucks and no sewers – often within feet of the other country from which the managers of their *maquiladoras* drive over in their Lexuses each morning. Frederick Engels, whose documentation of the working class of Manchester, England, in 1844, created the first awareness of proletarian life under industrial capitalism, would recognize the poverty of Juárez, for all

Capitalism

the differences in terrain, weather, and culture. However, Engels would certainly be startled by the degree of rootlessness in the city – even though rootlessness was also a feature of the Manchester workers – as well as by its violence – though violence, too, was certainly a feature of mid-nineteenth-century Manchester, as it would be in any rapidly transforming society.

Juárez, though, is something else. In the words of a local vendor: "Even the devil is scared of living here." As Charles Bowden puts it in his powerful witness to hell on the border:

> Juárez is different [from other, equivalently impoverished places] in a way that tables of wages and economic studies cannot capture: in Juárez you cannot sustain hope ... We tell ourselves that there are gangs and murders in American [sic] cities. This is true, but it does not deal with the reality of Juárez. We are not talking about darkness on the edge of town or a bad neighborhood. We are talking about an entire city woven out of violence.[9]

The fabric is made from certain elements unknown to nineteenth-century capitalist society: decay of religion, narco-trafficking, promiscuously available assault weapons, gangs (an estimated 250 in Juárez) arising from society's breakup and become a law unto themselves, along with the breakup of moral systems that comes from having a superpower suck a society's blood with instruments like NAFTA and the *maquiladora*, all played upon by capital's ever-present culture of commodified desire and eroticism. There is a nihilism that brings out the predatory remorseless killing potential in human beings, bred in conditions of extreme alienation such as appears in the surging world megacities – Lagos, Nairobi, Mumbai, Djakarta, and Manila – where those tossed up by globalized capital try to reconstruct life in appalling circumstances.

Just as the population of Juárez is unknown, so is the murder rate, though it is generally agreed to have at least doubled since the pre-NAFTA year of 1991. Hundreds of people simply disappear each year, but since many are just passing through and known to no one, their fate cannot be determined. Scores of others just show up as unidentifiable, badly decomposed corpses in dumpsters, or strewn about the desert. The majority of the corpses are of adolescent girls showing signs of rape and sexual mutilation. A mass sex murderer is sought; periodically, some gang or gangster is fingered and arrested – and then the finding of corpses resumes.

Debbie Nathan has identified a pattern to the killings. The wages paid by *maquiladoras* provide more than subsistence; they are also solvents through which traditional bonds of family and community break up. When these bonds patriarchally repress women, working away from home in a factory can be experienced as liberating. It is like the opera, *Carmen*, a male fantasy of the workplace sexpot, here readily seized upon by powerless young women. The teenage *maquiladora* workers have been raised on a cultural diet of *telenovelas* and *fotonovelas*, endless variations on the theme of the poor but worthy girl found by a rich and older man, and who, after the necessary travail, wins him. In the *maquiladoras*, the elements of this narrative are laid out and fully erotized. Often dressed to the nines under their chaste smocks, female workers vie for the attentions of the male supervisors, who flirt with them, ask them for dates, and set going a dense network of intrigue. The process is continued into beauty contests and swimsuit competitions that transform the dreary workplace into a fairyland of romantic fulfillment.

The fantasy extends into the hours after work. In the sexually charged nightstrips to which would-be Carmens repair after dark, opportunities abound for selling the only thing of value they possess besides labor power. Formal and informal prostitution flourishes alongside, or in place of, factory employment. To further sweeten the pot, the clubs advertise contests like "Most Daring Bra," or "Wet String Bikini," with prizes that generally exceed a week's salary. In these ways, hapless women may join up with their executioners, themselves suitably positioned by the macho barbarism set going in places like Juárez, whose murder rate becomes a grim index of capitalist nihilism.[10] Today, some ten years after these stories broke, the Juárez murders of young women continue and remain unsolved.

Speed-up, or the ever-decreasing circulation time of capital

The relentless expansion of capital occurs primarily in terms of *time*, whose equivalence to money is much more than metaphoric. This is shown vividly in the case of "fast food," whose penetration we have already observed. It stands to reason that what is "fast" about this food applies not just to its consumption, but also to the production process, as we see from a lead article, published in 2000 in the *Wall Street Journal*:

> "HimayItakeyourorderplease?" says the drive-through-greeter at Wendy's Old-Fashioned [sic] Hamburgers. This greeting takes only one second – a triumphant two seconds faster than is suggested in Wendy's guidelines – and the speed of it was clocked by a high-tech timer installed this January. In just three months, the timer – which measures nearly every aspect of drive-through performance – helped knock eight seconds off the average takeout delivery time at this restaurant. But manager Ryan Tomney wants more. "Every second," he says, "is business lost."

Wendy's, whose ads promote the avuncular image of Dave Thomas as the kindly, slow-moving, and somewhat befuddled boss, is the fastest of the fast-food chains ("Most chains would sell their first-born to get that speed," says a researcher). Its success translates into augmented profit at a time when the spatial expansion of these emporiums is running out of room: for every six seconds saved at the drive-through, sales increase by 1 percent. The enhanced profitability means an emphasis on drive-through windows (growing three times as rapidly as on-premise sales), which in turn reinforces the culture of automobilia (see below) while fostering waste of all sorts. Then there are the effects on those incidentals, human beings:

> The attempt to turn drive through into a science inevitably encounters two wild-cards: employees and customers. Manage-

ment at big chains insist that employees like the timer because it turns their work into a game – can I make 300 consecutive sandwiches in less than seven seconds each? But working in the new world of sensors and alarms isn't always fun.

Indeed. Mr Tomney wants to get the order fulfillment time down to 90 seconds from the current industry-leading 150 seconds. "The new timer will help. It emits a series of loud beeps every time an order isn't filled within 125 seconds." This does tend to take away some of the fun of working for fast food (an industry that averages as much as 200 percent turnover annually).

Certainly, the seven drive-through employees demonstrate incredible concentration and effort during a recent lunch hour. The griller keeps 25 square burgers sizzling on the grill ("Not enough," Mr Tomney says) and, within five seconds of a customer's order, places one on a bun. Once the meat hits the bun, the griller hands off to the sandwich makers, who have no more than seven seconds to complete each customized creation.

Watching the operation, Mr Tomney looks for ways to save time. The bun grabber retrieves buns from the warmer the instant she hears a customer order through her headset. But watching her wait for a customer order, Mr Tomney [notices something]. Her hands aren't positioned.

"Two hands on the bun-warmer door as the order is being placed, just like you're taking the frisk position," her manager demonstrates, hands against the wall, legs slightly spread.[11]

A nicely chosen image, one must admit, for this vignette of today's go-go society.

As we observed above, the exponential growth of capital is paralleled by the exponential rate of technological change, from the mechanical technologies of the early industrial period, to the electronic technologies (like the above timer) of the ill-termed "information age," on to the biotechnologies and nanotechnologies of the century now underway.[12] The commodities of this world are to capital only deposits of value, which will not be freed unless those goods are circulated, exchanged for money, and consumed, i.e. realized. For capital to "grow," then, its realization must speed up; and this routinely means a diminution of its circulation time, from the original investment at the point of production, to the speed up – i.e. "productivity" – of workers, to its release for the next cycle at the point of consumption.

The significance of time for capital is closely tied to its rupture from nature. Exchange-value and money have no natural ground; they can only be the abstraction of what enables one thing to be made equivalent to another, that is, of equivalences of ideas. Applied to labor, this means there is only one standard by means of which different human labors can be compared in monetary terms, namely, the time expended in production. Between this function and the equally important one of regulating its complex, technically coordinated productive apparatus, capitalism becomes the time-obsessed society. It could never have come to exist without profound shifts in subjectively experienced temporality, from a world regulated by the complex and interrelated temporalities of ecosystems to one in which a single, uniform and linear standard is imposed upon reality and comes to rule it.[13] The desynchronization between natural time and workplace time devolves, therefore, into a disarticulation of human being and nature, and is foundational for capital's efficient causation of the ecological crisis. We would say that capital *binds time*, yoking linear temporality and social control into a regime supervised by clocks and their personifications like Wendy's Mr Tomney.[14] As Marx put it in a poignant lament:

> If the mere quantity of labour functions as a measure of value regardless of quality ... It presupposes that labour has become equalized by the subordination of man to the machine or by the extreme division of labour; that men are effaced by their labour; that the pendulum of the clock has become as accurate a measure of the relative activity of two workers as it is of the speed of two locomotives. Therefore we should not say that one man's hour is worth another man's hour, but rather that one man

during an hour is worth just as much as another man during an hour. Time is everything, man is nothing; he is at the most, time's carcase. Quality no longer matters. Quantity alone decides everything; hour for hour, day for day.[15]

Bound time signifies life lived compulsively, estranged from natural cycles and indifferent to ecosystems under assault. Its acceleration is played out across many frontiers.

1. Intensification of the sales mentality, as everything, including the self, is reduced to commodity-form. Along with this, contempt for truth spreads throughout society. Lying is embedded in the pressure toward profitability, which depends upon convincing someone to buy something they don't really need at a price most advantageous to the seller. I recall once idly watching C-Span during the course of a Congressional hearing on some issue between telephone and cable-TV companies. One of the testifiers was asked what he did during the work day. The reasons for this question escape me, but the candor of his answer was unforgettable: "Oh, the same thing we always do," was the reply, "just hustling customers." No one took notice; why should they? The man was only expressing the logic of the system. Within capital's order, where advertising lies so blatantly that it has to make fun of itself and turn corruption into a joke, to question the hustling of customers is like questioning the need to breathe. The Budweiser corporation seems to have done the most with this, especially with their "Lite" beer, which turns the moral universe of alcoholism into a selling point, as in commercials where the lush professes "I love you, man" to his father, brothers, girlfriend of the moment – anything to get the drink – an exceptionally weak and tasteless concoction, it may be added.

The class system of capital conduces to endless permutations of deceit in order to conceal its elementary injustice. As persons become personnel, synthetic bonds replace the organic ones of traditional society. The ethos here is "managerial" and the techniques manipulative, a sign of our times backed by a vast apparatus for the engineering of human relations. As a recent

Capitalism

article by one such technician put it in the headline, "Show Humanity When You Show Employees the Door." The point is that companies should "reinforce their cultures and maintain trust even during cutbacks." This self-evident piece of hypocrisy is no problem for the managerial mind.[16] It goes without saying that people can be made to accept this morality – were this not the case, rebellion would have broken out long ago. Managerial science not only builds in the artifice of humanity even as it reduces workers to disposable things – it drills the workers to treat customers in the same way, training them to put on happy faces, to make prolonged eye contact, and to speak to each and every customer. This lesson, also, most workers internalize only too well. As one Safeway employee said: "It is just a pride that they have instilled in us that we should treat everybody like we would like to be treated. We talk about being positive all the time. We have classes on wiping out negativity and [having] enthusiasm."[17] Classes in enthusiasm! Not just classes at the job, it might be added: the classes in school do the same, as do the churches and of course, the television and movie screens.

2. In the speeding up of buying and selling, leading to the reduced utilization time of commodities, or, to put a more eco-logically evocative term to it, the systemic production of waste, that is, the throwaway society.[18] Among those wasted, we would have to give first place to human beings. Whereas in traditional society virtue is accorded to all phases of the life-cycle, and in-cludes the wisdom of the old, under capitalism, speed-up affects not only lives, but life itself. In this respect, an article from 2000 in *New York* magazine, titled "Washed up at 35," was revealing. The subtitle went on to ask: "Haven't made it yet? Feeling paranoid about the hyperambitious 23-year-old planning his IPO in the next office?" "'They're all worried about growing old,' says an 'anti-aging specialist' physician about his corporate clientele. 'They say that companies now demand a very youthful image, and if they can't fit in, they're not going to get the promotion. They might not even keep their job. We're talking about people in their late twenties.'" In sum, "youth has become an increasingly

valuable commodity." Now, of course, this has long been the case for capitalism, with its cult of the new and its denial of aging and death. But it is important to note that the trend accelerates, along with capital itself. As a thirty-one-year old tycoon puts it: "I only have three years left … three years before I burn out … It's a race; things are moving five, ten times faster than they used to . . . you have this very short window, if you are going to brand yourself" – the assumption being that becoming a "brand" is what life should be all about.[19]

3. Associated with the compression of time, we see a homogenization and compression of space; and with time and space so prepared, capital's penetration of all aspects of the life-world of individuals and communities accelerates.[20] This is not merely a function of population pressure, as its most remarkable feature is the growth of surveillance and behavior control. The totally administered society is the *telos* of capital, and engrained in its acceleration.

4. With the relentless speed-up afforded by advances in information technology, the boundary between work and domesticity is fast disappearing, along with that between body and machine. In this Brave New World, microcomputers and cell phones become bodily appendages forging semi-permanent linkages between workers and the productive system. It used to be that home was the "haven in a heartless world"; now that polarity is, if not reversed, largely erased: the archetypal person of the near future is entirely absorbed, day and night, into a space–time continuum for the reproduction of capital.

5. The relentlessly increasing rate of capital turnover devolves into an ever-more harried, crowded, and frantic pace of existence. Combined with the financial pressures of living the consumerist life, ordinary people have to work more and more to stay afloat. The specter of personal indebtedness becomes the fifth Horseman of the Apocalypse – it being said that the average worker is only two paychecks away from losing home and car. More and more, people scramble, becoming increasingly obsessed with money, and becoming slaves to the system. The vaunted capitalist

65

economy, with its endless opportunity, thus becomes a limitless sink for absorbing life-worlds into itself.

Not surprisingly, this condition is celebrated by the propaganda apparatus: how else could people be made to bear it? Here is a somewhat extended and delirious, but nonetheless paradigmatic specimen taken from the advertising pages of the major media, a full-page ad in the *New York Times* of June 26, 1996 (A20), taken out by the American Express Company. The ad is entirely given over to the following text, which sprawls over the page:

> *Whoever you are, whatever you're doing, we're here to help you* plan your children's education. And show you how you can still afford to retire when they get into college. We're here to help you negotiate a second mortgage, afford a second car or go on a second honeymoon. We're here to help you choose a mutual fund, a pension plan and a savings scheme. We're here to help you prepare your taxes. We're here to help you turn your idea into a business. We're here to help you turn your business trip into a vacation. We're here to help you with a few suggestions on where to go. We're here to help you with lawyers, accountants, doctors and bankers. We're here to help you with travel agents, theatrical agents and car rental agents. We're here to help you if you smash your rental car or if you smash someone else's. We're here to help you arrange a weekend in Paris for an anniversary. We're here to help you find the most romantic bistro, the most comfortable hotel. We're here to help you change your dollars into francs, your francs into sterling, your sterling into lira and your lira into any currency in the world and back again. We're here to help you climb the Odessa Steppes [sic] and look out from the Leaning Tower of Pisa. We're here to help you with visas, passports and other local customs. We're here to help you if your husband, your wife or your partner falls ill while abroad. We're here to help you cut your costs when you need to fill up on gas. We're here to help you splurge when you want to. We're here to help you save when you don't. We're here to help you ease your workload when it all gets too much. We're here to help

you see the world. And we're here to help you pay for a change of clothes if an airline loses your baggage. We're here to help you buy a Mexican sombrero, an Indian topi or one of those Australian hats with all the corks on it. We're here to help you if someone steals your Travelers Cheques. We're here to help you see the stars in Hollywood and the moonlight over San Francisco Bay. We're here to help you see Shakespeare in the park, Mozart in the open air and basketball at the Garden. We're here to help you get seats for football, for baseball, or for the charity ball. We're here to help you help the homeless. We're here to help you settle the bill on a credit card, a charge card or a combination of them both. We're here to help you spread your payments over time or clear a bill all at once. We're even here to help you pay from cyberspace. We're here to help you see your favorite rock group. And go again the next night. And the next. And the next. We're here to help you take up a new hobby or take out an old flame. We're here to help you save for a deposit on a new house. We're here to help you renovate an old one. We're here to help you understand your 401k and perhaps show you ways to save $401K. We're here to help you plan your future. We're here to help you arrange a trip down memory lane. We're here to help you say, "What the heck!" We're here to help you when you want to say, "Enough's enough." We're here to help you play more golf, more tennis, more of what you like. We're here to help you do less paperwork, less work and just plain less. We're here to help you spend more time away with your kids. We're here to help you spend more time away from everyone else's. We're here to recognize a foreign street sign, speak a foreign language and understand a foreign currency. We're here to help you out of a little local difficulty. We're here to help you whether you want to study Pavlov's dog or Schrödinger's cat. We're here to help you retire in some comfort. We're here to help you with cash at over 118,000 ATMs worldwide if you're caught short. We're here to help you at over 1700 Travel Service Offices worldwide. We're here to help you settle the bill at millions of restaurants, stores and hotels. We're here to help you 24 hours a day, seven days a week, 365 days a year. We're here to help you in every town, in every city, in every country all over the world. We're here to help you take advantage of the moment and help you plan for the next. We're here to help you do what you like, wherever you like, whenever you like. We're here to help you see more, escape more, learn more, find more and save more. We're here to help you *do more*.

The ad exhales the seemingly effortless, magical accumulation of the giddy epoch of speculative intoxication, and it does so by introducing a new demiurge: the omnipotent, omniscient financial corporation. The consumer just sits back and lets American Express (= money = finance capital = capital itself) magically provide all in interminable profusion. That such a bizarre idea should arise is a manifestation of the real yet spectral power of finance. With literally trillions of dollars flitting electronically each day through capital markets, with great fortunes made through manipulation of nothing more than numbers, with billions moving each day through gambling operations, including the supreme gamble of the stock markets, the whole world of capital takes on the character of a casino, in which the linkage between effort and outcome is ruptured, to be replaced by what is readily experienced as mere chance. It is a world in which the very materiality of existence can seem an inconvenient afterthought.

The handmaidens of chance are illusion and magic. That is why Las Vegas, rising inorganically from the desert in a jumbled mass of simulacra, becomes the city of our time. Once the province of the Mob, Vegas increasingly becomes Disneyfied into a spectacular site of fun for the whole family. There is the Sphinx and the Temple of Luxor, there is a building shaped like a bottle of Coca-Cola, here is Manhattan Island, with the stock exchange, the Empire State Building, the Brooklyn Bridge, even a replication of the great reading room of the Public Library. All is sign, representation, flows of value lighting up one form, now another, a city like a pinball machine.

In casino capitalism the operative word is "more," and augmentation expresses the accumulation process in its subjective as well as objective aspect. This signifier is nicely accentuated by American Express in its ad. The only thing left off its list of goodies is restraint. To be more exact, restraint is another item for which the omnipresent corporation can be of help: restraint itself is a commodity. Time and space are now corporate servants. Capital covers all; even "escape" is permitted so long as American Express sets the terms of escape. Thus less and more are integrated under the sign of finance. But in this calculus, less and more are not equivalent. The former, being incorporated under the sign of the dollar (for American Express – surprise! – will not do this for nothing, and if you do not pay your bill on time, they harass and fine you, then drop you like a leper and turn you over to the credit police), is subordinated to the latter, whose value consists of increasing. Less is therefore another kind of more: American Express will bring you more of less, not less of more. But more leads to still more. Thus it defines no end, only a self-reproducing expansion, the eternal growth of the capital system. A pure logic of power, insensate quantity and expansion, is offered to the sufficiently well off. The affluent get their munificent rewards, so great that the typical member of the wealthier classes lives better than any potentate in history. The others get the debris. And nature gets ruined.

The culture of advanced capital aims to turn society into addicts of commodity consumption, a condition "good for business," and correspondingly bad for ecosystems. The evil is twofold, with reckless consumption leading to pollution and waste, while the addiction to commodities builds a society unable to comprehend, much less resist, the ecological crisis. Once time is bound in capitalist production, the subtle attunement to natural rhythms necessary for an ecocentric sensibility becomes thwarted. This allows the suicidal insanity of ever-expanding accumulation to appear as natural. People with mentalities warped by the casino complex are simply not going to think in terms of limits and balances, or of the mutual recognition of all beings. This helps account for the chorus of hosannas from presumably intelligent authorities at the nightmarish prospect of a doubling of economic product in the next twenty years.

Thus capital produces wealth without end, but also poverty, insecurity, and waste, as part of its disintegration of ecosystems. As there is no single commodity (really, a vast system of commodities) more implicated in this than the automobile, we might round out this section with some thoughts about "automobilia"[21] and its related syndromes, including the newly discovered disease of Road Rage. Automobilia is a prime example of how rationality at the level of the part becomes irrationality at the level of the whole. Individually, cars are far better than a generation ago: they are safer, more reliable, more fuel efficient, longer lasting, and more comfortable. In the interior of a reasonably advanced car one encounters "all the comforts of home": luxurious adjustable seats, cell phone, splendid sound system, carefully controlled air – the whole package, as the salesman says. The interior of a car projects an image of a technological utopia, which is convenient, since so many people spend so much time inside them. Step outside the car, though, say on a busy road to fill up with gasoline, and the externalization of a disorder that more than compensates for the internalized order becomes clear. A horrendous cacophony assaults body and soul. Unlike a waterfall, even a train that organizes the human landscape, the cars just roar on; there is no pattern, no particularized, differentiated tale to be told. There is no integral ecology to it; it is just endless, consuming traffic – eons of stored sunlight converted into inertial momentum so that individuals can go their own way in capitalist liberty. And it is repeated in thousands and thousands of places, every day and night – carbon dioxide going into the air for global warming; other substances entering the chains that lead to photochemical smog or destruction of the ozone layer; fine particulate matter (think of the hundreds of millions of tires grinding down against concrete) entering lungs to help create a planetary epidemic of asthma, along with other heart and lung diseases; the above-mentioned noise adding another dimension of pollution; landscapes torn up and paved over, historically breaking down the boundary between city and country while blighting both with strip malls, thickets of garish signs (for how else can people in constant motion see where to shop?), and great swooping freeways on which we hurtle like so many corpuscles in the circulation of capital – the ensemble disintegrating, as has nothing else, the fabric of human ecology.

The ruinousness of automobilia is bound up with its absolutely crucial role in the global economy – combined, to be sure, with the ensemble of densely associated industries like oil, rubber, cement, construction, repairs, etc.; and equally, from its embeddedness in the entire landscape of lived life, indeed, the very construction of the self. Deep changes in needs accompany the growth of automobilia. If one is trapped within a stifling existence, then driving away from it, even if this is just to go round and round in traffic-clogged circles (contributing, of course, to the clogging), is experienced as a release. This is one reason it is easy for the automobilious giants to spin forth their greenwashed ads that show people blithely moving, no other car in sight, across the very landscapes they are actually wrecking, or to depict ecological advances in the production of cars that are, however rational in the particular instance, simply overwhelmed by the sheer quantity of cars produced.

Looming overcapacity hangs over the automobile industries, as it does for capitalist production in general, with the ability to make some 80 million cars a year, and but 55 million or so able to be sold. Those unrealized 25 million vehicles are a giant splinter in the soul of capitalism, and the goad to endless promotion of automobilious values. From 1970 to 2000, the population of the United States grew by some 30 percent – while the number of licensed drivers grew more than 60 percent, the number of registered vehicles nearly doubled and the total vehicle-miles driven more than doubled.[22] Notably, the miles of road added during this period has gone up but 6 percent. This figure is product of a set of hopeless choices: either perish in nightmarish traffic, or further destroy lived space with gargantuan roads (and eventually perish under even more traffic, which fills newly created highways like gas a vacuum). Even the relatively low figure of 6 percent translates into major changes in certain strategic locations. One is continually astounded, for example, by the numbers of lanes added to Los Angeles freeways (at some points, eight in either direction by my recent estimate, with additional ones now being added above the roadway).[23]

As the logic of automobilia unfolds, new levels of disintegration appear, and even people deeply acculturated into the ways of motorcars crack under the strain of contemporary vehicular life. Road rage, a new "mental illness," is one outcome, resulting directly or indirectly in some 28,000 traffic deaths a year caused by "aggressive behavior like tailgating, weaving through busy lanes, honking or screaming at other drivers, exchanges of insults and even gunfire." This figure, though provided by chief federal highway safety official, Ricardo Martinez, may be speculative; another survey, however, describes 1,500 homicides a year whose instigation is directly traffic-related. According to Leon James, a psychologist from Hawaii, "Driving and habitual road rage have become virtually inseparable. This is the age of rage mentality." James cites as contributing factors, a "tightly wound 'controlled' personality type" for whom driving provides a release from "normal, frustration filled existences" and gives rise to "fantasies of omnipotence." Observe that the personality type in question is itself an adaptation to the capitalist marketplace, while the second factor, the omnipotent release from frustration provided by driving, is a basic component of the use-value of automobiles, hammered home by car chases in movies, and the romanticization of auto advertisements. Road rage may be a mental illness, but one completely within the universe of capitalism's automobilia.[24]

Globalization, or the establishment of a planetary regime to supervise the expansionary process

The notion of globalization expresses the fact that capital's expansion, colonization, and penetration now take place on a planetary scale. From one angle this is simply the logical extension of its cancerous growth. It did not happen smoothly, though, but as the result of a severe accumulation crisis of the 1970s that signalled the end of the great post-Second World War expansion, and, with it, the end of the welfare state and the Keynesian liberal era. Under the revamped ideology of neoliberalism, capital set forth to reassert the hard core of its exploitation of labor and nature. With a political lurch to the right expressed by Thatcher, Reagan and Kohl, the system did what it could to restore "growth." This meant, among other things, granting an absolute priority to capital's boundary-busting tendency, in the course of which trade skyrocketed and the barriers to global ecological breakdown were removed even as the chorus of ideologues announced the new paradise.

Globalization is, then, both business as usual and a new level of accumulation, with new institutional forms, and, of course, new ecological as well as political implications. Capital's eternally restless, crisis-driven dynamism is bound to reach novel levels as boundaries are surpassed and recombine. The epoch of globalization reflects, then, the reaching of a certain world-wide stage on which the struggle is to be enacted, and the building of new instruments to operate on it. It is worth observing that, for all its power, the triumph of capital still has a ways to go, with considerable swathes of the world, for example, peasantries, still in the grip of traditional, precapitalist ways of production, and others engaged in the so-called "informal" economy, where the accumulation of capital can only partially take hold. The basic mission of the globalized system is to convert that rough half of the world's economy which still remains relatively outside the engine of accumulation into full, subaltern, participation: to achieve new, "lean" ways of production utilizing dispersed locations, to take over the natural resources, to consume the labor power cheaply, to keep commodities rolling so that the values embedded in them may be realized, and above all, to do whatever it takes to allow capital to move where, when, and how it wants.

The phase of globalization raises important questions as to just where the center of capitalist power resides. A common

Capitalism

view, for example, holds that corporations now rule the world, having supplanted nation-states. But while this view calls attention to some highly important issues (it helps focus the mind, for example, to realize that General Motors holds assets worth twice those of the Philippines), the conclusion does not stand up very well to examination. For one thing, corporations are as much the object of globalization as its subject. As we have seen in the instance of Bhopal, the corporation is itself moved by the gigantic force field of capital in which it is suspended, and is given life to the extent that it fosters accumulation. And for another, states play a role in the accumulation of capital which is just as fundamental as that of the corporation – only imagine what would happen if the process were entirely turned over to the latter, with no governmental presence to regulate and enforce.

So the questions really are about the changing forms of capital itself, along with the changing configurations of state power. As to the former, the epoch of globalization is in part a function of the growing importance of finance capital, i.e. capital in its money-form. Money was always closer to the heart of what capital is than anything else, and under capitalism the role of money always tends to grow faster than that of things or human beings.[25] Broadly speaking, then, globalization manifests the boundary-breaking effects of a surplus of capital-as-money confronting sluggish human and mechanical materials and striving to set them into motion on an ever-widening scale. In consequence, more pressure is felt throughout economy and society, and is translated into eco-destabilization on a world scale along the axes outlined above.

Finance capital is both more liquid and more hungry for immediate reward than any other kind, such as capital embodied in land, machines, or people. This is a property of exchangeability and reflects the fact that in its financial form, capital is much purer and closer to its essential being than in any other shape. To repeat, capital is no thing, but a relation that embeds ("invests") itself in things of one kind or another. As it achieves its money-form, then, capital comes closest to being pure relationship: it is coming into itself ... but not yet there: never there, yet always moving and dragging the world along with it. For even money has inertia, more in the early years when it was tied to material things like shells or gold, less and less as it becomes dematerialized and moved about by electronic means. Capital is eternally seeking to shed this burden; yet as it does so, becoming, in effect, less material, its effect on the material earth becomes greater. It spreads faster, farther, draws more of the world into itself, restructuring production, circulation, exchange, and consumption to accommodate its ever-growing pressure, in a logic that drives toward bringing the entire earth within the orbit of the dominant economic order.

This induces new modes of organization among existing states. It generates great regional blocs across Europe, Asia, and the Western hemisphere, and creates, so to speak, an office of Hegemon, presently occupied by the United States as the state strong enough to claim the role of global gendarme. But it also brings into existence new *trans-statal* formations to regulate the now expanded ecumene, in particular, through the supervison of trade.[26]

Capital achieves its global organization through a threefold trans-statal structure. First, trade itself achieves a scale requiring direct supervision. Second, lending institutions are needed to inject requisite funds into the dependent "periphery" so that trade and other instruments of capital can become stimulated and circulate properly. Finally, an agency is needed to police the debts and other financial irregularities that inevitably arise under this arrangement, and to keep all the parts of the gigantic machine in good working order – a financial cop to go out in advance of the flesh-and-blood, bullet-dealing police and armies. In sum: a trade organization, a global bank, and a financial enforcer – a World Trade Organization, a World Bank, and an International Monetary Fund – fused into an iron triangle of transnational accumulation, and serving the transnational bourgeoisie.[27]

There are, of course, important distinctions within this apparatus, and between different elements of the state system, just as there always are with any ruling class. The United States has largely called the shots (chiefly from the Department of the Treasury, along with the Federal Reserve Bank), and has been in essential charge since the "American Century" began with the close of the Second World War.[28] It was Richard Nixon who unilaterally took the world off the gold standard in 1971 and allowed exchange rates to float, which is to say, kept them pegged to the value of the dollar, the strongest currency. In this way the United States, which had become a debtor society thanks to imperial exertions in Vietnam, was allowed to remain so without penalty, indeed, became enabled to finance its expansion as the debtor in charge of the show. Not for it the "Structural Adjustment Programs" applied to lesser debtor nations by the IMF, that hammer which breaks down civil society and the local economy by selling off public assets, cutting back governmental expenditures and, by orienting the economy toward export, submitting peripheral societies to the WTO-sponsored regime of trade. One law for the lion and another for the ox remains in effect. So much for the simple-minded notion that globalization signifies the decline of the nation-state. *Which* nation-state, it has to be asked. The boss and enforcer, or the subaltern and provider?

In any case, trade, being a direct expression of capital's logic, conquers all. Before the abandonment of the Bretton Woods regime of fixed exchange rates in 1971, cross-border financial flows were some $70 billion a day. Thirty years later, the figure has grown more than twentyfold; while in the United States, trade has doubled its share of GDP, spurred by absolute bipartisanship of Democratic and Republican leadership. Quarrel the parties might about abortion and school vouchers; but where the free flow of capital is concerned, there is never any doubt as to what comes first.

As globalization propagates the mechanisms of accumulation around the globe, society after society is swept into the vortex of ecodestruction. Dependent and unequal development accompanied by massive debt becomes the midwife of this process. Wherever a debt is incurred, there will be pressure to discharge it by sacrificing ecological integrity. Indonesian President Suharto, a great friend of globalization, put this clearly after being slapped with a Structural Adjustment Program. No need to worry, said the amiable leader of the world's fourth largest nation, Indonesia could always exchange its forests for the money owed to the banks. The devastating effects of global debt on nations of the South[29] can be discomfiting to global capital. The scandal has led to a flurry of efforts to bring the load down, with some $50 billion in debts being retired in the year 2000. Alas, the South owed at the time about $2.3 trillion – twenty-six times as much – nor do the terms of forgiveness free them from the wheel of accumulation. As an account reported, "The IMF, the World Bank, the United States and others say that African countries must open up to the global economy – and control wasteful internal spending and inflation if debt relief is to be put to lasting use."[30] In other words: give us your forests and cheap labor by other means, and we will forgive the debt that you can't pay under any circumstances.

Because of debt's injustice, the IMF is usually considered the heavy villain in the regime of globalization. "Doctor Death," *Time Magazine* called it in 2000.[31] This is a reasonable assessment of the organization which has brought at least ninety poor nations under its spell. But the IMF, or "bad cop" of globalization, should not be singled out as the source of the problem, an impression fostered in a recent essay by Joseph Stiglitz, chief economist of the World Bank from 1996 to November 1999. We met Stiglitz, you may recall, in the last chapter, joining the chorus of world economic leaders extolling the wonders of unlimited growth. Now, however, he has become something of a whistle-blower, and caused something of a sensation by an article in the *New Republic* that confirmed all the worst suspicions as to how utterly secretive, antidemocratic, and ruthlessly attentive to short-term profitability is the IMF. Using as examples the handling of the Asian and Russian fiscal crises of 1997–99, Stiglitz left no doubt that the placing of "profits over people," as the saying has it, has caused calamities of Holocaust proportions throughout much of the world. However, he also showed no intention of calling into question the capitalist system as a whole, but would have us believe that this disaster was the fault of *bad* capitalists at the IMF and the Treasury department; more, that their sin lay in not taking the advice of the World Bank, with its superior economists and good capitalists, all of whom, it is well known, place people over profits.[32]

The fantasy is widespread that somewhere a virtuous and all-knowing capitalist can be found, a fairy prince who will rescue the mismanaged global economy. As the World Bank plays "good cop" in this scheme of things, and no doubt has some well-intentioned individuals working for it (just like any bank, or indeed, Monsanto, Chevron, etc., even the IMF or Union Carbide), many are disposed to believe that the Stiglitzes of the world can rescue us with their superior technical wisdom. When plain people go to Lourdes in search of miracle cures, the intelligentsia proclaim them superstitious. Yet many are willing to trust a profit-making bank that puts technical intelligence in the service of accumulation, a bank that helped finance enterprises such as Union Carbide's plant in Bhopal; and put into place the ecodestructive Green Revolution for which Bhopal was built, was a great supporter of Suharto, and has built huge fossil-fuel-consuming projects throughout the South while prating of the need to control global warming.[33]

Those persuaded by recent propaganda to think that this leopard has changed its spots might ponder the case of Bolivia, the poorest country in South America. Having been pressured by the World Bank to sell off its airline, electric utilities, and national train service to private interests, the desperate nation was at length coerced into selling chunks of its water system to a consortium headed by the US construction giant, the Bechtel corporation, along with partners from Italy, Spain, and four Bolivian companies – an authentic spectacle of globalization at work, commodifying an essential substratum of life. Thanks to the Bank, the investors only had to put up less than $20,000 initial capital for a water system worth millions. With Bank loans, the consortium set about to divert various rivers – no doubt with the ecological care that usually attends enterprises of this sort – and then, to cover the costs, attempted, again with the Bank's blessing, to force through price increases of as much as $20 a month – this in a country where the median working family income is $100 a month.

Major protests were the result. These catapulted new layers of indigenous resistance into prominence and forced the Bank and Bechtel to back off. They also led to military responses that killed eight people, prompting World Bank director James Wolfensohn to say that giving away public services inevitably leads to waste and that countries like Bolivia need to have "a proper system of charging." The highly cultured former Wall Street financier claimed that the privatization of the water supply was by no means directed against the poor, even though the Bank had stated in July 1999 that "no subsidies should be given to ameliorate the increase in water tariffs" and that all users, including the very poor, should have bills that reflected the full cost of the expansion of the local water system.

No further comment should be required, but this addendum is necessary: that Bechtel (which also has played a particularly disgraceful role in the "reconstruction" of Iraq)[34] was once the province of George Shultz, Secretary of State under Reagan, and that one of the soldiers firing into the protestors was identified as a man trained at the US Army's School of the Americas, an institution located in Georgia and designed to keep the Western hemisphere in good working order. This put him into the company of the President of Bolivia, the Governor of the province, and the mayor of the town – Cochabamba – where the action was centered, all of whom shared the same *alma mater*. Where, then, is the limit of the apparatus of globalization?[35]

Global capitalism exists along a continuum extending from the dignified chairman of the Federal Reserve Bank to the most vicious Russian mobster and Colombian drug lord. All are mandated by the great force field and under its spell. In a stunning *fin de siècle* article, Christian de Brie describes "a coherent system closely linked to the expansion of modern capitalism and based on an association of three partners: governments, transnational corporations and mafias ... [in which] financial crime is first and foremost a market, thriving and structured, ruled by supply and demand." Each partner needs the other, even if the need must be vigorously denied. In short, an honest look at the system takes us light years from the glowing promises of neoliberalism. Contrary to the official imagery, the actual corporate culture breeds a swarm of pathogens:

> restrictive practices, cartels, abuse of dominant position, dumping, forced sales, insider dealing and speculation, takeovers and dismembering of competitors, fraudulent balance sheets, rigging of accounts and transfer prices, the use of offshore subsidiaries and shell companies to avoid and evade tax, embezzlement of public funds, bogus contracts, corruption and backhanders, unjust enrichment and abuse of corporate assets, surveillance and spying, blackmail and betrayal, disregard for regulations on employment rights and trade union freedoms, health and safety, social security, pollution and the environment. Not to mention what goes on in the world's growing number of free zones, including those in Europe and in France, where the ordinary rule of law does not apply, especially in social, tax and financial matters.

"An incredible plunder, the full extent of which will never be known" arises, conditioned on one side by state connivance, and, on the other, by seepage into the underworld. Throughout the planet, but especially in the South, "workers have to contend with thugs hired by the bosses, blackleg trade unions, strike-breakers, private police and death squads." There is a hidden metabolism, in sum, between the shady practices of corporate capital and the organized criminality of gangsterdom:

> ... banks and big business are keen to get their hands on the proceeds – laundered – of organised crime. Apart from the traditional activities of drugs, racketeering, kidnappings, gambling,

procuring (women and children), smuggling (alcohol, tobacco, medicines), armed robbery, counterfeiting and bogus invoicing, tax evasion and misappropriation of public funds, new markets are also flourishing. These include smuggling illegal labour and refugees, computer piracy, trafficking in works of art and antiquities, in stolen cars and parts, in protected species and human organs, forgery, trafficking in arms, toxic waste and nuclear products, etc.

Occasionally a sign of this appears in some scandal over campaign contributions, a vicious African civil war, in the washing ashore of illegal immigrants from China or of a submarine purchased by the Russian mafia from disaffected naval officers. Often it devolves on to the rampant street crime of the cities of the South. There will never be a complete reckoning of the iceberg beneath this tip, though its magnitude can be estimated as an annual "Gross Criminal Product" of one trillion dollars.[36]

Setting aside the moral implications, the presence of this vast shadowland signifies capitalism's fundamental uncontrollability, and therefore its inability to overcome its crises of ecology and democracy. From this standpoint, the ecological crisis is the effect of globalization viewed from the standpoint of ecosystems, as great waves of capital batter against and erode ecological defences. Similarly, democracy, and not government, is the great victim of globalization. As global capital works its way, the popular will is increasingly disregarded in the effort to squeeze ever more profit out of the system. In the process, the instruments of global capital begin to take on political functions, breaking down local jurisdictions and constituting themselves as a kind of world governing body. But the regime lacks what normal states, even despotic ones, require, namely, some means of legitimation. In the post-aristocratic, post-theocratic world of modernity, democratic advances, even the pseudo-democracy that passes for normal these days, are the necessary glue that holds societies together. Capital's inability to furnish this as it moves toward its realization in the global society has made its operation increasingly look like

81

a global *coup d'état*. This is the great political contradiction of our time, and drives the present surge of resistance.

The men in charge

> Just between you and me, shouldn't the World Bank be encouraging more migration of the dirty industries to the LDCs [less developed countries]? I think the economic logic behind dumping a load of toxic waste in the lowest wage country is impeccable and we should face up to that ... I've always thought that underpopulated countries in Africa are vastly underpolluted: their air quality is vastly inefficiently low [sic] compared to Los Angeles or Mexico City. (Lawrence Summers, while at the World Bank)

> You know, there are some people who are just losers. There are some countries that are just losers. And if you forgive them the debt, it doesn't make a lot of difference. (James Wolfensohn, President, World Bank)

> You must cut costs ruthlessly by 50 to 60 percent. Depopulate. Get rid of people. They gum up the works. (Jeffrey Skilling, President, Enron Corporation)[37]

To draw out the broad ecological outlines of capitalist society is one thing; to prove that this will inexorably lead to ecocatastrophe unless capital is overthrown is another. Here the question becomes, not what capital is doing to ecosystems, human and natural, but whether it can adapt and change its ways, given the gathering breakdown of its natural ground – or to be more exact, whether it can do so in time to permit a mending of its relations with nature. Everyone appreciates how fabulously adaptable capital has been. It has eluded destruction time and again, so much so that the capacity to also adapt to ecological breakdown is pretty well taken for granted.

Market society has been fabulously successful in producing wealth. Why not, so the standard argument runs, will it not be just as successful in producing ecological integrity? But where this line of reasoning goes astray is in not realizing that this time, the lesion arises from capitalist production as such. The problem afflicting previous crises was how to resume a pattern of growth interrupted by one stress or another. Now, however, it is precisely the pattern of growth that causes the problem. Yes, capital can produce "green commodities," or anti-pollution devices; it can even recycle and conserve resources as well as energy. But because it does so as capital, it does so by producing itself before anything else; and this gathering sea of capital will have the effects documented above, essentially washing out the marginal gains achieved by efforts at recuperation. This proposition is no more provable than its converse, the popularly assumed idea that capital will work its way out of the ecological crisis. The question is, rather, whether it is more plausible, and for this purpose we may introduce yet another line of reasoning.

Capitalist production includes all those forces that enter into the generalized production of commodities. These include the prevalent human dispositions that enter into production. If it is true that capitalism induces a kind of mentality turned away from recognizing nature, we mean for this to be understood as one of the elements (in Marxist terms, a "force of production") making the ecological crisis more intractable. In plain language, one of the biggest ecological problems with capitalism is the capitalist.

If the ruling class – those persons who through ownership and/or control hold the reins of the system in their hands – were to prove capable of appreciating just how much trouble we are all in, then, just maybe, they could install necessary changes in time. If, however, they are *structurally incapable* of dealing with the crisis, then this greatly reinforces the indictment made here. I say, structural, because the behavior of elites cannot be reduced to ordinary motivations like greed or domination, as greedy or domineering as they may in fact be. When we are talking of class interest and of how individuals become personifications of great institutional forces, all the innumerable variations that make the human psyche interesting are subjected to a few basic rules, and a remarkable uniformity of behavior prevails. Of course, an individual member of the elite can rebel and step aside. But what

83

does it matter that a few capitalists think differently from their fellows if their ideas are drowned out by the preponderant force of class opinion? In actuality, a member of the elite who starts seeing things radically differently either gets back into line or is extruded from power; he simply ceases being a member of the elite, and gets replaced by someone more in accord with the needs of capital. For the remainder, the system imposes a powerful and uniform set of constraints, as the dominant social forces induce some psychological elements and inhibit others, while providing ideals, rationalizations, and norms of conduct, in short, a kind of moral universe within which behavior is shaped and given structure.

Each society selects for the psychological types that serve its needs. It is quite possible in this way to mold a great range of characters toward a unified, class purpose. To succeed in the capitalist marketplace and rise to the top, one needs a hard, cold, calculating mentality, the ability to sell oneself, and a hefty dose of the will to power. None of these traits is at all correlated with ecological sensibility or caring, and all are induced by the same force field that shapes investment decisions.

The three statements by elite figures given above are, of course, not representative of the public face put to the world by the ruling classes. In fact, Summers has claimed that his remarks were meant to be "ironic." If so, however, it is the irony that states a factual truth with a face-saving twist, for the substance of the remark, along with those by Wolfensohn and Skilling, holds a mirror to the actual trajectory of capital. Capital speaks through these powerful figures, in all its ruthless calculatedness, its willingness to jettison the unprofitable, and its reduction of nature to resources and sinks. What they are saying, then, is authentic even if it may be denied. Putting the matter this way removes us from thinking of the capitalist elites as being motivated by "greed," or some internally driven psychological state. Of course greed plays a role. How could it not when stupendous fortunes can be had for compliance with the rules of the game? But the question is how greed, or the drive for power, or cold and calculating ways of thought, conduces to blindness and rigidity. These are the salient traits, and they arise from the intersection of psychological tendencies with the concrete life-world of the capitalist. Consider some of the ways in which this works itself out anti-ecocentrically.

1. First, the bigger the system gets – which is to say, the more it fulfills its destiny of expansion – the more grandiose becomes the capitalist way of thought. And the more grandiose, the more removed. If you sit atop Manhattan's World Financial Center, fly in private jets, manipulate billions of dollars with the tap of a keypad, and control a productive apparatus capable of diverting rivers and sending missions to Mars, you are not likely to experience the humility of a St Francis or the patient tenacity of a Rachel Carson. And lacking this, you are no more likely to experience fellow-feeling for the web of life than for the poor people of Africa. In short, ecological consciousness is blocked by the ruling class position.

2. This grandiosity is greatly reinforced by a sense of personal invulnerability, which insulates capitalists from the consequences of their actions except as these affect the bottom line of profit. Ordinary people are not so protected. The reason that so many people of color, for example, have toxic waste dumps in their neighborhoods (estimates have run as high as 60 percent) is transparently that such people do not sit at the command structures of the corporations that pollute. Those who do, by contrast, see to it that the poisons they make stay out of their own neighborhoods and away from their own children. This keeps the elites from seeing the direct evidence of the destabilizing effects of capitalist production. And it feeds the fantasy that they can always surround themselves with protection against a nature out of balance.

3. Even if the elites screw up, their reward is ensured. Indeed, consolation prizes are given to executives who fail, a story which caught the attention of the press in 1997. As the *New York Times* put it: "For top executives, failure – once a wretched embarrassment disguised in corporate spin language or hushed up completely – now pays. Especially if they fail quickly." Failed top

executives at AT&T, Disney, Apple Computer, and Smith Barney were sent packing with, respectively, $26, 90, 7 and 22 million dollar payoffs – scarcely an incentive to worry greatly about what they are doing. (The reader will no doubt be impressed by the progress evinced by the system nine year later, when a golden parachute of $211 million was given to the CEO of Home Depot upon his firing.) The structural reason for this lies in the increasing turnover at the top – itself a function of the acceleration of capital – that leads executives to demand safety nets and in the same moment, undercuts loyalty, coherence, and larger vision at the upper level of corporations.[38]

4. Along with this, the ever-growing size of capitalist corporations removes them from contact with nature as an object of care. Insulated by dense and seemingly endless webs of bureaucracy, and presiding over enterprises that typically make anything and everything and throw off subsidiaries like Imelda Marcos changed her shoes, the capitalist bosses have every reason to neglect the immediacy and mutual recognition essential for ecological ways of being. Their order of interrelation is dominated by the entirely anti-ecological principle: the law of exchange. The more money-capital rules, the more is nature reduced to mere abstraction, and the more rationalized are the ruminations of a Lawrence Summers. According to the regime of finance, the economic logic is in fact "impeccable" to dump more toxic waste in poorer countries. That's simply how one makes more money, which is all that "counts."

5. Another core trait of the capitalist is the fetish of technology. Since technology raises the rate of surplus value extraction, it is a key to profitability, and so becomes invested with the godlike power of capital. The capitalist therefore not only overestimates the technological, he himself becomes like a machine. In his hard, cold calculatedness, he thinks "instrumentally," that is, reductively and in terms of parts rather than wholes. This is doubly useful in that it permits ready-made rationalizations of one's behavior, and the isolation and separation of such traits as could stir forth some ecological awareness.

6. Of course the capitalist does not only think; he is also a passionate, desiring creature. The problem is that capital selects for such passions as are recklessly ecodestructive, particularly, the desire to win at all cost. The main mechanism of this is the relentless competition built into the heart of the system, which assures that only the rabidly self-seeking and ruthless are elected to patrol the higher reaches of capital. There is nothing mysterious about this, but its significance is easily overlooked in the macho world of capitalist culture. This is a much more cogent factor in capital's anti-ecological regime than simple greed. The attitude was summed up by Coca-Cola president and CEO Douglas Ivester (deposed in 2000). Friendship, admiration and respect, said Ivester, is not "really my priority. This is what I really want. I want your customers, I want your space on the shelves, I want your space of the consumer's stomach. And I want every single bit of beverage growth potential that is out there."[39] Just as capital can never stop expanding, therefore, so can its personifications never have enough. How can people of this sort ever be expected to wake up to the ecological crisis?

7. The effect is accentuated inasmuch as the regime of finance capital places an emphasis on short-term profitability. The very fluidity sought by capital imposes ever-greater demands that profits be realized right away or sooner. This is the main reason why nothing substantial will be done about global warming under the present regime. Sure, all sorts of constructive measures are on the drawing board, but to take them seriously involves the unthinkable measure of cutting into immediate profits. If capitalists could all plan together, this might be possible. But that in turn runs against the law of competition.

8. One last tendency that keeps capitalists from dealing adequately with the ecological crisis deserves mention. Aside from logical styles or personal passions, we may assess the capacities for judgment of this ruling class. Needless to say, this has to be fairly sound in certain respects if an individual is to ascend the capitalist hierarchy. That is, the tycoon needs to be able to distinguish between his grandiose and aggressive desires and

87

what the real situation will bear. However, this principle applies only to those areas in which profitability is the criterion. Here the capitalist's powers are brought to bear and the results are usually impressive. But where, as with the ecological crisis, the capitalist is simply in over his head and his instrumental kind of thinking and mechanical materialism necessarily misconstrue the real situation, then he is prone to especially great distortions. This is because of his grandiosity, his immersion in the discourse of "spin control," public relations and other kinds of manipulation, and also from an induced character trait quite common among those who live by the market, namely, a kind of "optimistic denial." The capitalist has to be thoroughly realistic on one level, but insofar as he is immersed in commodity exchange, he is also subject to a high degree of wishful thinking. Success in the imponderable market depends a great deal upon instilling confidence and assurance that such and such will really sell, for whether such and such actually sells depends in part upon whether people believe in it. This attitude, so essential to huckstering and "hustling customers," is normally balanced by shrewdness of one kind or another. However, where, as with the ecological crisis, the shrewdness is misplaced because the situation is incomprehensible, then the all-too-human traits of denying reality and resorting to wishful thinking come to the fore. Since no one in fact can predict the outcome of the ecological crisis, or any of its constituent ecosystemic threads, the way is left open for optimistic denial; in short, minimization of the dangers, and inadequate responses taken for opportunistic motives rather than from a real appreciation of the problem.

The indictment

Capitalism bestrides the world because of its fantastic ability to produce wealth – and to induce the wealth-producing side of human nature. The result is the most powerful form of human organization ever devised, and also the most destructive. Capital's advocates claim that its destructivity can be contained and that capital, as it matures, will peacefully overcome the rapacity shown in its phases of primitive accumulation, the way Sweden advanced from its Viking past. Give us a little more time, they argue, and globalization will truly become the tide that raises all boats and not just the yachts of the wealthy, while the general increase in wealth will enable the earth which is harbor for these boats to be made snug and bright.

An opposite conclusion is argued here. I hold instead that with the production of capitalist wealth, and, as an integral part of it, poverty, eternal strife, insecurity, ecodestruction, and, finally, nihilism are also produced. These concomitants may be externalized and exported, so long as production is local and restricted. But as capital matures and becomes global, the escape routes are sealed and its cancerous character is revealed – penetrating all spheres of human existence, destabilizing the ecologies of space and time, and subjecting the earth to an increasingly authoritarian and corrupt regime.

The ecological crisis is the name for the global eco-destabilization accompanying global accumulation. Capital has shown a phenomenal resiliency and ability to absorb all contradiction in its logic of exchange – this is a main reason why various modes of revolt have come and gone, leaving only bitter memorials behind, as Che Guevara has become the name for a brand of beer. In the ecological crisis, however, the logic of exchange itself becomes the source of destabilization, and the more it is drawn into the picture, the more corrupt and unstable becomes the relation to nature. Capital cannot recuperate the ecological crisis because its essential being, manifest in the "grow or die" syndrome, is to produce such a crisis, and the only thing it really knows how to do, which is to produce according to exchange-value, is exactly the source of the crisis. In other words, it regards the ecological crisis through the distorting lens of the effect on accumulation; by seeking to remedy the latter, which is all, really, that capital can care about, it necessarily worsens the former. This is seen very clearly in the regime of emissions trading set up under the Kyoto Protocols.

And, finally, capital's iron tendency to produce poverty along with wealth and to increase the gap between rich and poor, means that capitalist society must remain authoritarian at the core and incapable of developing the cooperative space for rationally contending with the ecological crisis. Freeing up human creative power, which is our best chance to overcome ecological decay, is simply anathema to it.

The logic of this argument is not yoked to the appearance of some sudden overwhelming calamity, nor to the more likely concurrence of a great number of smaller weakening blows leading to collapse, nor even to the possibility that the system will muddle through. It is predicated rather on demonstrating the utter unworthiness of capitalism to shepherd civilization through the crisis it has engendered by its cancerous expansion. The above-mentioned contingent disasters may happen one way or another, or some or all of them may not happen at all, but we must be perfectly clear that they are primed to happen, and that capitalism, far from providing remedies, makes them more likely the more it fulfills itself.

That is why, in this excursion through the peculiarities of capital and capitalism, I have emphasized the anti-ecological features of capitalist production rather than the particulars of its relation to the crisis. Only the barest suggestion has been given of the innumerable instances of environmental assault; of the great propaganda system and its greenwashing campaign; of the betrayal of ecological responsibility by the established media; of the perfidy of individual politicians and parties; of the cooptation of environmental groups; of the complicity of the scientific establishment; of the tangled legal system; and of the efforts to suppress and intimidate environmentalists. Good books have been written about all of these things – and in Chapter 8 I return to some of them in assaying the adequacy of current ecological politics.[40] But we should not lose sight of the whole picture in attending to particulars: There is a single world-dominating order, and even though it still has not reached everywhere, it cannot be reformed, cannot be satisfied with less than everything, and has the institutions in place for its purposes. No set of individual reforms can encompass what capital means, nor drive it out by the root. Therefore, no matter how meritorious or necessary any particular reform may be, the fact remains that it is capital as a whole that has to be confronted and brought down, as daunting as that prospect may be.

Capitalism

Part II | The domination of nature

5 | On ecologies

To say that capital is ecodestructive is to claim that, under its regime, large swathes of the natural world are becoming undone. However troubling, this is straightforward enough. But we have also said in a number of places that it is "anti-ecological," which is not quite the same thing. The latter term introduces a new notion, that the word, ecology, signifies something to be valued in our relationship within nature, and that capital does not simply degrade one portion of nature or another, but violates the whole sense of the universe. Obviously, this obliges us to say a thing or two about what that sense might be, and, in a more general way, what it means to talk about nature.

The notion of nature is as elusive as any concept in the repertoire of thought. Nature palpably exists irrespective of what we say about it. And yet nature only exists *for us* insofar as we say anything about it. All propositions about nature, from the most esoteric investigations into cosmology, to the regulations for dumping waste, to the writings of ideologues left, right and center – including, to be sure, the thoughts written down here – are mediated by language, which, besides being an imperfect mirror of reality, is densely social and historical. Practically speaking, then, there are two layers of our imprint upon nature: first, the natural world has been substantively rearranged by human influence, to the extent that one would be hard-pressed to find any configuration of matter on the surface of the earth, and a good ways above and below it, that has not been altered by our species-activity;[1] and, second, that all propositions about the natural world are, first of all, social utterances. When we speak, or become aware, of something called "nature," we are apprehending something that also has a history, at the least, because the ways of speaking about it are social practices, and also, in the great majority of instances of interest to us, because the "natural" entity has itself received a human, historical imprint.

The term ecology and its various meanings also has a history, in this case conditioned by the gathering crisis that bears its name.[2] It stands to reason that when the integrity of the natural world is under ever-growing threat, the notions used to account for that integrity and its disintegration will come into prominence. In the century-and-a-quarter since it appeared on the intellectual landscape, ecology has managed to acquire a great deal of signification. As used here, the term has a fourfold meaning:

- A technical discipline within the natural science of biology devoted to the study of the interrelationships between living creatures and their environment. Here the crucial variables are usually the populations of diverse life-forms as they interact with the rest of nature.

- An object singled out for ecological study, that is, not populations as such but locations within the totality of the earth. We can talk of this as a more or less definite place, as, for example, the ecology of a local pond or of the Amazon basin – which at a certain scale may take the name of a *bioregion*. Or we may think of it as a subset of the natural world with certain internal relations, like the atmosphere, or the endocrine system of higher animals. Here the object in question has systemic properties, i.e. is a structure of interrelating elements defined both spatially and temporally; hence the name *ecosystem*, to define a principal object of our study. Ecosystems are bounded but also interrelated with each other (as, for example, the endocrine system is related to the circulatory system, or the oceans to the atmosphere). In fact, there is no such thing as an ecosystem-in-itself; all are interconnected, in ways that concern us greatly. We use the term *ecosphere*, to refer to the world regarded according to the principles of ecology, in other words, it is the earth as seen "ecosystemically." And from a still higher level of abstraction, we can think of nature itself as the *integral of all ecosystems*. This notion, of an integral, means also that we think of "wholes" composed of parts but distinct from the sum of those parts. In philosophical language, we are not developing a hierarchical systems-theory, but a dialectic of emergence.

- A dimension of the human world. This is essential, unless we take the nonsensical position that humanity is outside of nature. Needless to say, developing a social view of ecology may not be to every natural scientist's taste. And in any case it requires us to extend our method by introducing dimensions peculiar to the human world, such as language, meaning, and history. These attributes give us our identity as a natural species. Once we begin looking at things this way, moreover, there is no reason not to talk of the ecology of cities, of neighborhoods, of families, or, indeed, of minds.[3]

- Since values are uniquely human phenomena, we logically extend the scope by taking into account ethical positions with ecological content; and since an ethical position is a guiding orientation for action in the world, we talk of ecological politics as well. It is in this latter sense that we indict capital as "anti-ecological," just as the indictment of its "ecodestructiveness" refers to the second, ecosystemic, sense of the term. What it may mean to ethically act ecologically, or to hold "ecocentric" values, which is the term we will use here, is a problem integrating all dimensions of ecology, and the solution of which, to be termed "ecosocialism," is the aim of this study.

Ecological thinking concerns relationships, and the structures and flows between them. At one level, this is mere common sense; at another, it turns what we take to be reality upside down and commits us to a world-view and philosophy of nature very much at odds with the dominant system. Nature as such vastly exceeds the phenomena of life; yet life may be justly regarded as being at the same time both a special case of nature, and, in a way we only dimly surmise, as a potential of nature – something that nature generates under specific circumstances.[4] Life is unitary, in the sense that the basic molecular architectures of humans, redwoods and slime molds all indicate a common ancestor. Yet life is also inconceivably – to our dim awareness – multiform, in a profusion that has arisen over 3.5 billion years through ceaseless interactions between living creatures, and with their non-living surroundings. It follows that all ecosystems that contain living beings also relate to the rest of nature, whether this be other creatures, the immediate surroundings of the earth's macro-physical environment, i.e. the "environment," or the molecular, atomic, or subatomic realms, or the extension of nature into the cosmos. A slender, filamentous connection throughout the great reaches of nature, to be sure, and scarcely likely to ever be fully comprehended by our science, but existent so long as we take the relatedness of elements within nature with full seriousness. From this standpoint we think of nature as the integral of all ecosystems, extending in every direction and beyond the limits of the planet. Talking of integrals means talking in terms of organisms, and of Wholes – in other words, the systematic intro-duction of an ecological vision commits us to positing reality as an interconnected web whose numberless nodes are integrated into holistic beings of ever-exfoliating wonder – or would be so, until capital got hold of them.

What is life?

The boundary between the living and the non-living is not sharp, which is to be expected if life is a potential form of being hatched by nature. Nature is *formative*, that is, it has the dynamic potential to generate particular nodes of existence; and life rep-resents a way-station of its formativeness. Were nature a diffuse continuum with no differentiation among its parameters, such as pertained at the moment of the "Big Bang," and will return at the extended moment of its "heat death," then there would be no-thing at all, no particularized aggregation, no allocating of time and space, of dust, of energic differentials, of galaxies, stars, planets around stars, seas and land on the planet, rocks on the land, pools of water, concatenations of chemicals in the air and in the waters, cycles of temperature and light – in short, none of the differentiation that is the lot of the cosmos in the eons between its alpha and omega points. So the category of existence is occupied by the "some-things" that exist. These comprise *beings* insofar as they internalize their existence, that is, make their "is-ness" part of themselves. In this way, every-thing has being insofar as it is not other-things. This "being of beings" relates to and to a degree incorporates the other-things, making them internal to itself even as they become objects. Beings are temporal; they evolve as they come in and out of existence, and with their evolution comes a fuller internalization. In other words, a motion of inwardness toward subjectivity accompanies a more highly differentiated objective existence. In one line of development, this eventually results in the emergence of consciousness and mind. What we call "development" takes place on a terrain of being, and through greater subject–object differentiation – whether expressed in terms of the maturation of a child or as the evolution of life.

Life manifests a kind of being that self-sustains and replicates – that propagates its own form, through the presencing of definite individuals along with the capacity of said individuals to reproduce. But nature is not only formative, it is also dissipative of form – indeed, were it not, form itself could not exist. Thus it is that, for our universe, there is a trajectory between alpha and omega points, between an undifferentiated moment of origin and an end – unimaginably distant[5] – at which all beings cease to exist because differentiation itself has ended. The passage of this great loop is registered in the famous laws of thermodynamics, although not accounted for by them. The First Law expresses the insight of ancient natural philosophy, as in the Epicurean doctrine that "nothing comes of nothing"; it holds that matter and energy are conserved in physical systems. The Second Law surpasses this by introducing the notion of form and the dissipation of form. If "entropy" is a logarithmic measure of the probabilistic disorder of a given physical system, the Second Law states that for such a system, whether it be the air in a room, a living body, or the earth as a whole, so long as neither energy nor matter is added to said system – that is, so long as the system is "closed" – then its entropy will rise with time. An increase in the randomness of its elements, or from the other side, a loss of form, will therefore emerge in the absence of the input of energy. More, the direction of this change defines "time's arrow." Thus an ice cube melts, "with time," in a glass of water, replacing a relatively improbable state with a more probable one – that is, one corresponding to a greater number of system possibilities in what physicists call phase-space.[6] Similarly, when we die, the exquisite combination of molecules that has existed in this living form is returned to the great flux of the universe. It is living form that maintains that exquisiteness – to which we, as self-reflective living creatures, respond aesthetically.

There are a number of themes here that need a bit of unpacking. First, we understand life to stand in a degree of tension with the universe that gave it existence. The universe, or nature, has within itself to give birth to life, as a "natural" potential of the cosmos. But at the same time, and through the workings of the same nature in its Second Law, life stands against certain laws of the universe. Life must be . . . and life cannot remain. Poised between these poles, life must continually *struggle* for its existence; if it does not, it passes into death.

In the current orthodoxy the term "struggle" is endowed with Hobbesian and Social Darwinian meanings: struggle is the war of all against all, and the survival of the fittest in a regime of continual mutual aggression. This notion was not Darwin's, and it is not only ideologically distorted, but factually wrong. By no means do all creatures behave this way. In fact, no creature, not even the "king of the jungle," endures wholly through predation; while for the simplest creatures, those microscopic cellular beings on which the entire biosphere rests, the Social Darwinian notion is without meaning. As the British paleontologist Richard Fortey points out, the first "sustainable" systems, the mat creatures, or "stromatolites," whose lineage goes back 3 billion years to the Precambrian (roughly 2.4 billion years before the emergence of more complex multicellular organisms) and that still endure in certain protected locales, are composed of layers of prokaryotic bacteria, the topmost, "thin as a sheet of paper," doing photosynthesis, the lower layers breaking down the waste products of the upper by fermentation, the whole given structure and nutrient by trapped grains of minerals. "It was a sustainable system, an ecosystem in miniature. If this truly reflected the state of the nascent biological world it is clear that cooperation and coexistence were a part of life close to its inception. Existence at base can be thought of as reciprocal rather than competitive ... These humble structures are the birth of ecology."[7]

Given that for the considerable majority of the time life has been on earth, it existed as static mats of microorganisms undergoing biochemical exchange with the rest of nature, the meaning of "struggle" includes forms of cooperation as well as competition and predation, and indeed, the former would be more fundamental than the latter. The stromatolites had no organs, they gathered not, nor did they hunt, nor were they hunted, and for a period longer than the so-called higher life has existed. Yet they lived and had "ecologies." For the stromatolites – and, at bottom, ourselves – to struggle means therefore to engage in transfers of matter and energy required to sustain a certain formal organization in relation to the Second Law. Dead, the numberless atoms of our substance are essentially unchanged; their mutual positioning (including the positioning into more complex molecules), however, is drastically rearranged. The absence of life signals a reorganization in the direction of randomness and disorganization, mainly carried out in this epoch through the agency of other living beings who rebuild their substance from the elements of the old.

Life, then, is what sustains organization; to be exact, organization at low entropy. The ensemble of energic and formal processes required for this constitutes the specific life activity of a given creature or species. The hunting, gathering, etc., of "higher" organisms is a more elaborate way of proceeding down the path, grounded in the necessities of a more elaborate formal structure. Each creature must extract energy in order to struggle, so as to maintain its form, which is to say, to endure. And this means that each creature is insufficient in itself, for insofar as it individuates, it also separates, and that from which it is separated is therefore related to it, connected yet different. Those who do not come together so, are the non-existent.

All living beings have internal and external relations of parts to wholes. This quality, that life must exist in relation to other life and to nature as a whole if it is to contend with the Second Law, defines the notion of ecosystem, and on a far deeper level than that of a mere collection of bodies. Ecosystems constitute places of "putting together." They are the sites where creatures interact in ways potentially conducive to their emergence and sustenance. Ecosystems are the loci of nature's formativity, active ensembles where being comes into existence. Ecology in the larger sense is the discourse of such ensembles, and is built into the fabric of terrestrial life, from the infinitesimal microorganism to the ecosystems now being destabilized.[8]

Life emerges on this planet – we may set aside the question of alternate life on other planets – owing to a fortuitous set of circumstances within the range of cosmic possibility. Here nature originates life, which then, through struggle and in its ecosystemic places, proceeds to evolve. But evolution is conditioned at every step by the flux of ecosystems. Life's own activity, played out in ecosystems (along with other natural influences, e.g. meteorites, solar flares, etc.) is what prods living beings along, changing the terms of the struggle for existence and leading to evolutionary development. Ecology, therefore, is integrally tied to evolution – one may say that any given ecosystem is a synchronic slice through evolutionary time. Life is defined anti-entropically, insofar as its chief feature is the sustenance and creation of form. Living systems display degrees of order incomprehensible to the crude mind. Whether we look at the obvious proportions and symmetries of organisms or, more impressively still, the fine molecular structure wherein each atom seems to be positioned as in a tiny workshop, it would seem that life not only disobeys but positively flouts the Second Law. This is exactly what the struggle for existence is about. Dead, the corpse of a once-alive creature very quickly falls into line with the principle of rising entropy. The work of life, and the intricate dance of energy and form that goes into it, is essentially an enterprise to stave off and reverse the Second Law. Far from refuting the Second Law, then, life affirms its power by struggling against it.[9]

The struggle of life against entropy does not deny the Second Law, because living creatures are anything but closed systems. Whether they convert ambient sunlight into usable form through photosynthesis in the plant kingdom, or eat the products of this activity in the substance of animals, life is constantly taking in low-entropy energy to sustain its form. A considerable degree of evolved biochemical activity consists of the capacity of living beings to capture energy in small packets, principally of high-energy phosphate bonds, so that the fine structure of life's workshop can proceed. Here, in the astounding nano-factories of the cell, the principle permitting the emergence of life in the first place is institutionalized: reactants are held together, energy is transformed into small and usable amounts, and the whole tiny architecture is repeated trillions of times over, as life builds and propagates itself.

Through it all, the net entropic pattern remains very much in line with the Second Law: insofar as life can be put in the position of a (relatively) closed system, it will increase the entropy of the totality comprised by itself and its surround. For the earth as a whole, it is not so clear. It is very likely the case that life's capacity to draw down the energy of the sun (and to a lesser extent, that of more immediately gravitational sources like tides and geothermal hot spots) has so overriden the constraints of closed systems as to have produced, at least until quite recently, when the ecological crisis has reversed the pattern, an actual decrease of entropy on the planet. At least, that is the way I would regard the "Gaia" principle, according to which the earth itself is a super-organism, with the capacity to self-regulate and even to exhibit signs of a kind of consciousness.[10] It would seem to be the case that whatever Gaian tendencies are evinced by the global ecosystem are manifestations of the cumulative effects of evolution upon the planet, made possible by the genius of life to subject the globe to its ordering effects. In this scheme, the "closed" system is the earth + space, with respect to which the overall increase in entropy is accounted for by harmless re-radiation of degraded solar energy into the latter. Meanwhile, organic evolution achieved for the earth as a whole what the life process does for individual beings, namely, an increase in order and dynamic form.

If ecology is the readout of life's formal organization at any point in time, then evolution is its forward temporal motion. Therefore, the ecological state of things at any moment is like a snapshot of evolution about to happen. This should not be inter-preted, however, as a teleologically ordered process, pulled from beyond by God – or, in the more ideologically understood sense, that evolution awaits its fulfillment in an equilibrium under the guidance of the current ruling class or master race. The notion of formativeness in nature requires, rather, a more dynamic reading. For if ecology were ever in a steady state, then there would be no pressure to evolve, and nothing of the beauty and intricacy of living form. It is lack, and conflict, and the ceaseless interaction between living beings and their surround, that condi-tion the evolution of life. Equilibrium as such is not a property of life, while generally speaking, those functions within which a kind of balance obtains are better thought of as a metastable equipoising, i.e. the "holding together" of elements in creative formation. Heraclitus seized the root of things when he posited ceaseless motion, with its absencing and presencing, as the way of the universe.[11]

Therefore, when we talk of the "stability" of ecosystems, we do not imply a static condition, or even one of simple equilibrium. We mean, rather, a state of being with an irreducible indeter-minacy, within which one might say, "life goes on-ward": evolving new (though not "higher") species, and introducing those formal shapes and dynamic processes into the ecosphere that comprise its work on earth. Since it is in the nature of ecosystems to move and evolve, we do better to evoke their *integrity* than their stability. The notion of integrity includes stability as a rate of change and emergence compatible with the working of any ecosystem. Even at its "climax," the forest continues to evolve. At the physiological level, the immune system is stable if it is capable of changing by introducing new antibodies to meet new contingencies. Ditto for the circulatory system, which has to keep maintaining its existent vessels, and extending new ones into traumatized areas.

To speak of the integrity of something means recognizing that it exists as the integral of its parts. In a word, it is a Whole. Preserving ecological integrity is a matter, therefore, of preserving Wholes, and fostering their emergence and development. I say, fostering, meaning that in the human world we have a choice as to whether to do this or not – a choice that depends in part on whether we value the integrity of ecosystems. As to why we should do, one might say that our own survival depends on it, but also and necessarily, because to value this way means to fulfill our own nature, to find its integrity as well. The ordering effects of life on earth are not merely a matter of overcoming entropy. They also result in those entities and patterns that we find beautiful – and this sense of beauty is no indulgence, but the participation in that nature from which being arises. If we wonder at the beauty and elegance of nature, then, we are nature appreciating itself, and our wonderment is part of the form of nature itself. We have the choice as to whether to try to foster the continuance of life. By choosing "no," that is, choosing to continue on with the way of life that leads to ecological disintegration, we are also choosing against ourselves. And this leads us to ask, just who we are.

On human being

A natural creature, beyond doubt, the same basic set of molecules, including DNA, the same submission to the entropy principle, the same fundamental ground plan, caught up in evolutionary time and dependence upon ecosystems. Like all natural creatures, the human being has an imprint. The bat has sonar, the whale special capacities for diving (and its kind of sonar), the bee its quantum dance, the venus flytrap its signature form of carnivorousness. Each creature in nature has its "nature," its way of being, its point of insertion into the ecosystemic manifold, its peculiar mode of struggling. We regard "human nature," or "hummingbird nature," or "bee nature," or "maple tree nature," in this light – both holistically, as the species-specific way of struggle in an ecosystemic world conditioned by the entropy principle; and also at a more concrete level, as the ensemble of powers, potentials and capacities that enable this way to be expressed. There is nothing mystical about the fact of particular species-nature; it is simple logic. To be is to struggle, and each point of difference in being is a different mode of struggling. In this way, living forms arise and take their place in ecosystemic manifolds, each in their way, better, each *as* their way.

The notion of human nature is often unpopular with people of progressive persuasion, who see in it a system of essentialist chains: men *are* in essence like this (e.g. from Mars); women *are* like that (from Venus); blacks are this way; and Chicanos that way, etc. – always with the more or less unstated proviso that in a stable social order they will remain that way, generally at a subaltern rank. Nature – and human nature – in this view are essences, false reductions of what humanity is, and therefore a fetter on what it can be. But this point of view, however well-intentioned, is mistaken. Essentialism is undoubtedly wrong, both morally and philosophically, because it imputes to the object a thing-like inertia that violates its range of potential being; it is, we might say, a kind of reification. But there is no *a priori* reason to place the blame for essentialism on the idea of nature. The categories of nature need not inherently limit human freedom and potential, although they can be used in this way – and always will be drawn upon as such by ideologues of authority and repression. They need not, in other words, conflate humans with other creatures, any more than they reduce elephants to hummingbirds. The idea of social or cultural determination is often opposed to determination by nature, as though the former had a built-in reassurance of freedom. But there is no reason why this need be so. Essentialist views, say of blacks and Latinos, can just as well be expressed in culturalist as in racist terms. Classically, racism is a biological essentialism, the object being considered an (inferior) subspecies of the human type. But this essence can just as well be transferred onto ethnicities or other cultural structures, where it becomes the "culture of poverty," or the "black family," or, as the latest wrinkle has it, the culture of believing one's group to be racially oppressed, all of which allegedly traps the groups in question into a universe of self-defeating social assumptions.[12]

In any case, the notion of human nature is necessary for any in-depth appreciation of the ecological crisis; and its lack is a sign of the crisis itself. In the absence of such a view, humanity is severed from the remainder of nature, and a genuinely ecological view is replaced by mere environmentalism. If we have no nature, then nature is always outside us, a mere grab-bag of resources and instrumental possibilities. Nor can the ties linking humanity and nature be given as a set of physical transfers between people and their "environment." Creatures struggle as organismic totalities, that is, full beings who act in the ecosystemic world and are acted upon by the world, not as leaky bags of dull matter.

All creatures co-evolve with their surround, in the course of which they actively transform their surround. Nature gives rise to form, and living creatures are trans-forming forms. That is why to talk of environment instead of ecologies violates the nature of things. Life actively changes the world, from other creatures to the very configuration of the rocks and the composition of the air. The atmosphere we breathe was made by living creatures, and so was the soil. The form of every creature is determined by other creatures.

Humans are also trans-forming, but with a core difference that defines human nature: we have evolved the inwardness, potentially inherent for all beings, into a subjectivity, or self, which has the capacity for an *imagination* – an internally represented world – and we act upon and transform reality through this imagination. I do not mean that we live only in the imagination, as that would be tantamount to not living at all, nor that the imaginary world is more important than the world it represents; but only that the capacity to represent the world internally, to work it over in thought, and to remember and anticipate it as well as to actually inhabit it, is what makes us human. The specifically human is a whole motion, encompassing inner and outer worlds and mutually transforming both. The signature of human nature lies in this motion as a whole, while the various powers that comprise our nature are the components necessary for this motion to occur. These powers and their various substrata all evolve ecosystemically, just like the rest of nature, with the highly important distinction that a co-evolving human sphere, mediated by the imaginary world, arises alongside the sphere of non-human existents – alongside of, then interpenetrated with, colonizing of, and, in the time of ecological crisis, destructive of the non-human order. Still, we never escape nature and do or become just as we please. Everyone has to eat, pass urine, to rest and sleep; everyone gets sick, and everyone will die. Our lives remain conditioned by the realities of nature, from quantum flows, to coarse Newtonian mechanics, to the hegemony of the entropy principle. No matter how ingeniously we may fashion nature – including the manipulation of the genome and the creating of new kinds of life – we are still doing no more than learning its laws so that we may use them for human purpose. Nor, it must be emphasized, does this remarkable capacity make us the high point or end point of evolution, for every creature standing at the end of its line of evolution is, with respect to the genealogy of nature, as high as any other. However, it does give us a kind of power such as no other creature has remotely possessed, and, with this power, various delusions and opportunities.

Teasing apart some of the threads of human nature, we find the following.

- An ensemble of somatic elements, rapidly evolving owing to the marked selection advantage conferred by human nature: a relatively huge brain, elaborate voice-box, opposable thumb, upright posture, and the like, providing the material substratum of specifically human ways of being.

- Of special importance was the emergence of language as the specific human mode of communicating and representing the world. This involved "hard wiring" of the evolving brain, coordination with the evolving speech apparatus, and, decisively, integration with evolving forms of sociality, the result being that the powers of individuals could be combined.

- Human sociality implies *society*, as a kind of super-body, with a *culture*, transmissable through generations as a shared system of meanings. Society and its culture become the locus of that parallel, imagined universe which comprises the human order in its varying relationships to nature.

- The boundary of the super-body with pre-existing nature is made by means of *technology*. Tools are extensions of the body as well as transfer points of the body into material nature, and of nature into the body. Technology is always socially determined and the bearer of meanings constructed through language. It is not a collection of tools but a fabric of social relations, certain threads of which are nature transformed into tools for the transforming of nature.

- Human being entails a new order of subjectivity. All beings, we have observed, possess a potential interiority implied by their difference with other beings – the fact that they are some-thing and not others. Human nature appears as that development within which this interiority acquires internal structure through the particular forms taken by our consciousness under the influence of language. All creatures are present to each other. Language involves *re-presentation*: a sphere of interiority arises where what is presented is presented back – re-presented – owing to its signification with language. Hence the real is, so to speak, doubled. This re-presenting is formative of the imaginative space of subjectivity. The imagined world is just as much a part of human ecology, as are chemical messengers for dog ecology or moth ecology.

- As this space of interior representation attains identity, it becomes a *self*. Its form is given by a degree of consciousness of itself, clothed by language with the words, "I" (as the subject phase) and "me" (as the object phase). The radically augmented power of the human species is generated here, in the space where the world is created within the self, which then defines a social collectivity that acts upon the world.

• An ensemble of relations is involved here – not just intelligence, and the practical skills, but desire as well, which conditions and drives the practical intelligence. This arises from the radical formlessness of human instinctual structures, which is reshaped according to culture. Correlated with this are the processes of separation and individuation that occur out of the matrix of childhood. Culture implies intergenerational transmission, which rests upon the facts of childhood, something no other species remotely undergoes.[13]

• The sociality of humans is unique – though neither more nor less so than that of bees, coyotes, baboons, dolphins, etc. It cannot be reduced to that of any other social animal, no matter how many amusing parallels may be found. This is because of the centrality of the self in human existence, and also because this self is always and necessarily a social product, formed through language and mutual *recognition* between the developing person and others. This foundation gives the human self a permanently dialectical quality – that is, it is formed in and lives through a set of contradictions that arise as the self is formed in mutual recognition of others, and, later, in contradiction between individual interest and social bond. The mark of the other is always upon the self, and so is its aloneness and fear of solitude, facts that are to loom large in our relation to nature.[14]

• The unique relation of human being to desire, along with the dialectics of the self and recognition, mean also that sexuality and gender play a uniquely powerful role in human existence compared with all other creatures. The significance of this for the ecological crisis will be explored in the next chapter.

There is an inescapable tension between humanity and nature. From one side, a fully embodied creature, obeying all the laws of the universe; from the other, a stubborn, proud and will-full creature who distinguishes the self from nature and even chooses to protest the natural. We can say it is a facet of human nature to *quarrel with nature and even to reject the purely natural given*. This notion may serve to signify human nature as a whole. It appears in phenomena as ubiquitous as the need to cook food, and to adorn the body, and as fundamental as technology – for each tool, as an extension of the body, is also a kind of protest against the limits of the natural body. And it marks the deepest stratum of our psyche as we relate to the ends of life. Every creature fights for life; but only a creature defined by selfhood will ponder death, fear death, deny death, or develop religion as a reaction to the perceived limits of existence. Thus, one of the most distinctive features of humanity in the archeological record is funerary evidence. Even the simplest trace of a burial condenses all that is specifically human: an awareness of death, that is, of the finitude of the self; a protest against death; care for the person who died, along with grief and sense of loss; the technologies of burial; and as a condition for the whole ensemble, society and culture. Nothing of the sort obtains for other creatures.[15]

Defining human nature as a tension with nature enables us to avoid essentialist positions that confine the human being in a prescriptive staitjacket. It allows for the quirkiness of human beings, and our playfulness, and aesthetic side. It also says something about human creativity, as the restless need to remake the world and to make other worlds, and about the sense of beauty that uniquely marks the species. And it does this while yet rooting us in nature and allowing for the immense range of ecological modes of being that characterize us, including those leading to and potentially leading out of the ecological crisis.

The general function we have been describing may be identified as *production*, as the term for what human beings do, as part of nature, to express the formativity of nature by mediating it through the human world. When we produce, we *trans-form* nature. We use the term "labor" to express in a general way the human propensity to produce, being careful to distinguish this meaning from the degraded (or "alienated") sense of toil that characterizes the products of domination, as we discuss below. Similarly, an economy enters the picture when production is socially organized, and there is a division of labor, and a wide exchange of what is produced, so that human powers are more elaborately expressed.

Both social production and consumption are direct extensions of human nature, in that each transforms nature through an engagement with the imagination and the ensemble of human powers. Production – and the human capacity of labor – is, as Marx insisted, a matter of looking ahead: every object which gets made exists in the imagination before it does so in reality. Every commodity is defined by its *use-value*, and this, too, is necessarily a function of need, which in turn is a function of want, which in turn can be a function of desire. No purely mechanical or utilitarian accounting can give a sense of the use-values of commodities, and, therefore, of the economy itself: the imagination needs to be invoked.[16]

But we are not done with human nature. There are other, more complex qualities to be noted.

- The emptiness that always shadows the self and the peculiar set of powers conferred by human nature creates for humanity a capacity not seen elsewhere in nature, namely, a reaching beyond itself, along with the potential – by no means expressed in all instances – of achieving a universal perspective, and of reaching toward the Whole. Broadly speaking, this refers to our spiritual life, the forms taken by which, or lack thereof, enter into the ecological crisis.[17]

- In addition, we recognize that the peculiar position of the self, poised as it is between the form-dissolving entropy principle and the looking-forward of production, leads to a special, socially conditioned temporality specific to each society, and produced in its myth and narrative. Human nature, by rejecting the given and making its world, configures an account of itself according to time: it produces *history*.[18] We have said something already about the special temporal conditions of capitalism, with its speed-up and binding of time. However, every society has a special temporality, wrought from the arrow conferred by the entropy principle, and manifesting the tension with nature that will always be an aspect of human being.

- All of the powers of humanity, spiritual and practical, are available for addressing the social order and have the potential for transforming it. The extremity of social transformation we call revolution. If nothing in nature stands still, how much more so is this the case for human beings and society! All things pass, and, for us, the relevant question is whether the capitalist order will pass away before it causes humanity to pass away. But capital cannot pass away of itself; it has to be ushered out, through a conscious transformation into an ecologically rational society.

Ecosystemic integrity and disintegration

Ecosystemic boundaries provide structural scaffolding for what is within an organism (the "organs" and other internal ecosystems – nervous, endocrine, immune, etc.), as well as the point of differentiation between ecosystems. The nature of the ties between organisms in a particular ecosystem is given by the specific activity of each being, and is never singular. Trees in a forest are linked through the myriad of creatures who relate to them as food, shelter, nesting place, etc., as well as through their access to water, air, sunlight; and also directly between each other, through a subterranean network of fungi, root hairs, and the like that effectively link all the trees into a superorganism.

Existing systems theories, including informational theories, tend to posit a mechanical and crudely hierarchical set of relations between ecosystemic elements. This leads to hopeless contradictions in the relations between humanity and nature, which

113

have prevented the emergence of an integral view; for the human relation to nature is immensely subtle and dialectical – i.e. proceeding from negation – and cannot be neatly or hierarchically packaged. So long as mechanistic reduction holds sway, the set of ecosystems will be put together essentially like a motorcar, with each system being a part like the starter, the tires, etc. What is needed is recognition of the fact that the formativeness of life introduces a radically different element, which we here simply call the Whole, and is manifest in the dynamic fluidity that obtains within and between ecosystems. Elements of living ecosystems do not exist as separable parts; they also exist in relation to the Whole, which is formative and non-reducible to any of its parts, and which plays a role in determining them, and cannot exist without them. What is individual exists in relation to the Whole, therefore, and this relationship must be included in any concrete account of things. Our very being is given this way, which for humans, endowed as we are with deep interiority, appears as *spirit*. The Whole is the formative notion of the ecosystem: it is a kind of *logos* that constitutes the intelligence of the ecosystem, which intelligence is drawn upon by individual beings within the ecosystem and, in our case, eventuates in consciousness. When we, or any other creature, are truly thinking, we are thinking in respect to the Whole; there is a sense in which it can also be said that the Whole is thinking through us.

The boundary-processes between elements in an ecosystem determine its integrity. These processes are as varied as life-forms themselves, and cannot be reduced to any common property beyond the interplay between formativeness and the constraints of entropy and other fundamental physical laws. Yet we can say that the integrity, or "health" of an ecosystem is a function of how these boundary processes, of whatever kind, relate organisms to each other internally, to other ecosystems externally, and to the Whole. The integrity of an ecosystem can be expressed in relational terms; we might say that it depends upon the degree of *differentiation* between its elements, where this term describes *a state of being that preserves both individuality and connected-*

ness. From another angle, to the extent that organismic beings *recognize* one another, they are both distinct and connected: they become themselves through active relation to the other. In this usage, recognition need not imply any defined subjective element. It is rather any mutual signalling that preserves both connection and individuality. Nor does differentiation always imply harmony or equilibrium. It can allow for interactions between organisms that result in the death of one or more of them; but a death, nevertheless, that provides for the preservation of the Whole.[19] The ecosystem consists of the comings and goings of all its constituents; this ceaseless motion builds up the Whole, within which, therefore, the death of individuals is just as important as their particular lives.

If differentiation is the key to understanding ecosystemic integrity, what makes for ecosystemic disintegration? Here we introduce a formal process that interrupts the dialectic of individuality and connectedness, and leads to the *separation* of elements, or, from another angle, of their *splitting*. What splits apart the elements of an ecosystem, either from each other, or, what amounts to the same thing, from the Whole, will impede the development of that Whole, block the evolution of new forms, and eventually destroy the individuals within it. Splitting entails a breakdown of recognition. Whatever fragments an ecosystem, separating its constituents and depriving them of the range of their mutual interactions, will block the formation of the Whole, and to that degree impoverish the development of the organisms within that whole, cause a deterioration of their internal state and even, perhaps, lead to their extinction.

This can be viewed in terms of physical separation – the so-called "island effect" by which ecosystems sink below the size that permits the optimal interaction of their organismic elements[20] – but also as the introduction of disruptive elements into the ecosystem, either new organisms ("pests" and pathogens), or new substances that block the life-processes and so annihilate ecosystemic existence. The introduction of methyl isocyanate into Bhopal was an example of splitting as annihilation: it literally split apart bodily integrity. A similar discussion could be resumed at a more subtle level for pollutants that have been inserted into the biosphere – as, for example, by organochlorines that mimic hormones and fragment the integrity of the endocrine ecosystem.[21] The same, however, applies to capital, which *separates the producer from the means of production*, as well as through the effects of money, to be discussed below. All of these modalities introduce self-perpetuating splits into ecosystems, which eventually disintegrate them. What is split away leads not to a renewal of being but to emptiness and withering, physically but also subjectively, as when traumatic memories are split-off, or parts of the self become alien. From the other side, the appropriation of split-off parts of the self, accompanied by the letting-go (as against the splitting off) of desires, is a sign of the development of the human being, and the core gesture of healing.

The ecological crisis is a great and proliferating set of ecosystemic splits, both natural and human, subjective as well as objective – a fraying of the fabric of the ecosphere. But what was frayed can also be mended, the way a broken arm can be mended. Here the break in the bone splits apart the functional unity of the limb, which the healer mends by figuring out how to hold together the broken parts so that nature's reintegrative process can resume. So it is with damaged ecosystems: ways must be found to restore and hold together elements to create a flourishing ecosystemic boundedness. There are important homologies to this in the ordinary functioning of nature, for example, the structural dynamics of the cell, where small packets of energy are deployed through the exquisite arrangement of ribosomes in mitochondria, "holding together" the intricate array of molecules so that the synthesis of low-entropy compounds – and structures composed of these – can go forward. It is not too far-fetched to claim that these conditions formally reproduce those attending the origins of life itself. Another example, in which I should hope every human participates, is the holding of children, the animate communication with them, and, then, necessarily, the letting go when the child is capable of moving on her own. This is the way individuality and connectedness become integrated in a human life. The great intricacies of raising children are variations on this simple theme; they amount to the provision of safe spaces in which an entropically unlikely interaction of elements can take place. Nothing fancy, yet more than three billion years of evolution enter into it.

It is important to recall in this time of despair that humanity, the greatest pest in nature, is not necessarily pestilential. All production – our giving form to nature – is an ensemble of order and disorder, and an entropic gamble. By "producing production" ecologically, we bring the odds of that production in the direction of ecosystemic integrity. The artist's fury to rearrange the given is akin to the gardener's tearing of the soil. "The cut worm forgives the plough," wrote Blake, knowing that destruction and production are conjoined sides of a dialectic.

Gardening, taken at large, can vary from a crude appropriation of capitalist consumerism (pesticides, heavy equipment, etc.), to inspired modes of "organic" intervention, including the practice of "permaculture," which engages a conscious effort to design gardens as full ecosystems.[22] All good gardening consists of differentiating a pre-existent given by the holding-together of disparate elements (seeds, water, good soil, compost, mulch, light, etc.) so that ecosystem development can occur. Conscious preparation is necessary, along with culturally transmitted knowledge. Thus gardening is a social process, enhanced to the degree that a fully realized association enters the picture. In fact, a community garden is an excellent model of a pathway toward an ecological society, as we will discuss later on.

The whole of history enters into each garden plot, and is perennially reopened there. These filaments extend back to the origins of humankind, and reveal the authentic core of our nature – which is to creatively intervene in nature. Long before the neolithic revolution had opened a path toward hierarchical society, humanity had learned to read the book of nature and to follow its generative way. It was a hard learning, whose lesson is lost in a facile romanticization of "first peoples." For the very first humans were by no means always kind to nature, nor should we expect this of them. Marauding bands of archaic peoples, for example, were quite likely the exterminators of mastodons, along with many other species. And why not? Why should the powers of collective action and technology afforded by human being not have gone haywire again and again under the circumstances of paleolithic existence, just as they have since? There is no surprise in that. The wonder is, rather, that at least some of the same creatures learned from their mistakes, learned to care for nature, and to divine the essentials of an ecocentric way of being.

If we look back to those forms of production that are not only precapitalist but essentially pre-market (in that the elements of private property, money, and exchange are peripheral), we find humanity capable of the whole range of ecological relations, creative as well as wanton. The latter is written in many extinctions and false starts, while the former may be summarized as follows: *That under original conditions, the human being is not merely capable of living in "harmony with nature"; more fundamentally, an un-alienated human intelligence is itself capable of fostering the evolution of nature even as it itself evolves.* In this sense, what we call "nature" is to some degree a human product itself, so that ecology and history have a common root. If evolution is mediated by the activity of creatures through ecosystems, should not the consciously transformative activity that is the human trademark, also be an evolutionary force?

Consider the Amazon basin, a hotly contested zone of the ecological crisis. It is recognized that an immense proportion of living species – including innumerable as yet undiscovered by us, along with many that are extremely useful – are found in this great womb. What accounts for this prodigious diversity? There is no single "efficient cause," in the sense derived for the ecological crisis as a whole; but there are distinct efficient causal patterns, a major one of which involves human intervention. The principal mode of species diversification is known as "allopatric speciation," briefly, the divergent paths taken by common gene pools as the creatures bearing those genes are separated and undergo divergent development under varying ecosystemic conditions. The famous example is the varied evolution of finches in the Galapagos Islands, discovered by Darwin. As different populations from the stem species moved to different islands, they ceased interbreeding and divergences began to appear under the different island conditions – which had been further changed by species activity – until eventually new species appeared.

In the hot and moist Amazon basin, the immense, varied yet relatively unbroken terrain, some 6 million square kilometers in area, creates an exponentially greater gene pool for the purposes of recombination. However, the very unbrokenness of the terrain can be seen to work against the project of speciation. For despite the great range of soils and habitats, there are few islands, or mountain ranges, or insurpassable bodies of water to provide the ecosystemic differentiation to allow allopatric speciation to "naturally" take its course. One would think, rather, that the oceanic scale of the rain forest would cause related gene pools to constantly intermix, thereby inhibiting the profusion of new species. Such reckoning omits, however, to take into account a creature able to create new ecosystems and demarcate them from others in a fluid and shifting way. More, this creature, left to its own devices, will for a few millennia live in small communities and as a result build a great number of micro-ecosystems.[23] The indigenous peoples of the Amazon not only created new ecosystems, they deliberately made these in a way that encouraged diversity of species, as by planting different configurations of trees that would attract varying patterns of game species. Moreover, they engaged, like many Indians of the Americas, in the controlled burning of the landscape. Utterly unlike the mass burnings by alienated and desperate workers and peasants that have been destroying the rain forest for the past two generations, this kind of burning is conducted in small batches, at carefully controlled times and rates, and by the individuals who directly inhabit the land. As Susanna Hecht and Alex Cockburn comment for the Kayapó (who at the height of their society tended an area roughly the size of France), the burning "is coupled with activities that compensate for its potentially destructive effects."[24] The result is actual enhancement of fertility (necessary given the peculiar conditions of the rain forest) and the provision of micro-ecosystems for rapid speciation.

Here humanity writes with its labor on the surface of the Amazon basin to bring forth new and richly varying life-forms. Far from being a congenital enemy of nature, then, humans can be a part of nature that catalyses nature's own exuberance. This ecologically creative activity is reserved, however, for those whose human ecology is closely configured to the varying natural ecologies with which it interacts, so that the combined human–natural ecosystem is integral and differentiated rather than disintegrated and split. It needs be realized that this kind of behavior requires that the earth not be treated as private property, or, what comes to the same thing, that the labor which undertakes it is freely differentiated, or as we will be calling it, freely associated. It is under such "original" conditions that human intelligence and consciousness learned to take an ecocentric form. This way of being creates people who differentiate nature and know the individual plant species one by one,[25] who live in the small, collectively managed communities that provide an immense range of opportunities for allopatric speciation, and who develop the existentially alive culture whose lessons are ours to learn.[26]

6 | Capital and the domination of nature

The pathology of a cancer upon nature

What is the root of capital's wanton ecodestructivity? One way of seeing this is in terms of an economy geared to run on the basis of unceasing accumulation. Thus, each unit of capital must, as the saying goes, "grow or die"; and each capitalist must constantly search to expand markets and profits or lose his position in the hierarchy. Under such a regime the economic dimension consumes all else, nature is continually devalued in the search for profit along an expanding frontier, and the ecological crisis follows inevitably.

This reasoning is, I believe, valid, and necessary for grasping how capital becomes the efficient cause of the crisis. But it is incomplete, and fails to clear up the mystery of what capital *is*, and, consequently, what is to be done about it. For example, it is a commonly held opinion that capitalism is an innate and therefore inevitable outcome for the human species. If this is the case, then the necessary path of human evolution travels from the Olduvai Gorge to the New York stock exchange, and to think of a world beyond capital is mere baying at the moon.

It takes only a brief reflection to demolish the received understanding. Capital is self-evidently a possible outcome given the potentials of human nature, but despite all the efforts of ideologues to argue for its natural inevitability, no more than this. For if capital were natural, why has it only occupied the last 500 years of a record that goes back for hundreds of thousands? More to the point, why did it have to be imposed through violence wherever it set down its rule? And most importantly, why does it have to be continually maintained through violence, and continuously reimposed on each generation through an enormous apparatus of indoctrination? Why not just let children be the way they want to be and trust they will turn into capitalists and workers for capitalists – the way we let baby chicks be, knowing that they will reliably grow into chickens if provided with food, water and shelter? Those who believe that capital is innate should also be willing to do without police, or the industries of culture, and if they are not, then their arguments are hypocritical.

This, though, only sharpens the questions of what capital is, why the path to it was chosen, and why people would submit to an economy and think so much of wealth in the first place. These are highly practical concerns. It is widely recognized, for example, that habits of consumption in the industrial societies will have to be drastically altered if a sustainable world is to be achieved. This means, however, that the very pattern of human needs will have to be changed, which means in turn that the basic way we inhabit nature will have to be changed. We know that capital forcibly indoctrinates people to resist these changes; but it is a poor and superficial analysis that would stop here and say nothing further about how this works and how it came about. Capital's efficient causation of the ecological crisis establishes it as the enemy of nature. But the roots of the enmity still await exploration.

A great deal of ink has been expended in trying to decide just what is the core of our estrangement from nature, but little of it has any real explanatory value. It is perfectly possible and quite desirable, for example, to identify, as do the Deep Ecologists, certain central and controlling ideas that define a pathological relation to nature, notably the "anthropocentric" delusion that sees nature, in all its intricate glory, existing like so many planets around the human sun. No understanding of the ecological crisis would be complete without such a dimension. But it is a dimension only, that outlines the subjective shape of an ecodestructive complex without connection to the objective side of things, and with no clue as to how it arose – nor, therefore, with how it can be overcome. A mental attitude explains no more than some of the internal circuitry of a phenomenon, and until its origins and relationships with the world are spelled out, is just an empty and vague abstraction.

The domination of nature | 6

122

Similarly, many authors are ready to talk of "technology," or "industrialization" as the active elements in the crisis, since it is obvious that it is through such means nature is being laid waste. But to stop at this point is not only incomplete, but also evasive and politically opportunistic, since it is patently the case that the industry in question, and the tools it uses, are instruments of capital accumulation, and have been so since the beginnings of the modern world.[1] No tool, nor any large-scale organization of technology, can exist in itself; industry, and all the qualities internal to it, are products and expressions of a given mode of social organization, and cannot be conceived apart from it. The world teems with brilliant innovations that deserve application as ways of checking the ecological crisis but will not be used because they run against the exigencies of accumulation. The same can be said for "science," also routinely hauled out as the culprit responsible for our estrangement from nature, which is said to be reduced "scientifically" to a mere object for dissection. Well, yes, this does happen, but the questions must again be posed: which science, in the service of which interests, and shaped by which social forces? No doubt, an estranged science plays a tremendous role in the domination of nature. But estrangement of this kind must itself be explained, and in the explaining, we push back the origins of domination.

Science, technology, and industry are today all subsumed into the capitalist system. Yet capitalism as we know it did not spring full-grown into the world. It combined many precursors, which took root in peculiar cultural soils. The economies that resulted were not the bearers of any particular essence, but reflected, like the personalities of individuals, specific integrations, some of which have been more deadly to ecologies than others. For example, our variety of ecodestructive capitalism was a peculiarly European concoction, and, as such, deeply influenced by the dominant Christian religion, spiritual edge of an extremely powerful and by no means ecologically friendly world-view.[2] The attitude of Christianity toward nature long predates capitalism, and extends from its Judaic roots, as in the passage in Genesis

(1–27) where Yahweh gives Adam "dominion over the fish of the sea, and over the birds of the air, and over the cattle, and over all the earth, and over every creeping thing that creeps upon the earth" – all of which is not only compatible with but mandated by the belief that "God created man in his own image, in the image of God he created him" (28).

No other world religion, and certainly no tribal religion, incorporates the domination of nature so directly into its *Logos*. It bears emphasis that this attitude was strongly contested within Christianity – indeed, some of the greatest saints, Francis and Teresa of Avila being the most famous, are defined by rebellion against it, just as the Church itself would strive to contain the capitalist monster once it arose from European soil. Religions are dialectical; they express domination as well as the protest against domination, and even the release from domination. Nevertheless, there is a definite balance of forces at play; and for Christianity, the preponderance of these forces was expressed in what would have to be called an anti-ecocentric direction. This is best shown by the striking hatred of the body that marks the history of Christendom, along with its obsessive preoccupation with feelings of guilt.[3]

Many societies could have led the way into the capitalist era, including China and India, which were more highly developed by far than Europe in the fifteenth century, while being more at home with nature. It is impossible to say whether their accession to capitalism would have resulted in an ecologically friendlier outcome. But the luck was with Europe, which had its shipping lanes along the trade winds that led to the "undiscovered" Americas. And so the civilization whose previous development had primed it for the domination of nature became capitalist in the sense that we recognize the beast, especially after emergence into harsh and life-denying Calvinism.[4]

Yet this relationship does not entitle us to declare Christianity the villain of the piece, either, since the crisis is quite capable of being reproduced without it; indeed, in its current phase, virtually all traces of the religious origins of capital have been effaced. In the final analysis, a religion is itself the ambivalent product of a certain kind of society. Thus the evocation of Christendom again raises the question of origins and pushes back the quest until it disappears into the mists of human beginnings. Here, however, we reach a ground that can enable a reasonably coherent – if highly attenuated and schematic – image of how the domination of nature arose, and what led it to mutate into capitalism. It goes without saying that what follows is adapted to the purposes of this work and does not represent a full rendition of the story and the many questions attached to it. The reader must decide for him- or herself whether the light it casts will compensate for the brevity of treatment.

The gendered bifurcation of nature

The first map of the human species was drawn according to "him" and "her," in that produced configuration of sexuality known as *gender*. Gender is the original dividing line within humanity; and the constructions of humankind, whether within humanity or between humanity and nature, are inscribed by it. There is nothing more "material" (including the common origin of the words, *material* and *mother*). Sex is of the earth, and the primary dividing lines between genders were expressed in earth-transforming labor. Out of this matrix (there is that root again) arose the beginnings of domination; and all future dominations, including that effected by capital, are shadowed by that of male over female.

This is not an exercise in politically correct male-bashing. However, a candid look at the history of domination would be radically incomplete unless the role played in it by the construction of the masculine gender were acknowledged. The actual origins must remain shrouded in an impenetrably distant past. Nevertheless, everything that is known (though all-too-often ideologically denied) about the human species compels the reconstruction of the following, which we state baldly and according to the ideas already developed about human nature, so as to bring out the essential points: [5]

125

- In the original, hunter-gatherer, phase of society, the first differentiation of labor occurs according to sex, generally speaking, with males hunting and females gathering – along, needless to say, with their work of reproduction. Note that this labor produces the gender itself, and that its origins were a genuine differentiation, with mutual recognition, fluid social relations, and self-determination. This can still be seen in the cultural remnants we have of these peoples, and by the reconstruction of the quality of self-experience derived from it: thus the "dream-time" of Australian first peoples, the wandering of souls, the manifestations of Trickster, and so forth.[6] The phase encompasses the great span of human prehistory, and entails a great range of human–natural transformations, including the domestication of animals and the origins of agriculture. Though without domination, the original division of labor set forth males as the takers of life and females as life's giver. Moreover, the death-dealing tools of the hunt, and the fact of its often being carried out by roving bands, prepared a way for something worse.

- Here a sporadically occurring event may be postulated of whose existence we are certain even though no concrete first instance can be brought forward. Its agent was masculine, not as individual hunter, but as a subset of the collective: a group, or band of hunters; and its stimulus would vary, being composed, however, of subjective as well as external forces: the latter being, say, a threat to survival, like disease or drought, which compelled a search for new resources; while the former was a function of the psychodynamics of the male group. In any case, the event in question was a transformation of the hunt to a raid, with the object being now not the obtaining of food, skins, etc., from animals, but the expropriation of productive labor from other humans, i.e. taking not just the life of another creature, but the life-giving and building power of one's own kind.[7] This necessarily involved the seizure of women and children from a neighboring collective. We suppose a threefold violence: killing or driving off the males from the attacked collective, denying the self-determination of the seized women and children, and the forcible sexual violation of the captives.

- This act was a profound mutation in human being. It created a whole new conjuncture, which in time became a structure. First, the possibilities of exploiting another's labor are introduced, always in the direction of male over female. Second, the potentials for enduring social divisions are grounded in this, again male over female; these are to extend from the hunting band, to the warrior band, and to the ruling class, with any number of intermediate and modern variations, e.g. the Vatican Curia, the NFL Superbowl champions, corporate boards of directors, the Joint Chiefs of Staff, the Politburo, secret societies like Yale's Skull and Bones (in which George W. Bush participated). Indeed, there is a sense in which the whole world has been run by male bands since the beginnings of history. Third, the genders are further produced by this, with sharply opposed identities constituted by master and slave. And fourth, violence – physical force along with the culture glorifying this – had to become institutionalized in order to hold onto what had been stolen.

- The structures imposed by the original seizure of female labor had dramatic expansive possibilities. Social violence entered the lists of the dangers to which societies are exposed, along with those of natural cause. The violence invited retaliation and/or defense; and it came to define ever-larger social aggregates with expansive dynamics, as each particular group underwent a compulsion to achieve power relative to others. Internally, the drive toward power caused struggles for leadership and social control. The result, after innumerable twists and turns we are unable to detail here, was the emergence of the Big Man, the Chieftain, the King, the Shiekh, the Emperor, the Pope, the Führer, the Generalissimo, and the CEO.

We would emphasize again that these principles would be variously applied across a vast range of situations. There is no need, either, to imagine a single such event radiating outward to encompass the rest of humanity. But what has to be underscored is the absolute dynamism of this event, and the fact that it amounted to a real mutation of human society as potent as anything from the realm of genetics. Out of the nexus of original male violence arose codified property relations, as a way of holding onto what had been taken: thus the notions of property and legitimacy follow that of violent seizure. Similarly, the institution of patriarchy emerged, as a system of apportioning women and assuring ownership and control over children – a never-ending dilemma for the man who sows his seed and moves on, as the Big Man must. Property in this sense is not primarily that which attaches to the self, like clothing or jewellery (though in stratified and wealthy societies, the control over personal consumption is quite significant); but rather the power of producing – and re-producing life – and the means for life. The control over labor originates civilization; and this originates in the forcible control over women.

The control over labour enables civilization to emerge and shapes it,[8] and this means that a basic estrangement, or *alienation*, is introduced at the foundations of society – alienation being the reflex, at the level of human being, of ecosystemic splitting. The dominant male identity is formed in this cauldron. From the beginning, its reference point is the other males in the hunting/warrior group, with whom it associates and identifies; coordinatively, it comes to shun and deny recognition to the subjected female. A purified male-Ego comes to define the dominant form taken by the self, which enters into the exfoliating system of splits constituting the emergent civilization. Subjectively, this alienation becomes inscribed as a progressive separation from the body, and from what the body signifies, namely, nature.[9]

A polarization between the human and the natural worlds ensues, with masculinity occupying the human (= intellectual, far-seeing, spiritual, powerful, and active) pole, and femininity the pole of nature (= instinctual, limited and body-based, inconstant, weak, and passive). The *gendered bifurcation of nature* has been set going, to configure the relations between genders, and between humanity and nature, all the way to the ecological crisis once it takes capitalist form.

The path leading from the first violent expropriation of labor to the heights of capital passes through the solidification of property and the appearance of class as a defining element of society. Class institutionalizes property and emerges *pari passu* with the introduction of splitting into human ecosystems. Though violent expropriation is a necessary step in domination, it is insufficient in itself as a way of producing and reproducing life. Secondary forms of recognition become essential to hold the social ecosystem together and harness its forces. Class is one such, operating in the sphere of production as patriarchy does in that of reproduction. Class codifies the formal arrangements for the ownership of productive property and the control over labor. The rule of law is layered over that of violence, and internalizes violence. Labor has become unfree.

Class is not grounded in physical difference or biological plan like gender, but in the formalization of the productive core of human being. Since the free exercise of transformative power expresses human nature, class is a violation of human nature, and with it, of nature itself, even if it is not grounded in the physical body. Class relationships never appear in pure, unadulterated form, however, as the splits they impose would tear society apart. They occur, rather, embedded in a further institutional turn, which emerges and takes the form of the *state*. It is the class–state nexus that comprises the decisive leap between archaic society and what we call civilization. With this, history as such begins, and the cyclical, differentiated time of original society is transformed according to the hierarchical ground plan of class. Now society has a controlling agency to tell its story to itself – a story, however, given over to conflict because of the institutionalization of class. States impose writing, through their cadres of technicians; and they impose universalizing religions like Christianity through their cadres of priests;[10] and they impose laws through their judges and courts; and they impose violence and conquest with their armies, and also the legitimation of violence and conquest. Everything thereafter is marked with contradiction, stemming from the state's original dilemma, that it stands over the whole of society, but is for society's ruling classes.

States carry forth all those notions we call "progress." They also, however, implement the domination of nature, in all the forms taken by nature – women certainly; but also, the other peoples conquered by those states which achieve imperial status. As enslaved and dominated peoples become incorporated into the domain, they acquire the status of Other – barbarians, savages, human animals, and, eventually (with the growth under capital of science), ethnicities and races – all of which categories cluster with the female at the "nature" end of the bifurcation within humanity.

This discussion may help clarify a vexing issue on the left, namely, as to the priority of different categories of what might be called "dominative splitting" – chiefly, those of gender, class, race, ethnic and national exclusion, and, with the ecological crisis, species. Here we must ask, priority in relation to what? If we intend, prior in *time*, then gender holds the laurel – and, considering how history always adds to the past rather than replacing it, would appear as at least a trace in all further dominations. If we intend, prior in *existential* significance, then that would apply to whichever of the categories was put forward by immediate historical forces as these are lived by masses of people: thus to a Jew living in Germany in the 1930s, anti-semitism would have been searingly prior, just as anti-Arab racism would be to a Palestinian living under Israeli domination today, or a ruthless, aggravated sexism would be to women living in, say, Afghanistan. As to which is *politically* prior, in the sense of being that which whose transformation is practically more urgent, that depends upon the preceding, but also upon the deployment of all the forces active in a concrete situation; we shall address this in the last section of this work, when we deal with the politics of overcoming the crisis.

If, however, we ask the question of *efficacy*, that is, which split sets the others into motion, then priority would have to be given to class, for the plain reason that class relations entail the state as an instrument of enforcement and control, and it is the state that shapes and organizes the splits that appear in human ecosystems. Thus class is both logically and historically distinct from other forms of exclusion (hence we should not talk of "classism" to go along with "sexism" and "racism," and "species-ism"). This is, first of all, because class is an essentially man-made category, without root in even a mystified biology. We cannot, in other words, imagine a human world without gender distinctions – although we can imagine a world without domination by gender. But a world without class is eminently imaginable – indeed, such was the human world for the great majority of our species' time on earth, during all of which considerable fuss was made over gender. Historically, the difference arises because "class" signifies one side of a larger figure that includes a state apparatus whose conquests and regulations create races and shape gender relations. Thus there will be no true resolution of racism so long as class society stands, inasmuch as a racially oppressed society implies the activities of a class-defending state.[11] Nor can gender inequality be legislated away so long as class society, with its state, demands the super-exploitation of woman's labor.

Class society continually generates gender, racial, ethnic oppressions, and the like, which take on a life of their own, as well as profoundly affecting the concrete relations of class itself. It follows that class politics must be fought out in terms of all the active forms of social splitting. It is the management of these divisions that keeps state society functional. Thus though each person in a class society is reduced from what s/he can become, the varied reductions can be combined into the great stratified regimes of history – this one becoming a fierce warrior, that one a routine-loving clerk, another a submissive seamstress, and so on, until we reach today's personifications of capital and captains of industry. Yet no matter how functional a class society, the profundity of its ecological violence ensures a basic antagonism which drives history onward. History *is* the history of class society – because no matter how modified, so powerful a schism is bound to work itself through to the surface, provoke resistance (i.e. "class struggle"), and lead to the succession of powers. The relation of class can be mystified without end – only consider the extent to which religion exists for just this purpose, or watch a show glorifying the police on television – yet so long as we have any respect for human nature, we must recognize that so fundamental an antagonism as would steal the vital force of one person for the enrichment of another cannot be conjured away.

The state is what steps forward to manage this conflict so that the ruling class gets its way without causing society to fly apart. It is the state's province to deal with class contradiction as it works itself out in numberless ways – to build its armies and use them in conquest (thereby reinforcing patriarchal and violent values), to codify property, to set forth laws to punish those who would transgress property relations, and to regulate contracts, and debts between individuals who play by the rules, to institutionalize police, courts and prisons to back up those laws, or to certify what is proper and right in the education of the young, or the marriage of the sexes, or establish the religions that justify God's ways to mere man, or to institutionalize science and education – in sum, to regulate and enforce the class structure, and to channel the flux of history in the direction of the elites. The state institutionalizes patriarchy as well as class, and hence maintains the societal ground for the gendered bifurcation of nature. Furthermore, inasmuch as the modern state is also a *nation*-state, it employs the attachment of a people to its land as a source of legitimation, and thus incorporates the history of nature into myths of wholeness and integrity. All aspects of the domination of nature are in fact woven into the fabric by means of which the state holds society together, from which it follows that to give coherence to this narrative and make a difference in it, we have to attend to the state and its ultimate dependence upon maintaining the class structure. All of this is to play a basic role in the unfolding of contemporary ecological struggles, as we discuss in the next section.

The rise of capital

> Capitalism only triumphed when it becomes identified with the state, when it is the state.[12]

Class relationships separate people from their vital power. Capital goes further: it separates our vital power from itself, and imposes a double estrangement. The arena within which this occurs is the labor market, and the instrument of its occurrence is that most strange and interesting concoction of the human mind: money.

As the saying goes, money makes the world go round. But there are three different aspects to money, which ascend in mystery, though all are bound together in reality.[13] The first, simplest, and most rational as well as the most ancient, would be money *as an instrument of exchange and trade*. We say, rational, because without some independent element that enables goods to be compared to each other, economic activity, indeed, society itself, would remain paleolithic. At this level, the money-function allows raw materials, instruments of production and finished goods to be brought together from varied sources, making a wider human intercourse possible.

The second way we know money is *as a commodity*, something that can be acquired, traded, and, crucially, accumulated. There is, from this angle, a history of money that passes from common concretions like shells or exchangeable possessions like cattle,[14] to metallic coin, to the abstraction into paper notes of one kind and another, onwards into the ever-increasing dematerialization taken by the money-form until today, in the digital age, it covers the globalized world with a shower of bytes. To explore these aspects would distract us from the task at hand. However, one of them, namely, the propensity for dematerialization, is of absolute importance, as it leads to the third and most puzzling, as well as most relevant, aspect of money.

What installs our system as the enemy of nature is the property of money as *the repository of value*. The notion of value, so difficult to grasp, yet so compelling for civilization, provides a window onto the pathology of power. Where money is concerned, value is an abstraction of the exchange function: thus from the particulars of exchanging one item for another, we arrive at "exchangeability-in-general." But it is also the convergence of exchangeability with desire. Value is the projection of human want into nature – including human nature and the qualities of the self. It is the setting up of an alternative, monetized world, with no fixed connection to the original world.[15] Thus value does not exist in nature, though the creature who devises it does. As Georg Simmel put it in his magisterial work on money:

> The series of natural phenomena could be described in their
> entirety without mentioning the value of things; and our scale
> of valuation remains meaningful, whether or not any of its
> objects appear frequently or at all in reality ... Valuation as a real
> psychological occurrence is part of the natural world; but what
> we mean by valuation, its conceptual meaning, is something
> independent of this world; is not part of it, but is rather the
> whole world viewed from a particular vantage point.[16]

There are distinct universes of value, by no means all economic. The infant values the breast, the child her dolls, the Buddha, contemplation, the ecocentrically minded, the biosphere, the fetishist, a stiletto heel, and so forth. Nor are all abstractions evil, to say the least, else we would regard mathematics as a crime, or the abstracting of Marx when he developed his notions of value in order to emancipate labor. Abstractions – including quantification – need not be pathological so long as there remains a differentiated path back to the sensuous-concrete, such as we see in fruitful science; or when, as in the case of "pure" mathematics, abstractions are bracketed away from the external world. That is, the mathematician does not confuse his abstractions with reality – unless he is psychotic, and even if he is psychotic, he lacks the means to bring reality under the sway of his abstraction. Not so for capital, which converts the sensuous world into abstraction for the purpose of value. Since the sensuous world remains in touch with the plenum of nature, this conversion can become a splitting of devastating proportion and leads to a new order of domination.

Whatever is produced tends to serve some purpose, even if this be frivolous, destructive, or fantastic. Thus a kind of value adheres to all made objects according to the needs these meet, or, to choose another word, their utility. For produced things, *use-value* represents the conjugation of labor and nature, and occupies the boundary between human nature and nature at large. And because human nature entails participation of the imagination, there is no use-value that does not include some subjective and imagined dimension – whether this be the coziness of a good blanket, the taste of wine, the anticipation of the potential life lying embedded in a seed, and so forth.

Use-value is essentially concrete; it is a *qualitative* function, composed of sensuous and intellectual distinctions with other aspects of the world, including other use-values. Being qualitative, it retains the essential feature of differentiation, that distinct elements can recognize one another and form links and associations. Use-values can be deformed when they come to express alienated ways of being – what else can be said, after all, about use-values such as are expressed by a TV game show, or any of the commodities that reflect false needs – sports utility vehicles, lite beer, fashion magazines, hand guns, and so on. But because they are also concrete, they can be restored, as a "used" article can be mended and made to shine. Indeed, the mending of the ecological crisis requires precisely such a restoration.

Not all use-values are attached to commodities. However, all commodities have a use-value, since no one would purchase anything or exchange it for something else unless it has some utility.[17] But they also have another kind of value, arising from the fact of exchangeability that attaches to all commodities: *exchange-value*. Here, in sharp contrast to use-values, the sensuous and concrete are eliminated by definition and *a priori*. All that is

135

retained as the mark of exchangeability is quantity: this item, x, is exchangable for so many of y, which in turn is exchangeable for so many of z, and so forth, with no intrinsic end. Any concrete quality will break the chain; only number suffices, and money becomes the embodiment of that number. Hence money is fundamentally quantity, which becomes its use-value. Simmel again: "The quantity of money is its quality. Since money is nothing but the indifferent means for concrete and infinitely varied purposes, its quantity is the only important determination so far as we are concerned. With reference to money, we do not ask what and how, but how much."[18]

There is nothing else in the universe like it. Use-values require the participation of nature, but exchange-values are made by quantifying nature. The ascension of quantity over quality gives these relations the capacity for evil once the value function is advanced to the center of the social stage, as in capitalism. In this loss of the sensuous and concrete, the abstracting function is abandoned to the delusions of power. Precisely because nature has been detached, with its limits and inter-relations, in short, its ecosystems, there is no longer any internal limit to the value function. It can expand effortlessly. Pure quantity can swell infinitely without any reference to the external world, even though the quantity-using creature remains very much in that world. And if there is some will-to-power in the creature who makes for himself this value function, carried forward from traditional modes of domination, then that, too, can go to infinity.

Along the way, possibilities for recognition are sundered. Simmel points out two aspects: that valuation takes place in the human being, i.e. "part of the natural world," and that it is not the world in itself, but "rather the whole world viewed from a particular vantage point." The abstraction into money sets loose these two formally distinct parts of value to wander their separate ways – and the creature who subsumes both those ways, *Homo œconomicus*, or the capitalist personification – is split internally and from the world. Hence the value that stalks forth in the economy is also the route that turns our differentiation from nature into a regime of splitting, which is to say, into one of self-perpetuating ecodisintegration.

The transformation of capital from an ancient part of the economic system into the world-devouring monster reproduced by capitalism occurred when the value function became attached to labor itself. For this to have taken place, an extensive series of prior developments, affecting the history of money as well as labor, was necessary.

Long before capitalism arose as such, rulers appreciated the power of money and foisted it upon the masses – who proved significantly reluctant to take the bait. In a far cry from Adam Smith's ideological notion, that the species has an innate propensity to barter, truck and exchange (in other words, that capitalism is part of human nature), the use of money was distinctly an acquired habit, often requiring coercion. With regard to Europe, which as the cradle of the capitalism we know deserves special attention, Alexander Murray has pointed out a kind of turning point occurring around the first millennium, in which a society not simply unacquainted with money but actually resistant to it was converted into one whose wheels were to become increasingly lubricated with lucre.[19] In Carolingean times, coins were introduced from above into a matrix that had no "use" for their exchange-value, and where they were treated primarily in their second function, as a commodity to be exchanged along with others. Many coins were melted down for bullion, others were given directly to the poor, others were converted into ornaments and silver chalices, while others still have been found unused in various storage sites. Fines and penalties such as flogging had to be imposed to rouse the people of the "Dark Ages" into the glories of exchange. Murray concludes that money was considered "strange and suspect," and holds "psychic inertia" responsible. But I would think that said inertia was grounded in an intuition of the wreckage inherent in the strange function of value, a prescience, shared for a time by the Catholic Church, that the same money could become a wedge breaking down the integrity of communal life-worlds. In any case, there can be no doubt that medieval monetarism eventually

137

speeded up economic activity and prepared the way for capitalism. By facilitating exchange, money increased its own value,
fostered avarice, led to usury, and created demand for its own
accumulation. The production of money surged – thus England
had ten mints in 900, and seventy a century later – and banking
– which first occurred to people in the ancient era – came into
Europe with the founding of the Bank of Venice in 1171.

The expansion and centralization of trade, banking functions, and urbanism fostered rationalization and technological
progress. As the location of Europe's first bank in Venice suggests, this side of the process was advanced in the Mediterranean
and mostly in the Italian city-states. Venice, along with Genoa
and Florence, became the leading centers of the early manifestation of finance. Later the Luso-Hispanic plunder of the Western
hemisphere (opened by the Genovese Columbus) provided bullion for the finance capital that allowed Europe, whose economy
had remained backward with respect to Asian centers until the
mid-eighteenth century, to buy its way into hegemony.[20]

As for the labor relation, this was furthest developed in Northern Europe and especially through agricultural transformations
in England. Here the critical factor became the separation of the
worker from the means of production – which in precapitalist
society meant the land above all else, and, more generally, nature.
In one of Marx's many summaries of this he puts it as follows:

One of the prerequisites of wage labour and one of the historic
conditions for capital is free labour and the exchange of free
labour against money, in order to reproduce money and to
convert it into values, in order to be consumed by money, not
as use value for enjoyment but as use value for money. Another
prerequisite is the separation of free labour from the objective
means of its realisation – from the means and materials of labour.
This means above all that the worker must be separated from the
land, which functions as his natural laboratory ... the relationship
of the worker to the objective conditions of his labour is one of
ownership: this is the natural unity of labour with its material pre-

requisites. [Under these circumstances] the individual is related to himself as proprietor, as master of the conditions of his reality. The same relation holds between one individual and the rest.[21]

The separation required violent expropriation.[22] The rate of dispossession began accelerating after the mid-sixteenth century, as bullion from the Americas began entering the European economies. It took place most systematically in England in the form of the "enclosure" of the commons, i.e. of commonly owned land; it took place elsewhere in Europe as the precondition for the coming of capitalism to that subcontinent; it took place throughout the "New World" and Africa as millions upon millions became dispossessed so that the great capitalist enterprises and slave trades could fatten; and it continues to take place today, with the expropriation of community gardens in New York City, or wherever peasants stand backwardly in the way of accumulation, as, for example, in Mexico, where NAFTA fosters their being driven by cheap imports of corn off the *ejidos*[23] and into the *maquiladoras* or across the border – and also across that half of the world which lies vulnerable to globalization. The separation of peoples from the means of production and their communal heritage transfigures the notion of property and creates the social foundation of the capitalist mode of production; it is a gesture continuously reproduced as capital penetrates life-worlds. Separation in this regard has two aspects: the physical and juridical removal of producers from the appropriation of their own lives; and alongside this, the alienation or estrangement between the worker and the product made, the method of work employed, relations with other workers (and, by extension, all social relations), and, finally, from their own human nature. The fourfold sense of alienated labor was drawn by Marx in his early philosophical writing; later, in the mature synthesis of *Capital*, it became amplified as the famous concept of commodity fetishism, an insight into the way value-driven production mystifies the nature of things, so that commodities relate as persons, and persons as things, in a veritable frenzy of estrangement.[24]

Separation/alienation/splitting is the fundamental gesture of capital. It applies to the expropriation of peasants, but also forcefully to the industrial system, where technological prowess in the service of value-expansion puts the finishing touches to the domination of nature. The industrial revolution brought in its wake work-discipline, as individual human labor had to become integrated with machinery and coordinated on an ever-expanding scale. Just as early-medieval people were coerced into accepting the logic of money, so were early-modern people coerced into accepting the logic of the bound time of accumulation. Wages are convertible to capital only if placed in a rigid schema of linear temporality, inasmuch as an abstract interval is the only way of computing the exchange-value of labor-power, or of measuring the surplus value wrung from it. For this computation, technology in the form of clocks was required, along with new modes of socialization and a religious and moral culture to put it all together and justify the whole arrangement in the eyes of God.[25]

Science, technology, and industry, therefore, are all bundled together with the dominant religion and, under the aegis of capital, come to express its powers of splitting. In capital's early phase, the inner connection to the gendered bifurcation of nature was strikingly revealed in the great witch crazes of early-modern Europe, and through ideologues of science like Francis Bacon. As the system matured, its latent powers of ecodestruction would come to the fore under the aegis of industrialization.[26]

Industrialization is not an independent force, then, but the hammer with which nature is smashed for the sake of capital. Industrial logging destroys forests; industrial fishing destroys fisheries; industrial chemistry makes Frankenfood; industrial use of fossil fuels creates the greenhouse effect, and so forth – all for the sake of value-expansion. Most important, the technically driven production of the industrial order demands an expanded energy supply, for purpose of which fuels such as coal, natural gas, and petroleum are by far the most likely candidates. Such fuel represents past ecological activity: numberless residues of chemical bonds developed by living creatures in interaction with sunlight over hundreds of millions of years, now turned to heat energy to propel the instruments of industrial society. Each drive to the mall to buy wasteful plastic junk made from fossil fuel degrades eons of ecological order into heat and noxious fumes. I have read somewhere that in a single day the industrial world consumes the equivalent of ten thousand years of bioecological activity, a ratio, roughly, of 3–4 million to one. With this squandering, and the associated tossing about of materials of every sort, the entropic potentials inherent in social production reach levels of eco-destabilization on an expanding scale. The staggering pace of entropic decay has only become noticeable recently because the earth is sizable enough to have buffered its effects until the past thirty years or so, since when we have had a clogging of the "sinks" along with an ever-rising level of production.

The phenomenon of separation expresses the core gesture of ecodisintegration, for separation in the physical and social sense corresponds to splitting in the ontological sense. Splitting extends the separation of elements of ecosystems past the point where they interact to create new Wholes – or, from another angle, to the point where the dialectic that constitutes ecosystems breaks down. It follows that the ecological crisis is not simply a manifestation of the macroeconomic effects of capital, but reveals also the extension of capitalist alienation into the ecosphere. And as this alienation, and the whole structure of the system, is grounded in the relation between capital and labor, it also follows that the ecological crisis and capital's exploitation of labor are two aspects of the same phenomenon.

The historical matrix for this occurred when persons of the nascent ruling class subjugated labor into the system of exchange-value, turning human transformative power into a commodity on sale for a wage. The wage-relation, in which one's capacity to work is given a money equivalent and sold on the market, is much older than capitalism itself, nor was it the only form of labor within emerging capitalist markets,[27] nor, needless to say, is it a necessary evil in each and every instance where it appears. But its generalization into the means by which capital itself is produced permanently alters the landscape of human being in an anti-ecocentric direction.

Capitalism became a full-blown system when the political, economic, legal, and cultural conditions were finally put together into a self-expanding machine for turning human beings into salaried workers on the fertile plains of labor markets. There were many turns in this road, but the definitive one came when the class of capitalists took full control of the state during the various bourgeois revolutions. Then all the state functions mentioned above were subsumed into the purposes of capital. The goal of production became accumulation of value, use-values became subordinated to exchange-values, surplus-value production became the alpha and omega of the economy, and ecological relations were abstracted away from their mutual differentiation and fragmented. In its latest, neoliberal-globalized stage, increased gender exploitation becomes the rule for the great masses of humanity, even as upper-class women within the metropolis achieve substantive gains within the bourgeois order. Racial and ethnic schisms persist alongside of, and as a defense against, the ultimate atomization which is capital's *telos*. Non-recognition of fellow creatures is built into society, which thereby undergoes a motion toward nihilism; human nature becomes separated from itself, and what has been only a logical potentiality has become a historical actuality whose logical outcome is the complete submission of the globe to the regime of value.

Philosophical interlude

No more than an extended set of notes, really, since to do justice to the topic requires another volume, while to ignore it completely leaves too many threads of the argument dangling. In fact, we have been intervening throughout in philosophical debates, without explicitly saying as much; here we need only say a little further, so as to round matters out before launching into the question of how to transform capitalism.

The Australian eco-philosopher Arran Gare develops the notion of a kind of "wrong turn" taken by civilization, one manifestation of which was the postulation of a higher realm of being over the world of mere matter. We might call this the philosophical reflex of the domination of nature. That it took at first the shape of Neoplatonism, that is, at the cradle of Christianity, is less important for us than the fact that an idea of this sort keeps reproducing itself according to specifics of different epochs. This was the mutation that engendered Christianity's flight from the body, leaving in its wake a space of abstraction from which the line to capital can be drawn. As Gare's account makes clear, offshoots of this attitude remain active in many non-religious intellectual ideologies, for example, as *mechanical materialism*, which enshrines the deadening of matter by neglecting nature's formativity, or *Social Darwinism*, which naturalizes capitalist competition, seeing it as a fundamental principle of life.[28]

While it is nonsense to reduce ideas to material interests (after all, material interests include ideas and are shaped by ideas), it is necessary to regard all thinking as conjunctural, as no philosopher can do other but try to make sense out of the world as he or she has been thrown into it. All thinkers have positions, and take positions, of which their philosophies are necessarily expressions. Before there was Neoplatonism there was Platonism, which first elaborated the idea of essences; and we know enough about Plato to recognize the impulse behind his thought to establish philosophers as rulers, in the meantime subduing the common people with a strong state that condensed class relations into abstract principles while mystifying them with propaganda. Wherever, then, there is postulated a "higher reality" standing over mere reality, we may expect the thinker in question to have somewhere in mind, the installation of a class system with higher people over mere helots, needless to say, with himself on the side of the rulers. This went for Plato and, in recent times, for the great Martin Heidegger, whose ontology cannot – and more to the point, should not – ever be separated from his explicit Nazism.[29]

Heidegger is of special importance, as his thought is regarded very seriously by deep ecologists, particularly in regard to the critique of technology, where he even takes to task the notion of efficient cause.[30] He asks: is not the notion of efficient cause itself a concomitant of technological domination? Does it not therefore perpetuate the estrangement from nature and ultimately the ecological crisis? For Heidegger, the efficient cause does not stand apart from the instrumental cause, but is essentially instrumentality writ large.

Why, he argues, seek a *"causa efficiens"* which "brings about the effect that is the finished [product]," and that becomes "the standard for all causality," but at the same time drowns out the other Aristotelian causes: the *causa materialis*, or material out of which a thing is made; the *causa formalis*, the shape or form into which it enters; and the *causa finalis*, the end to which it is put? To Heidegger, the authentic technological attitude does not privilege any aspect of causality, but rather sees all four as "the ways, all belonging at once to each other, of being responsible for something else." From another angle, Heidegger posits a much more intimate and nonlinear relation between cause and effect than is conveyed in the notion of efficient cause, seen as a kind of demiurge standing behind the world and moving it.

The notion is developed in relation to a silver chalice made as a sacrificial vessel. Using terms such as "indebtedness," "considering," and "gathering," Heidegger conveys how a tool-using human can take responsibility for the "bringing-forth," or *poiesis*, of new being. In his later period (this essay was first composed as a lecture in the early 1950s), Heidegger saw the truth of being as a "presencing"; hence, "Every occasion for whatever passes beyond the nonpresent and goes forth into presencing is *poiesis*, bringing-forth." Far from being anti-technological, then, Heidegger sees technology as, ideally, an elementary form of the "coming into being" that is the human contribution to the real; it is to be set alongside nature's bringing-forth, or *physis*, by which is meant "the arising of something out of itself," like the "bursting of a blossom into bloom."

Bringing forth gathers the four modes of causality; hence revealing, or presencing, is the highest mode of technology. Following the Greek sense, Heidegger locates this true meaning as *techne*, and groups the technical approach to reality with "the arts of the mind and the fine arts."

> Whoever builds a house or a ship or forges a sacrificial chalice reveals what is to be brought forth, according to the terms of the four modes of occasioning. This revealing gathers together in advance the aspect and the matter of ship or house, with a view to the finished thing envisioned as completed, and from this gathering determines the manner of its construction. Thus what is decisive in *techne* does not lie at all in making and manipulating nor in the using of means, but rather in the revealing mentioned before. It is as revealing, and not as manufacturing, that *techne* is a bringing-forth. (295)

Under conditions of our estrangement, things have not worked out this way: "the revealing that holds sway throughout modern technology does not unfold into a bringing-forth in the sense of *poiesis*." Instead, it is a "challenging . . . which puts to nature the unreasonable demand that it supply energy which can be extracted and stored as such." The earth is now reduced to a repository of resources; and this degrades both mineral and agricultural practice. It is an "expediting" directed toward "driving on to the maximum yield at the minimum expense." There is a "monstrousness that reigns here," for the description of which Heidegger sets out another set of ontological terms, to go along with challenging: "setting-upon," "ordering," and "standing reserve" (this being a kind of hypostasis, in which "everything is ordered to stand by, to be immediately on hand, indeed to stand there just so that it may be on call for a further ordering.")

Heidegger integrates this critique in the term, "en-framing" (*Ge-stell*). This accounts for the dependence of modern technology on physical science; more deeply, it suggests the way in which being is frozen and constrained under the spiritually desolate condition of modernity. From this point, Heidegger derives many of the phenomena inherent to this way of technical being, from the reduction of God to a mere *causa efficiens*, to the self-estrangement of "man." "Where this ordering holds sway, it drives out every other possibility of revealing." Thus, enframing technology becomes hegemonic, and the very possibility of truth withers.

Heidegger concludes his essay optimistically: there is a "saving power" growing in the midst of the danger posed by enframing. For there is a "granting," too, in the midst of technology, and this can be gathered as a saving power. How? If we "ponder this arising," and, in recollection, "watch over it." In this way we can get beyond the notion of technology as an instrument, not through "human activity," but by "reflection": we can "ponder the fact that all saving power must be of a higher essence than what is endangered, though at the same time kindred to it." Specifically, Heidegger calls for the enhancement of an artistic dimension, not for aesthetic purposes alone, but as his Greeks did, for the purpose of revealing: "The closer we come to the danger, the more brightly do the ways into the saving power begin to shine and the more questioning we become. For questioning is the piety of thought" (317).

Taking his cue, let us question Heidegger, though perhaps not with piety. Begin with the question of universality. A thinker of Heidegger's magnitude, one of the philosophical luminaries of the twentieth century, must, one should think, stand for the *whole* of humankind if he is to command respect. And indeed he claims to do just this, if only through his continual reference to "man" as the subject and object of his discourse, viz: "Who accomplishes the challenging setting-upon through which what we call the real is revealed as standing-reserve? Obviously, man. To what extent is man capable of such a revealing?" (299). We may translate this: who is the agent of the pathological relation to technology that is causing the ecological crisis? The answer to this is, self-evidently, man. At this point the questioning of Heidegger may commence. For the usage of an undifferentiated "man" as the subject of technological degradation is a highly dubious way to confront the ecological crisis.

Who is this "man"? Logically, it is either somebody or everybody, and if the latter, it is either all of us as an undifferentiated

146

mass, or all of us in some kind of internal relation – a hierarchy like patriarchy or class, in other words, some articulation of the social world.

The articulated view opens onto an effective understanding of the crisis. But it is not the one chosen by Heidegger, who, instead of articulating the real character of humanity, splits it into two equally unsatisfactory moieties. Manifestly, he speaks for an undifferentiated notion of "man"; concretely and practically, however, he speaks only for the Northern European elites. Heidegger really speaks just for some people, but as this would absolutely violate the spirit of his discourse and the supreme abstraction of his language, he ascends into the fuzzy realm of a falsely universalized subject.

How do we know that Heidegger speaks just for the dominant classes of Northern Europeans? There is the matter of his personal history, which was only evaded and never repudiated during the years when this essay was gestated. The younger Heidegger was acutely aware that philosophical syntheses are reflective of real struggles and cannot be fulfilled unless the philosopher intervenes in these struggles. In this spirit he connected his philosophical project of curing the malaise of modern society to National Socialism, and saw the Nazi Party as capable of healing this lesion by taking state power in Germany.[31] The Nazi career of Heidegger was one of the great intellectual scandals of the twentieth century, and the shame of it undoubtedly contributed to a certain gnomic tendency in his later thought, such as we see in essays of this kind, where elliptical phrases, neologisms, and scurrying through the language of antiquity for authenticity, maintain the illusion that no specific program for transformation need be enunciated. But Nazism was nothing if not a specific project. Whatever else can be said about the Third Reich, there can be no doubt that whoever signed up to its principles (and Heidegger was a party member and a major official at Freiburg, one of Germany's leading universities) affirmed a radically racist view of the world, within which, of course, the Northern European elites occupied the master role.

We can see directly within the present text how Heidegger refuses to define a specific agent for the crisis, however much its logic may demand this – and also why the question of efficient cause is distasteful to him, as this methodology, used faithfully, would disclose his dreadful partiality. And so Heidegger talks movingly of the revealing expressed in the making of a silver chalice, but glosses over the reality that has degraded craftman-ship and its spiritual associations. For who makes chalices any more? Why not address the people who make Barbie dolls, or methyl isocyanate, or overpriced sneakers, or cluster bombs – and who can stop doing so if they are willing to starve, or lose their health insurance, or not make the mortgage payments on the house?[32] Are not the real conditions of their labor the causal elements in the deterioration of their *techne*?

Heidegger talks elsewhere of the "forester" who no longer "walks the forest path in the same way his grandfather did" because he is "today ordered by the industry that produces com-mercial woods" thus making him "subordinate to the orderability of cellulose." Yes, yes, excellent to talk of this, but why not go on to the "industry" as a causal mover – not because of the essence of "industrialization" that it bears, but because it is going to serve the lord of capital that reduces trees to cellulose? Nor should this be talked of in strictly metaphorical terms: Who is this industry? There are real people involved, who personify the great forces of the capital system yet must also be held morally, politically, and legally responsible, as the management of Union Carbide should have been held responsible for Bhopal.

Similar reflections are in order for the peasants whose down-fall Heidegger laments – and who fell, and continue to fall all over the world, because of the encroachment of the same profit motive. And of course, the same goes for one of his most impor-tant insights, that there is something active at work in the world which "puts to nature the unreasonable demand that it supply energy which can be extracted and stored as such." Does this something simply arrive, like Athene, from the head of its father? Or is it the product of a vast transformation only understandable in terms of the inexorable force of capital? Is it the self-generated exfoliation of an original estrangement, carried out without any mediations in the real world? Well, then, one still has to explain the many forms of said mediations, like stock exchanges, oil pipelines, credit cards, police, and armies.

If one draws all the appropriate inferences that point to such a conclusion, but refuses to name it as such, then one is mystifying, and as with all mystifications, supporting the status quo. It is striking how closely Heidegger's critique of technology can be applied to the capital system, yet never bridges across to this most obvious point. This is not to deny that his critique runs far beyond the ordinary insights derived from political economy. Heidegger's insights are, as he intended, profound: they advance our view of what is wrong and what has to be done to right it in a way that no political-economic analysis of the ecological crisis can touch. But what is merely profound swims at an inaccessible and meaningless depth. More, it can be used for malignant purposes. We dwell on Heidegger not just because of his philosophical eminence, but essentially because reasoning of this sort has been repeatedly used for malignant purposes. Behind the discourse of "ecology" can lurk, therefore, a specter of fascism. We return to the theme below.

Philosophy can and should be an active force extending the reach of political economy. In this regard, it seems to me necessary to postulate a methodological principle that embodies the paramount goal of reintegrating ecosystems. We have seen how the world of capital is riddled with the sequelae of splitting, and how ecosystemic integrity is critically dependent upon differentiation. It follows that we need to overcome splitting with differentiation, in thought as well as practice. We need, therefore, a method incorporating the notion of differentiation.

Let us recall some conditions for this. A differentiated relationship is one in which elements of an ecosystem are brought together in a process of mutual recognition that respects their wholeness and integrity. There are three terms here, each needing explication: the elements are presumed different, yet capable of

149

entering into a relationship; the entering upon this relationship requires the specific activity of an agent; and, finally, the mutual recognition implies identity-in-difference: entities are what their being is, yet this being is defined in the relationship to the other. In this case, we are speaking of bringing different ideas together, and, as we have seen for other aspects of differentiated production like gardening, holding them so that the life within them can be expressed as the formation of an integral whole.

A moment's reflection will tell us that we have been speaking here of a process broadly defined as *dialectical*. And since we may claim some lineage from the ancient Greeks too, we may recall that for these progenitors of philosophy, dialectic meant the bringing together of different points of view for the purposes of argument, and in the interests of arriving at truth.[33] Dialectic was not a mere pluralism but a consciousness of the radical unfulfillment of the merely individual mind, or ego, and of the hidden relationships of differing points of view. Dialectics recognizes both the limits and powers of the mind: that we are limited in our knowing, owing to the unfathomable reaches of nature which can be grasped intuitively at best, and owing, also, to the peculiarities and illusions of human selfhood, with its "dialectic" of separation and attachment ... but it also recognizes that we are powerful because of the capacity of the imagination to remain open to nature and to its shape in other human beings. Hence dialectics as practice is the bringing together of minds in a dialogical spirit of open discourse – a process the fulfillment of which requires a free society of associated producers, that is, a society beyond all forms of splitting, in particular, those imposed by class and gender or racial domination. Without this, the genius of those forced into the subaltern position will wither into ignorance, superstition, and apathy, while the logic of the masters will be fatally corrupted by power.

There is, in addition to dialectics as practice, the question of dialectics as logic, which we can only barely pursue here, except to say that it must be an abstraction from practice that remains in contact with practice – i.e. differentiated and not split-off from it.

Here the prime dialectical category is *negation*, as that which both is and is not itself. In line with this, dialectic must be capable of guiding practice as well, so that for dialectical realization, theory is practical, and practice is theoretical – a condition known generally as *praxis*.[34]

Finally, in this highly compressed account, we need to inquire as to the "dialectics of nature."[35] It is plain, first, that any such notion cannot privilege the "higher reality" over mere being, as this aggrandizes ecosystemic splitting into a metaphysic. The notion of dialectic is grounded in the formativeness of nature – it is, one might say, nature's formativity refracted through the human mind, the flux of nature, its absencing and presencing, made word. As differentiated ecosystems will tend to bring forth life, so is dialectic the location of human creativity. But we do not project the laws of dialectical logic into nature, for the twofold reason that these laws are abstracted from *human practice*, and that human practical activity, including the workings of thought, is conducted at a great remove from the ultimate workings of the universe. For the great majority of humankind, there is simply no elaboration of this into consciousness beyond a sense of awe – although it must be said, and left at that for now, that the greatest minds, including a considerable number of modern physicists, assert the participation of their thinking in the great reaches of the cosmos and the fine grain of matter and energy.[36]

The precondition of an ecologically rational attitude toward nature is the recognition that nature far surpasses us and has its own *intrinsic value*, irreducible to our practice. Thus we achieve differentiation from nature. It is in this light that we would approach the question of transforming practice ecologically – or, as we now recognize to be the same thing, dialectically.

On the reformability of capitalism

The monster that now bestrides the world was born of the conjugation of value and dominated labor. From the former arose the quantification of reality, and, with this, the loss of the differentiated recognition essential for ecosystemic integrity; from the latter emerged a kind of selfhood that could swim in these icy waters. From this standpoint one might call capitalism a "regime of the Ego," meaning that under its auspices a kind of estranged self emerges as the mode of capital's reproduction. This self is not merely prideful – the ordinary connotation of "egotistical" – though under capitalism it certainly exhibits *hubris*; more fully, it is the ensemble of those relations that embody the domination of nature from one side, and, from the other, ensure the reproduction of capital. This Ego is the latest version of the purified male principle, emerging millennia after the initial crime and reflecting the absorption and rationalization of gender domination into profitability and self-maximization (allowing suitable "power-women" to join the dance). It is a pure culture of splitting and non-recognition: it recognizes neither itself, nor the otherness of nature, nor the nature of others. In terms of the preceding discussion, it is the elevation of the merely individual and isolated mind-as-ego into a reigning principle.[37]

Capital produces egoic relations, which reproduce capital. The isolated selves of the capitalist order can choose to become personifications of capital, or may have the role thrust upon them. In either case, they embark upon a pattern of non-recognition mandated by the fact that the almighty dollar interposes itself between all elements of experience: all things in the world, all other persons, and between the self and its world. Hence nothing really exists except in and through monetization. This setup provides an ideal culture medium for the bacillus of competition and ruthless self-maximization. Because money is all that "counts," a peculiar heartlessness characterizes capitalists, a tough-minded and cold abstraction that will sacrifice species, whole continents (viz Africa) or inconvenient subsets of the population (viz black urban males) who add too little to the great march of surplus value, or may be seen as standing in its way, or simply are suitable objects of demonization to distract the masses. The presence of value screens out genuine fellow-feeling or compassion, replacing it with the calculus of profit-expansion. Never has a holocaust been carried out so impersonally. When the Nazis killed their victims, the crimes were accompanied by a racist drumbeat; for global capital, the losses are regrettable necessities or collateral damage.

The value-term that subsumes everything into the spell of capital sets going a kind of wheel of accumulation, from production to consumption and back, spinning ever more rapidly as the inertial mass of capital grows, and generating its force field as a spinning magnet generates an electrical field. This phenomenon has important implications for the reformability of the system. Because capital is so spectral, and succeeds so well in ideologically mystifying its real nature, attention is constantly deflected from the actual source of eco-destabilization to the instruments by which that source acts. The real problem, however, is the *whole mass* of globally accumulated capital, along with the speed of its circulation and the class structures sustaining this. That is what generates the force field, in proportion to its own scale; and it is this force field, acting across the numberless points of insertion that constitute the ecosphere, that creates ever-larger agglomerations of capital, sets the ecological crisis going, and keeps it from being resolved. For one fact may be taken as certain – that to resolve the ecological crisis as a whole, as against tidying up one corner or another, is radically incompatible with the existence of gigantic pools of capital, the force field these induce, the criminal underworld with which they connect, and, by extension, the elites who comprise the transnational bourgeoisie. And by not resolving the crisis as a whole, we open ourselves to the specter of another mythical creature, the many-headed hydra that regenerates itself the more its individual tentacle-heads are chopped away.

To realize this is to recognize that there is no compromising with capital, no schema of reformism that will clean up its act by making it behave more greenly or efficiently. We shall explore the practical implications of this thesis in our final section, and here need simply to restate the conclusion in blunt terms: green capital, or non-polluting capital, is preferable to the

153

ecodestructive breed on its immediate terms. But this is the lesser point, and diminishes with its very success. For green capital (or "socially/ecologically responsible investing") exists, by its very capital-nature, essentially to create more value, and this leaches away from the concretely green location to join the great pool, and follows its force field into zones of greater concentration, expanded profitability – and greater ecodestruction.

There are crises within capitalism, which both generates them and is dependent upon them. Crises are ruptures in the accumulation process, causing the wheel to slow, but also stimulating new turns; they take many shapes, have long or short cycles, and many intricate effects upon ecologies. A recession may reduce demand and so take some of the load off resources; recovery may increase this demand, but also occur with greater efficiency, hence also reduce the load. Thus economic crises condition the ecological crisis, but have no necessary effect on it. There is no singular generalization that covers all cases. James O'Connor summarizes the complexity:

> Capitalist accumulation normally causes ecological crisis of certain types; economic crisis is associated with partly different and partly similar ecological problems of different severity; external barriers to capital in the form of scarce resources, urban space, healthy and disciplined wage labor, and other conditions of production may have the effect of raising costs and threatening profits; and finally, environmental and other social movements defending conditions of life, forests, soil quality, amenities, health conditions, urban space, and so on, may also raise costs and make capital less flexible.[38]

But capital gets nature whether on its way up or its way down. In the United States, the boom-boom Clinton years witnessed grotesque increases in matters like the sowing of the ecosphere with toxic chemicals;[39] while the sharp downturn that accompanied the advent of George W. Bush's presidency was immediately met by rejection of the Kyoto Protocols. From the standpoint of ecosystems, the *phase* of the business cycle is considerably less relevant, then, than the *fact* of the business cycle, and the wanton economic system it expresses.

Economic problems interact with ecological problems, while ecological problems (including the effects of ecological movements) interact with economic problems. This is all at the level of the trees. For the forest, meanwhile, we see the effects on the planetary ecology caused by the growth of the system as a whole. Here the dark angel is the thermodynamic law, where mounting entropy appears as ecosystemic decay.[40] The immediate impacts of this on life are what energizes the resistance embodied in the environmental and ecological movements. Meanwhile, the economy goes on along its growth-intoxicated way, immune to the effects of ecosystem breakdown on accumulation, and blindly careening toward the abyss.

The conclusion must be that, irrespective of the particulars of one economic interaction or another, the system as a whole is causing irreparable damage to its ecological foundations, and that it does so precisely as it grows. And since the one underlying feature of all aspects of capital is the relentless pressure to grow, we are obliged to bring down the capitalist system as a whole, and replace it with an ecologically viable alternative, if we want to save our species along with numberless others.

Part III | Paths to ecosocialism

7 | Introduction

Let me summarize where the argument stands:

- the ecological crisis puts the future at grave risk;
- capital is the reigning mode of production, and capitalist society exists to reproduce, secure and expand capital;
- capital is the efficient cause of the ecological crisis;
- capital, under the charge of the present transnational bourgeoisie and headquartered chiefly but not exclusively in the United States, cannot be reformed. It can only grow or die, hence reacts to any contraction or slowing as to a mortal threat;
- as capital keeps growing, the crisis grows, too: civilization and much of nature is doomed. Indeed, it is not unwarranted to ask whether this will prove to be the way of our extinction as a species;
- therefore, it is either capital or our future. If we value the latter, capitalism must be brought down and replaced with an ecologically worthy society.

Let me add two conditions to this assessment, the first very well-known but numbing to contemplate; the second, scarcely appreciated but profoundly important:

- Capital rules the world as never before; no substantial alternative to it now commands the interest, much less the loyalty, of any significant body of people.
- Capital is not what most people take it to be. It is not a rational system of markets in which freely constituted individuals create wealth in healthy competition. It is, rather, a spectral apparatus that integrates earlier modes of domination, especially that by gender, and generates a gigantic force field of profit-seeking that polarizes all human activity and sucks it into

itself. Capital is spectral because its profit is the realization of a "value" deriving from estranged human power. This has been instituted in private ownership of the means of production, along with a peculiar system of domination – exploited wage labor – in which persons are split internally and between each other and nature. The implication is simple, if profound: in order to overcome capital, two minimal conditions need to be met: first, there must be basic changes in ownership of productive resources so that, ultimately, the earth is no longer privately owned; and, second, our productive powers, the core of human nature, have to be liberated, so that people self-determine their transforming of nature.

These two conditions go together: capital's power is so uncontested, because the conditions for seriously changing it are far too radical for the great majority of people to contemplate, much less support. We should be under no illusion whatsoever: the scale of the envisioned changes, and the gap between even a dawning awareness of what would be entailed and the presently prevailing political consciousness is so enormous, as to make a person want to forget the whole thing. Why, it is reasonable to ask, bother to burden us with ideas so off the scale of what society now proposes, that to raise them would seem the work of a lunatic?

I am not insensible to this line of reasoning. The fantastic unlikeliness of an ecological transformation has often occurred to me – say, during a walk through midtown Manhattan, loomed over by the "cloud capp'd" towers of corporate capital, the mighty banks, the whole gigantic symphony in stone, steel, and glass consecrated to the god of profit – or when I look around at the hundreds of thousands of scurrying people set into motion by that great force field like so many wind-up toys in the game of accumulation, and am led to wonder whether any of them is ready to think in the terms drawn here. Faced with the appalling evidence of just how far we have to go – not just the direct strength of the system but its indirect strength deriving from the weakness of its adversaries, and the way the crisis burdens the mind and drains the will . . . the idea of dropping the whole affair and settling back into creature comforts has often come.

But then one thinks of the stakes, and the compelling argument that leads to capital's indictment as nature's enemy, and there is no question of whether to continue. Nor can we allow the current imbalance of forces to sow doubt, or to confuse or vitiate the issues. When a physician deals with a grave illness, s/he must not waste effort in brooding about how difficult the case is, but work instead to see as clearly as possible what is the problem and what can be done. In a word, one does what one can.

It is time to concentrate on making changes, first on the wide range of what already exists; and then on possibilities for radical transformation. There is no point in wringing our hands and backing away from this task, and everything to be gained, literally, a world to be won, by pursuing it conscientiously.

General conditions of anti-capitalist struggle

It goes without saying that capital cannot be eliminated *tout court*. Even if this were possible it would be undesirable, indeed, monstrous. It would be akin to what can happen to an individual who awakens too precipitously from a deep sleep: he knows that he exists, but not who or where he is. The world makes no sense at all, and the effect is terror. The fact is, capital has come to define our existence, which is to say, our world. It may mean the end of this world, but that is not for now, when the problem is to ascertain lines of struggle so that a new and ecologically rational world may gestate in the midst of the old.

Here the notion, introduced toward the close of the previous chapter, that capital defines a way of being and not simply an economic system, becomes useful. For it leads us to widen the ground, and think in terms of the innumerable interstitial points at which capital's force field is inserted into the fabric of our existence, each one of which is at hand as a point of intervention. Our investigation has already shown that capital will not be overthrown unless labor is freed, and that the practical antagonist to this end is the capitalist state, which enforces and rationalizes

161

the system. Between, therefore, each of these points of intervention and the final outcome of bringing capital down there will lie a lengthy and often torturous path, as the individual points of development both grow and converge with others, defining in the doing, great movements and, eventually, structures which can take over for a collapsing system.

It matters practically that this notion of converging and reinforcing paths be given clarity, consistency and direction – and that these means do not violate the end of an ecologically rational society. In practice this will be a formidable task, given the facts, first, that the struggle is necessarily global and entails innumerable conjunctures "on the ground"; and, second, that any radical path – and no path can be more radical than this one – is constantly adapting itself as it goes along, and always working with a degree of uncertainty. But the study of capital and nature does enable us to think through certain points of definition to guide struggle:

- that the process needs to be revolutionary and not reformist, and that its goal, or *telos*, is a society beyond capital in harmony with nature;
- that the means not violate the ends: to take one example, that as the gendered bifurcation of nature is to be overcome, radical ecopolitics needs to incorporate an emancipated notion of gender, and work to define this from the outset. Closely related, as there can be no ecological society that violates human nature, and as human nature involves the free association of creative powers, so do authoritarian means violate ecologically rational ends;
- further, that the struggle needs to define the kinds of paths it takes up so that these hew to an anticapitalist *telos*. Certain features of this spring immediately to mind. Thus, as capital is a regime of the Ego, we need to attend to those portions of nature claimed by the Ego – to put it plainly, *private property*. We know this to be crucial in respect to private ownership of the means of production by the class of capitalists. How-

ever, the notion expands all over the place and configures the line of struggle in its concreteness. The history of capital may be viewed as a never-ending battle to take over collective and organic relationships and replace these with commodity relationships, which is to say, to create private property by destroying the *Commons*, and to embed this in the accumulation of capital. This rages today in matters as vital as the regime of carbon trading or the licensing of the genome. It is the continually shifting form of that history of class struggle in which Marx recognized the history of human society itself. It comes into fruition in a million particular battles, each of which is there to be addressed and all of which are there to be combined into a transformative vision of the new world. And it is to the exploration of this that the final section of this work is devoted.

The name given in what follows to the notion of a necessary and sufficient transformation of capitalist society for the overcoming of the ecological crisis is *ecosocialism*.

8 | A critique of actually existing ecopolitics

In this chapter we consider approaches to the ecological crisis that do not consider it essential in mending the relationship with nature to replace capitalism by a system grounded in the restoration of the means of production to freely associated producers. In other words, we assess what is non-ecosocialist in the politics of nature. Given the general acceptance of capitalism as having a kind of divine right to organize society, and the coordinated refusal to face up to its essential ecodestructivity and inability to correct itself, what will be discussed comprises the great majority of present-day ecopolitics. According to the argument offered here, therefore, these approaches either have to be given an ecosocialist content, or made compatible with it, or abandoned if we are to resolve the ecological crisis.

It goes without saying that the existing approaches are in many cases admirable, and comprise real points of attack. But if capital is the efficient cause of the crisis, we urgently need a new strategy that sees beyond them. This should be borne in mind during what follows, the occasionally sharp tone of which is sounded in order to radicalize current discourse.

There are a number of ways of thinking about the many sides of ecopolitics. Bearing in mind that we are dealing with different levels of abstraction, and much overlapping, it is useful to consider the subject from four angles: logics of change, economic models, ecophilosophies, and political models.

Logics of change
Working within the system The "system" here means various arms of the state, including regulatory agencies and the judiciary, as well as the extensive and varied set of established non-

governmental organizations (NGOs), and elements of capital itself. Obviously, it is a life's work to keep track of so large and complicated an apparatus, and we can do no more than set forth certain underlying principles in discussing it here.

It is unnecessary to detail once more how corporations and politicians are in bed with each other, and just how inadequately the state takes care of ecosystems. But these facts say nothing about whether or not it is desirable to work within them to make a change. After all, everything in capitalist society is conditioned by capital, from the EPA to the raising of children, and the writing of this book. Similarly, degrees of resistance to capital can be found in the strangest places. While it is a safe bet to conclude that the legal system is stacked to benefit the rich and powerful, it is not true that the law is reducible to economic interest, nor that it is impossible to secure real gains through the courts. By the same reasoning, corporate executives and other personifications of capital are only relatively consumed by it. In each of them, therefore, there may be glimmers of conscience, or, if not that, at least common sense.

The case of Al Gore is particularly instructive. Gore has gone as far as anyone in the system to challenge its ecological implications. He is the first – and still the only – instance of a kind of ecocentrism breaking into the consciousness of an official in capital's stronghold. For whatever reasons – he himself emphasizes the shock of his sister's death from lung cancer induced by the consumption of tobacco, a crop from which his family had grown wealthy – Gore became sensitized to the large-scale environmental effects of the economic system. He began to see these in ecological terms, and to focus on the overarching menace of global warming. He wrote a noteworthy book, which first appeared as he became vice-president in 1992 and called for a transformational approach to the growing crisis between humanity and nature. He was an important agent in the passage of the Kyoto Protocols in December 1997. Since the presidency was stolen from him in 2000, Gore has become a kind of evangelist preaching the necessity of taking climate change with the utmost seriousness. His 2006 film (and book), *An Inconvenient Truth*, has probably done more than any other single intervention to sound the alarm about global warming. It has opened a way, some twenty years after the danger first surfaced, to the beginnings of serious public debate.[1]

History will be kind to Gore, then, for his role in the ecological crisis – only, however, if his side of the debate loses. For throughout this whole process of awakening and evangelism Gore has never ceased carrying water for global capital.[2] As valuable as his advocacy of serious change to combat global warming undoubtedly is, by setting the logic of that change within the dominant system Gore commits an error of literally fatal proportions.

As vice-president, Gore took charge of environmental policy and, for all the visionary rhetoric, was spineless when it came to standing up to big business. His tenure in office, a time of resurgent economic expansion, witnessed the highest rates of growth of CO_2 emissions in history. He did nothing to stand against the ruinous trade agreements, such as NAFTA, and the emergence of the WTO. Very modest efforts to improve fuel economy for American cars were shot down by the oil industry without a peep from the White House. The Justice Department under Clinton/Gore reduced by some 30 percent effective prosecution of environmental crime compared to that of the first Bush administration. And Dr Sidney Wolfe, perhaps the most knowledgeable individual on the subject, reported that the Food and Drug Administration (FDA) and the Occupation Safety and Health Administration (OSHA), chief watchdogs protecting the health of the American citizenry, sank under Clinton to the lowest level of morale and competency that he had witnessed in his twenty-nine years of studying these agencies.[3]

It should come as no surprise, then, that *An Inconvenient Truth* fails to mention the word "capitalism," that it oozes with technological determinism,[4] does not take into sufficient account the global South, never questions the industrial model, promises that his approach will generate a lot of wealth, and offers no real way out beyond voting the proper people, i.e. people like himself, into office. Thus neither capital, nor the capitalist state, is at all questioned, nor is any authentic democratization offered. Salvation for the troubled bourgeois masses will come through choosing the best representatives among liberal politicians and technocrats, then letting them guide the people to the ecological Promised Land. Any other outcome from a Gore would have taken a miracle, as seers of his kind are carefully vetted for their reliability. It is as if the system keeps in its pocket a useful fellow or two who can be pressed into service as a voice for reform in times of crisis – reform whose deeper purpose is to ward off fundamental change.

We would conclude that whatever good may come out of the system needs to be, so to speak, triangulated with what is outside of the system if we are to be saved from capital.

Voluntarism At the end of *An Inconvenient Truth* is an embarrassing recital of "things you can do to save the planet," viz: use compact fluorescent lightbulbs, set the thermostat down, etc. We call these "voluntarisms." A voluntaristic act is one that arises from good intention and more or less stays there, without special connection to social movements consciously directed, in this case, toward the ecological crisis. Thus it is an action taken toward an individual manifestation of the crisis, and carried out primarily on moral or psychological grounds.

Such actions are understandably popular, as they comprise a risk-free way of feeling good about oneself in the face of overwhelming crisis. But they stand as much chance of overcoming the ecological crisis as handing out spare change on the subway does of overcoming poverty. I put this bluntly, not to question the virtue of voluntarism, but as a challenge for it to go further and build linkages necessary for effective action. A voluntaristic act is a point of potential, something available for connection to other acts, and other frames of reference. If it stays in itself, it will tend to be drawn off into individualism, which is to say, to remain split-off, isolated, and transient. If, on the other hand, it connects itself to a larger project, then it can enter into a gathering that is the heart of ecosystem formation and integrity.

While there is nothing wrong with any ecologically voluntarist act so long as it is done with a good heart and a mind toward restoring the earth, there is nothing inherent to it, either, that leads anywhere. Moral exhortations may *feel* as though they generate larger purposes, but this is an illusion. There is no *solidarity* inherent to the moral impulse; and unless that which makes for solidarity is added, voluntarism will stop at its own border. Certainly the world is better off because of recycling, but it is not that much better off, nor does the range of improvement much exceed the localities in which these acts are taken. This raises questions concerning localism itself, so widely held as a value by the green movements. Yes, local movements are capable of reproducing themselves and spreading to encompass the whole ecosphere. But that simply begs the question of what will suffice to make this universalization happen, which in any case is not voluntaristic action.

On the contrary, market forces have been applied to configure voluntarism according to the demands of capital. Thus recycling is reinforced by various sanctions and rewards, for example, laws in places like New York City, or incentives to avoid dumping costs in smaller localities. In this way, citizens are induced to provide free labor to the huge and growing industries that profit from "waste management," and voluntarism becomes ancillary to the capitalization of nature.[5]

However admirable individual acts of charity or ecological sanity may be, they tend to either be co-opted or to remain merely local and lose the thread of effective collective action. A lovely garden is a wondrous thing, and indicates the species potential for fostering ecosystem development and bringing new life into the world. But given the current predicament, it is a signpost and not an end. Voltaire's advice, *"Il faut cultiver nos jardins"* – in other words, let us tend individually to immediate and concrete satisfactions and ignore large-scale projects of social transformation – made sense in a world whose dominant forces were religious absolutism and fanaticism. In a world organized by global capital's force field, it rings with defeatism.

Ultimately, the touchstone of voluntarism is this: that it is an ecopolitics without *struggle*, struggle against the inertia and fear within, and the great weight of capitalist rationalization and repression without. It is the easy path at a time when sacrifice and heroism are called for.

Technological limits As we have seen, Al Gore is a techno-enthusiast (having claimed credit at one point for developing the internet). It is a widely held assumption that technological means of overcoming the ecological crisis are at hand. With the cracking of the genome, with astounding feats of information technology and telecommunications, with the emergence of extremely low-polluting energy devices like fuel cells (the product of whose combustion is water vapor), with the whole broad advance of science – and with a nice boost from the propaganda machine – the conflict between humanity and nature can be made to seem eminently resolvable. In an important sense, this is, if not absolutely true, at least operationally plausible – for if the technology did not, or could not, exist, then it would make no sense at all to agitate for an ecologically rational world.

But this is only a truism. Those old enough to recall the launching of the atomic age will recall how nuclear energy was going to be "too cheap to meter," just as the discoveries of antibiotics were supposed to herald the eradication of infectious disease. If we know better now, it is a sign of growing ecological consciousness that events in nature are reciprocal and multi-determined, and, across such a broad scale, never neatly predictable. What remains much less appreciated is that technology cannot be appreciated outside of its social relations. Ross Perot's 1992 campaign dictum, "If it's broke, fix it," was sign of the crudity that regards social problems as essentially mechanical and susceptible to tinkering, that is, to manipulation from the outside by a disinterested expert, as a mechanic would fix the transmission on a car. This is mechanical materialism of a vulgar sort, which sees technology as something applied to society and not an integral part of society.

In the specific case of capitalism, technological innovation has been the *sine qua non* of growth, and, because it cheapens the cost of labor, indispensable to surplus value extraction. The more technology, roughly speaking, the more growth under a capitalist regime – and since growth, capitalist-style, is the efficient cause of the ecological crisis, it shouldn't take a genius to sense the ambivalence of technological solutions to the crisis. If, for instance, energy were suddenly made free and unlimited and inserted into the capitalist system as it now exists, the results could be as catastrophic as giving an alcoholic unlimited drink. Free energy would, for example, so lower the costs of producing and operating motor vehicles, that the world would rapidly fill up with as many cars as Los Angeles, collapsing infrastructure, tremendously increasing resource depletion, paving over much of the remainder of nature, and leaving humanity to kill itself off in a spasm of road rage. Limits of energy and materials are, in this sense, brakes on rampant growth, but capital, nature's cancer, tolerates neither limit nor boundary. It goes where the profit is, and the more cars (and the more gas-guzzling the cars), the more profit.

The above example is revealing but also conceals the fact that, barring some kind of Buck Rogers breakthrough,[6] the prospective energy reckoning is not a happy one, and moots all fanciful predictions. In short, "limits to growth" exist, no matter what the director of the IMF thinks, and the current energy brouhaha is a sign of their drawing near. As a result of this, certain good things are being stirred up, such as the search for more fuel-efficient cars like hybrids, even if this has for its chief motive the putting of more cars on the road. Along the same lines, resource substitution is always on the agenda, but this, too, requires great inputs of energy, and, in the case of plastics and other synthetics, the direct transforming of petroleum and coal. It is simply propaganda that the informational commodities on which modern, "post-industrial" capitalism has learned to thrive sit more lightly on the earth.[7] The infrastructure for the information age is as impressive in its way as the railroads, and much less likely to be recyclable – for the simple reason that informational commodities require the miniaturization of highly complex assemblies involving many substances, in contrast to the relatively homogeneous components of older industrial processes. How, pray tell, are we to reclaim the many rare metals joined together in even modest personal computers, as these become obsolete the day before they are made? Do we burn them down in huge numbers – as takes place in China and India – and thereby release yet more dioxin into the ecosphere?[8]

So long, therefore, as growth is the alpha and omega of the economy, we will be eternally chasing our tail in an ever-widening circle of accumulation. Meanwhile, the industrial system remains utterly dependent on fossil fuels inputs that are radically non-renewable. I say, radically, to underscore the fact that the whole of capitalist society runs on high-energy chemical bonds laid down by living beings and concentrated over hundreds of millions of years. Thus we rob the past. The only substitute within the capitalist system for this needed concentration is the utterly unacceptable alternative of nuclear power, with its indisposable toxic wastes. Other modalities, principally, the vaunted solar alternative, are undoubtedly a good thing. But it is hard to imagine it as a replacement for a hydrocarbon economy at current rates of growth. Solar energy is simply too diffuse, and too expensive to concentrate, to serve the needs of contemporary society, much less one that continues to grow according to the plan of the capitalist elites. It is too easily forgotten that in using solar power one is starting with what nature had long-ago concentrated into the low-entropy fuels that end up at the gas station.[9] Hydrocarbons, noxious as they are, remain life's gift of low-entropy, essential to the industrial system and irreplaceable except at ruinously high expenditures of energy. Electric cars may be non-polluting, but the generation of electricity is not – nor should we forget that even before the vast increase in electrical generation required to propel our motor vehicle fleet, there is tremendous pressure to expand the electrical generation grid, now stretched to the limit. Again, hydrogen fuel cells offer a non-polluting energy supply of great promise – but how are we to obtain the hydrogen except by splitting water molecules, once more requiring prodigious amounts of electricity?[10] In their haste to excoriate the admittedly barbaric energy schemes of the Bush administration, environmental liberals often overlook the fact that the president is simply being candid and stating, in effect, that what he asks for is only what capital demands.

It is certainly the case that all measures of increasing the renewability and efficiency, and decreasing the pollution of energy sources – that is, all "soft-energy paths"[11] – are to be endorsed, and for the same reason one endorses recycling. What cannot be supported is the illusion that these measures of themselves can do more than retard the slide toward ecocatastrophe under conditions of capitalist growth – a fall that may become precipitous once fossil fuels become uneconomical to extract, or the greenhouse effect becomes too catastrophic. Only a basic change in patterns of production and use can allow ecologically appropriate technologies to have their beneficial effect. But this means a basic change in need patterns and in the whole way life is lived, which means an entirely different foundation for society. To the extent that expectation of technological fixes blinds us to this, technology may be said to stand in the way of resolving the ecological crisis.

In truth, technology does not stand in the way; it is part of the way. Technology is not a collection of techniques and tools but a pattern of social relationships centering on the extension of the body as an instrument for transforming nature. This can be seen by comparing patterns of producing foodstuffs – the prevalent capital-intensive industrial farm, and the so-called "organic" alternative.

An organic farm is no more "natural" than agribusiness, but it is predicated on certain kinds of relationships that are at least potentially foreign to capital as well as resonant with the ways of spontaneously evolving ecosystems. For example, instead of using chemical inputs to control pests or accelerate growth, other organisms are introduced or composting is employed – in each instance, a conscious enhancement of an original process is chosen instead of a substitution for it. From another angle, this introduces a certain indeterminacy and complexity into the practice of agriculture. Smaller and more intricately put-together systems, configured to the concrete contours of the land, replace the monocultures that homogenize landscapes. Thus the specificities of sites are developed rather than written over, as under capital. Finally, there is a great deal of intense personal engagement, with strong aesthetic and even spiritual potentials. This results from organic agriculture's surpassing of the homogenized and quantified monocultures of agribusiness, with its reliance on high inputs from fossil fuel and alienated labor. In other words, the organic farm exhibits the ecocentric potential of constituting itself as an integral ecosystem.

Organic agriculture surpasses voluntarism inasmuch as it reflects a deep and sustained commitment – or, what comes to the same thing, as it manifests highly developed social production. But this same fact also points toward the great vulnerability of organic farming to the vicissitudes of capital. Submission to the terms of markets, where price structures, interest rates, etc., are set by the benchmarks of big business, greatly hems in the organic farmer, and will continue to do so so long as he or she repeats the error of voluntarism by not challenging the market and struggling to transform it. Absent this transformation, the market, that is, capital, will simply adulterate, and finally expropriate the organic farm, enclosing yet another bit of the Commons. This is unhappily already well underway.

All of which leads to a look at non-socialist efforts to reform the economic system.

Green economics

Given the collapse of twentieth-century socialism and the hegemony of neoliberalism, it is not surprising that an influential and diverse body of opinion would arise claiming that a reformist economic path can be found out of the ecological crisis that does not require the overthrow and supersession of capital.

This "green," or ecological economics echoes a number of the economic points made here – that our system suffers from a kind of gigantism, that its values, in particular the espousal of quantity over quality, are severely flawed, that it misallocates resources, promotes inequity, and generally has made a botch of the global ecology. But green economics goes on to insist that the system has recuperative powers. It would not be entirely fair to say that the people who espouse it are part of the system,[12] for they have at times suffered one sanction or another. But green economics is not really outside of the system, either. Its proponents want rather to stretch and reorganize the system to realize ecologically sound potentials, and they believe that the means are at hand for doing so.

We can identify four strands woven into this tendency: The first, *ecological economics*, represents the ecological wing of mainstream economics; it speaks with an authoritative and technical voice toward the entirety of economic relations with nature. Ecological economics comes packaged as a professional association with a refereed journal. As a recent quasi-official volume asks:

> Can we … reorganize our society rapidly enough to avoid a catastrophic overshoot? Can we be humble enough to acknowledge the huge uncertainties involved and protect ourselves from their most dire consequences? Can we effectively develop policies to deal with the tricky issues of wealth distribution, population prudence, international trade, and energy supply in a world where the simple palliative of "more growth" is no longer an option? Can we modify our systems of governance at international, national, and local levels to be better adapted to these and new and more difficult challenges?[13]

Clearly, ecological economics is uninterested in social transformation, and accepts the potentials of the present system to absorb the crisis, that is, to "adapt." To this means, which has in effect become an end, ecological economists employ a great variety of instrumental measures, from "incentive-based" regulations (such as tradeable emission credits) to various ecological tariffs and "natural capital" depletion taxes, as well as penalties against polluters. There is one very definite common denominator underlying all the various interventions of ecological economics, which ties this discourse firmly into the mainstream of capital, and that is the commodification of nature in all aspects, its quantification into a system of value.

The trading of pollution credits began in the United States in 1989 with the effort to control sulfur dioxide emissions, and was smoothly applied to the carbon trading regime in the Kyoto Protocols. The United States government under George W. Bush has refused to go along with this on the grounds that Kyoto would be bad for the economy, but not all American capitalists agree; and the main body lie in wait licking their chops for the huge market which will result if Kyoto is generalized. A trading credit is a license, granted by the state, to exploit some part of nature, like a mineral right over a certain territory.

There are actually two lines by which the Kyoto process is tied to accumulation. In the first, pollution credits are traded with a modest reduction in emissions and potentially a great deal of value being added to the transaction. In the second, named the Clean Development Mechanism, Northern firms are given license to create carbon sequestration projects in the South, for example, eucalyptus tree farms. This frees them to continue polluting in the chimerical hope that their carbon will be recycled in some future time. At the same time, more of the Southern Commons is enclosed and more people are displaced from their traditional life and forced into the chaotic megalopolises.

That anyone would believe this scheme capable of containing global warming is testimony to the intense brainwashing that goes on these days. Of course the jargon of tradeable permits uses all the latest buzzwords of the rationality that would allow business to have its cake and eat it as well. And it is a fine idea, except for two problems: that it cannot work, especially for global warming; and that if it did work, it only perpetuates the kind of world that gives us the ecological crisis in the first place.

As for the first, the notion presupposes a rational marketplace of nations in which rich developed ones pay poor developing ones for the right to emit greenhouse gases. But this kind of market requires an orderly world-society of cooperating nations – exactly what imperialism-as-globalization has made impossible, and what the sequestration projects, with their indeterminate outcome and neocolonial impact, will make even more chaotic. Finally, to the extent that the project succeeds, so does it fail, for the new wealth which has been created remains like capital everywhere, constantly seeking investment outlets and placing yet more burdens on ecosystems. Under capital, with its ceaseless pressure to expand, wealth necessarily turns into ecological disintegration.

The idea of tradeable credits owes a great deal to Stephen Breyer, who was rewarded by Clinton with a Supreme Court seat,[14] as well as to major environmental NGOs, most notably, the Environmental Defense Fund, which see no contradiction in rationalizing pollution and turning it into a fresh source of profit.[15] The story offers useful lessons in the co-optation of the mainstream environmental movement as this passes from citizen-based activism to ponderous bureaucratic scuffling for "a seat at the table." Capital is more than happy to enlist mainstream enviros as partners in the management of nature. Big environmental groups offer capital a threefold convenience: as legitimation, reminding the world that the system works; as control over popular dissent, a kind of sponge that sucks up and contains the ecological anxiety in the general population; and as rationalization, a useful governor to introduce some control and protect the system from its own worst tendencies, while ensuring the orderly flow of profits. Ecological economics stands squarely midstream in this gigantic process of rationalizing capital, and provides a kind of *lingua franca* with which technocrats of all stripes – NGOs, foundations, environmental studies programs in academia – can gather around the table and discuss ways the ecological crisis can be kept from getting out of hand while preserving the integrity of accumulation. With ecological economics defining nature in the terms of private property, the experts are given an extensive playing field on which they never have to contemplate the fact that unlimited accumulation and ecological integrity form an iron contradiction.

Mainstream ecological economics is relatively unconcerned about the size of economic units. However, there are also those who cluster about a second strand of green economics and regard this question as primary. These may roughly be described as *neo-Smithian*, the Smith in question being the great Adam, father of modern political economy. Adam Smith's advocacy of free markets was in the interest of an end distinctly different from today's neoliberalism. Smith's vision – which in good measure also became Thomas Jefferson's – was of a capitalism of small producers, freely exchanging with each other. He feared and loathed monopolies, and felt that the competitive market of small buyers and sellers (where no single individual could by himself determine prices) would self-regulate to keep these at bay. Smith argued that state intervention, the *bête noire* of neoliberalism, leads to monopoly and economic gigantism. Neoliberalism, needless to say, has no difficulty at all with these latter ends.

The ambition of neo-Smithian thinking is to restore small, independent capitals to pre-eminence. For this purpose, as David Korten, one of the leading exponents of the view, puts it, Smith's assumption, "*that capital would be rooted in a particular place*," must be met.[16] Korten's ecological society, the essence of which he describes as "democratic pluralism," is based upon "regulated markets," in which government and civil society combine to off-set the tendencies of capitalist firms to expand and concentrate, even as these same capitalist firms, now reduced, continue to provide the mainspring of the economy.

Korten has achieved prominence in presenting these views, a number of which parallel those argued here. However, he does so without any concentrated critique of capital itself, neither does he look into questions of class, gender, nor any other category of domination. This is because Korten sees the primary lesion in philosophical or religious terms, as a suddenly appearing colossal kind of mistake identifiable as the "Scientific Revolution,"

177

whose "materialism" stripped life of "meaning" and crushed the spirit of "generosity and caring." He regards this grandly: "Failing to recognize and embrace their responsibility to the whole [human beings] turned their extraordinary abilities to ends ultimately destructive of the whole of life, destroying in a mere 100 years much of the living natural capital it had taken billions of years of evolution to create."[17] Note the reference to "natural capital," as though nature had toiled to put the gift of capital into human hands, who then abused this through false science and materialism. Since capital – or class, or the capitalist state – is no big deal to Korten, and even, when nature produces it, a good thing, he has no difficulty in seeing it checked by "globalizing civil society," who will restrain and effectively domesticate the animal, leading to the neo-Smithian Promised Land. This is essentially an upbeat fairytale standing in for history. If it were true, the world would be a much easier place to change; indeed, without capital and the capitalist state, we wouldn't have a problem in the first place.

It is so short a step from neo-Smithianism to *community-based economics* as to make one inclined to include them under a single rubric. But to introduce the latter as a third strand of ecological economics is serviceable as a way of indicating the breadth of the community economics movement, which includes, alongside neo-Smithians, followers of E. F. Schumacher, who called for a "Buddhist economics,"[18] or defenders of the "Commons," grouped about the *Ecologist* magazine, where the emphasis is on small producers from the South or indigenous communities; or major portions of the green movements, along with Social Ecologists (see below). The entire community economics tendency has roots in the anarchist tradition of Proudhon and Kropotkin, who emphasized mutualism as a defense against the forces of modernity and gigantism.[19] As proponents of this point of view are usually hostile to socialism, they oppose public ownership of the means of production and espouse a diverse mixture of economic forms.

Cooperatives are frequently mentioned among the elements of

community economics. But the *cooperative movement*, whether of consumers or, more significantly, producers, deserves mention as a separate, fourth strand of green economics because of its implications for the organization of labor and the advance of democracy. Because its essence is ownership by producers, the very notion of cooperation seems to cut to the core of capitalist social relations, replacing hierarchy and control from above with freely associated labor. As Roy Morrison has written, "Cooperation ... is both *social creativity* – the growth of new lifeways, of neighborhoods and communities – and *economic creativity* – the ways of making a living through the growth of community-based business enterprises ... Such cooperation is a matter of necessity. It is a key response to the crises of modernity. In this sense, the industrial state becomes the catalyst for the creation of its antipode, the dynamic cooperative commonwealth."[20] Marx at first thought well of cooperatives, speaking of them as "a greater victory [for workers, which he compared to achieving the ten-hour workday] of the political economy of labor over the political economy of property ... The value of these great social experiments cannot be over-rated ... they have shown that production on a large scale, and in accord with the behests of modern science, may be carried on without the existence of a class of masters employing a class of hands."[21]

Cooperatives are properly deemed private, in that they are owned by their workers and not society as a whole. But this meaning needs to be configured against the backdrop of a system that constructs the rules of property. It is here that the limits of green economics come into view. The fact of the matter is that cooperatives are both attractive and, so far as the transformation of society in an ecological direction goes, no more than a very halting and isolated first step. Picking up on Morrison's point, above, we could say that the *principle* of cooperation can be no more than partially realizable within the *institutions* of cooperatives in capitalist society. Actually, a significant portion of the capitalist economy, from farmer cooperatives, to credit unions, and even some HMOs,[22] is already in cooperative hands.

But this has not stopped the ecological crisis from maturing, just as it matures with leaded gasoline, recycled newspaper and other worthy palliatives. No doubt, were the entire economy in cooperative hands, matters would be different – but for that to happen, capital itself would have to be shoved aside and replaced, and that is quite another, and revolutionary, matter, which will not come from the cooperative movement.

The great error of assuming that cooperatives – or community economics, or green capitalism, or any of the reforms in themselves – will stem the crisis arises from confusion about their relation to capital. Capital will tolerate any number of improvements and rationalizations so long as its basic expansion is secured – and, indeed, many of the reforms succeed in doing just that, and are encouraged by the state or progressive elements of the bourgeoisie on that account, even if reactionary elements of the class may resist. Thus some cooperatives and green capitalism are allowed or even encouraged to join the club so long as they add modestly to accumulation, or at least keep out of its way.

However, it is this expansion which tears up ecologies – and, at the same time, suppresses cooperatives and other forms of green capital. If we examine capital's force field more closely, we see it as a demand for the growth of profits extended across the entire surface of society. This pressure at first seems transparently obvious; yet on inspection certain puzzling features appear. Profit is obviously a function of price, but prices are fickle and variable, while profits need to be much more structured. How, for example, are the great variety of economic price signals – stock quotes, interest rates, exchange rates, commodity prices, etc. – interpreted by economic agents in the capitalist marketplace? Through their monetary amounts, to be sure. But what function of money is involved – money as pure exchangeability, as a commodity itself to be traded, or as the embodiment of value? Clearly, the third: it is value that stalks forth in economic considerations of profitability. Money-as-exchangeability has no substantial existence – it is like writing on water; while money-as-commodity is itself to be traded and cannot stand for anything beyond that. Value, on the other hand, is the active relationship that pervades all transactions of capitalism.

If the force field is extended across the surface of society, then value is, so to speak, implanted throughout that surface to attract the force field; wherever exchange-value is inserted, there arises a commodity. Capitalism is generalized commodity production, and value is the all-pervading vector the installation and maintenance of which is the actual function of capitalism. Profits are the increasing of values (as manifested in money), and values link all elements of capitalism according to profitability.

As every cooperative manager knows, the *internal* cooperation of freely associated labor is forever hemmed in and compromised by the force field of value expansion embodied in the market, whether this be expressed in dealings with banks or an unending pressure to exploit labor in order to stay afloat, or through hierarchies or bureaucracies, or any of hundreds of mediations. In Marx's words (written at a later occasion after the idea had soured) cooperatives within capitalism, however well-intentioned they may be, necessarily reproduce "the shortcomings of the prevailing system" in forcing workers to become "their own capitalist ... by enabling them to use the means of production for the employment of their own labor", the standards of which are then set by the capitalist market. Therefore, whether cooperatives like it or not, capital, with all its atomization and competitive pressure, hems them in, and forces coops to become like the other capitalist enterprises – as, in the most egregious cases, happens with HMOs or United Airlines, the largest firm with substantial employee ownership.[23]

In every case, the pressure of value must be contended with; and the ecological success of a cooperative, or, indeed, any economic formation within capitalist society, may be judged strictly by the degree to which this force is neutralized or overcome. But what is the real force of value within capitalism? To revert to the previous discussion, it only arises as the world-destroying form of capital when *human labor* – the productive power essential to economic activity – is commodified in the wage relationship through the separation, or splitting, of producers from the means of their production. This becomes generalized, hence, under capitalism, exploitable labor is a ground for all economic activity, green or otherwise, since it determines the general market parameters to which green economics must conform. So long as the main institutions of capital endure to set the basic terms of the market, they continually force the separation of producers, i.e. humanity, from the means of production, including nature, and force labor to be exploited.

Viewed against the reality of capital, community economics seen as an end in itself becomes incoherent. In fact, it does so on logical grounds. For all economic activity is local – in that it involves somebody doing something somewhere – and it is global as well. Even in the most localized instance – say, some youngsters in Southern California picking lemons from the tree in their backyard and making lemonade for sale in front of their house – the final, local act rests upon a deep and widespread foundation. Did lemon trees grow immemorially in what is now San Diego? Are lemon trees, or any food-producing entity, just found in nature, or were they developed over centuries by past labor? Where did the water come from to grow the tree and mix with the lemon juice, and what struggles took place that it could be delivered so cheaply? And the sugar, what is its history?[24] Was this home-grown, or as likely, purchased with money from what source? And the house which becomes the marketplace, how is this owned – and built? From local materials . . . ?

A pure community, or even "bioregional" (see below), economy is a fantasy. Strict localism belongs to the aboriginal stages of society. It cannot be reproduced today, and even if it could, would be an ecological nightmare at present population levels. Imagine the heat losses from a multitude of dispersed sites, the squandering of scarce resources, the needless reproduction of effort, and the cultural impoverishment. This is by no means to be interpreted as a denial of the great value of small-scale and local endeavors: any flourishing ecosystem, after all, functions by differentiated, which is to say, particular, activity. It is, rather, an insistence that the local and particular exists in and through the global whole; that there needs to be, in any economy, an interdependence whose walls are not confinable to any township, or bioregion; and that, fundamentally, the issue is the relationship of parts to the whole.

Therefore, the vision of an ecological society cannot be purely local, and neither can it be a neo-Smithian system of small capitalists. For Smith's reasoning, like that of Jefferson, was strictly contextualized by its gestation in a transitional form of capitalism, primarily agrarian and based on hand-made commodities, before industrialization rewrote the map of society and tore great masses of people away from the earth and from control over their productive activity.[25] Smith's agents of transformation were members of a class of enlightened small landowners, whose freedom of function was given by their control over their land. Only under such circumstances does it make sense to even dream, as David Korten does, "that capital would be rooted in a particular place." That was a dream unrealized, as new class formations made accumulation possible on an expanding scale. Today, when to root capital is tantamount to rooting mercury, it is a nostalgic fantasy. And just as Smith's political economy needs to be historicized, so are his basic categories a-historical and essentialized. Yes, if people have Smith's famous innate propensity to truck and barter, then they should be given capitalist firms to realize this. But since when are the impulses of capitalism directly derived from the innate repertoire of human nature? Since the coming to power of capital, that is all. Why should we submit today to the model of small capital, which, however less murderous than large capital, is still based on the exploitation of labor, that most crucial of ecological insults, and is therefore inoculated with the virus of capital's cancerous growth, as well as other parochialisms?

Does this call, then, for the immediate abolition of money, wage labor, and commodity exchanges, along with all market relations and businesses? Absolutely not; measures of this sort recapitulate the Pol Pot or Stalinist solution, and they ride as heavily over humanity and nature as did slavery. They are forms of violence that tear apart ecosystems human and natural alike. An ecocentric people will not need to repress the accumulation of capital because the drive to accumulate will not arise from the ground of freely associated labor, and such a people will be free from exploitation. The problem is to get to that ground, in the course of which present ways of production need to be traversed and transformed, and not knocked over. But first it must be envisioned. To create that vision, a radical rejection of capitalist ways is necessary. We should reject, therefore, the phony tolerance espoused by green economics toward preserving a "diversity" that gives a substantial role to capitalist firms. One might as well try to raise weasels and chickens in the same pen. In this real world, all forms of capital, including the oxymoronic "natural capital" that is supposed to rescue us, are swiftly caught up in the flood-tide of accumulation.

My intention is not at all to disparage the virtue of a small economic or community unit. Quite the contrary: as we shall explore in the final chapter, small-size enterprises are an essential part of the path toward an ecological society, as well as the building blocks of that society. The question, rather, is one of perspective: whether the small units are to be capitalist or socialist in orientation and intention; and whether they are seen as ends in themselves or integrated with a more universal system. For both of these sets of choices, I would argue for the latter position: the units need to be consistently anti-capitalist, and they need to exist in a dialectic with the whole of things. For human beings are not rodents, who live in burrows. Nor are we insects, creatures who thrive at a small scale, because of which they cannot use skeletons or lungs, or any of the organs necessary for larger organisms. Humans are, by nature, large, expansive, universalizing creatures. We need different degrees of realization to express our being, grandeur as well as intimacy, the large grain as well as the fine. We need the equivalent of skeletons to support us, and specialized organs to meet our species need. Thus I should think that in an ecologically realized world there would exist significant sectors of large-scale activity, for example, rail and communications systems and power grids, just as world cities would flourish as sites of universality. I hope I may be forgiven for insisting that New York, Paris, London, and Tokyo not be taken down in an ecological society, but more fully realized; and that the nightmare cities of global capital – cities like Jakarta, Lagos, and São Paulo – will be restored to similar states of being.

This restoration in its many forms comes back to the question of the emancipation of labor, and not just waged labor, but all compulsive forms of our creativity, including most definitely the alienation of women's household work, and the stifling of children in schools. The fact is that the great bulk of human-kind are throttled in their humanity, and overcoming this is far more significant than any tinkering from above with a corrupt economy. This truth is either lost on the ecological economists or mystified out of existence. Any sense of real people, and real popular struggle, are abstracted from mandarin texts like *An Introduction to Ecological Economics*. Yes, the authors do call for a "living democracy," which is certainly a good thing. But life is struggle, especially in a class society where antagonisms are built into the social process. Yet for *Ecological Economics*, living democracy is "a broad . . . process to discuss and achieve consensus on these important issues. This is distinct from the polemic and divisive political process that seems to hold sway in many countries today." Thus we need "to engage all members of society in a substantive dialogue about the future they desire and the policies and instruments necessary to bring it about."[26] The image evoked is reminiscent of the official murals that decorate US post offices in which the European settlers/invaders are solemnly greeted by the Indians to deliberate on matters of mutual concern. Where sweatshops reimpose slavery within the capitalist system while untold millions of people in the middle classes are consigned to mall culture and the rat race, consensus is not exactly an illuminating term, and some divisive polemics, well-chosen and coupled with proper action, can do a great deal of good. False reconciliation is not the path out of a world as unjust as this. The demand for justice is the pivot about which labor will be emancipated; just so, must it be a foundation of overcoming the ecological crisis.

In bringing this section to a close, a few words may be added about Herman Daly, in my view, the best of the mainstream ecological economists. Daly, formerly with the World Bank and a student of Georgescu-Roegen, has done more than anyone to question the pathological growth inherent to the system. He has stood firm, in the teeth of elite opinion to the contrary, to the thesis of limits to growth and attempted to redefine economics accordingly. Nor has Daly hesitated to call for fundamental change, or to use strong, non-technocratic language in doing so.[27] I would see Daly as a bridge-builder between the established thought, the folly of which he appreciates keenly, and the more radical approach chosen here.

To this end, Daly has gone a considerable way (beyond, say, David Korten) toward a basic critique of capital. He was not afraid to advocate a maximum wage, and caught the predictable amount of scorn for his troubles.[28] He is willing to use Marx's framework for use- and exchange-value and the circulation process underlying capital formation.[29] And he has a keen awareness of the dehumanization of labor endemic to the capitalist system, and calls for widespread worker ownership as a remedy. He has even shown flexibility on the question of socialism, being an admirer of Karl Polanyi and Michael Harrington, who opened his eyes to the democratic potentials within socialism.

But these insights do not translate into praxis, especially on the all-important subject of labor. Yes, Daly would have worker ownership, but kept firmly within a capitalist market. His sensitivity to the predicament of labor is vitiated by an odd reading of history, in which the opposition between capital and labor is seen as the "dominant situation of the *past* ... [when it] was supposed that the interests of labor and management were in conflict more than they were in harmony. This was true when capital treated labor as a commodity ... It is much less true today."

A startling insight. As a result, "the goal should be to increase communications between labor and management so that the situation would be improved for both." Daly here repeats the ideology of Fordism, which has been scrapped since the crises of the 1970s, and was basically a mystification to begin with.

More pointedly, Daly does not believe in it, either. For example, he – and Cobb – would "insist that [trade policy] be accompanied by greatly increased competitiveness among American producers." For the purposes of competitiveness, of course, capital has to treat labor just as it always has, namely, as a commodity whose cost can be ruthlessly driven down – or shifted to the dirt-cheap overseas sources provided by globalization. In any case, the day when capital ceases treating labor as a commodity will be the dawning of a new, socialist era. In the meanwhile, Daly stays with the *ancien régime*, unable to cross the bridge he is building. He does "not want to see the renewal of labor militancy directed toward increasing its share of the pie over against capital and the general public" (as though the workforce were not a main portion of the general public). On the other hand, neither would he and Cobb "encourage continued interest in global domination," for which we may all offer a modest round of gratitude.[30]

Ecophilosophies

An "ecophilosophy" represents a comprehensive orientation that combines the understanding of our relation to nature, the dynamics of the ecological crisis, and the guidelines for rebuilding society in an ecocentric direction. These positions are not simply contained in texts, but inform social movements as well. All such "philosophies" – Christian, Marxist, the views espoused here as well as those mentioned below – are efforts to make sense of the dilemmas of being human at a particular time and place, in this case, in relation to the ecological crisis. They necessarily set themselves up against others. But any system can fall into the traps of egoism and sectarianism. The Tower of Babel still holds power over us, as each defends his little space, his cave. There is always a range of adherents to any doctrine, each end of which often ends up loathing the other in a spectacular demonstration of human folly. Across these spectrums one can find surprising cross-overs between doctrines, and deep internal contradictions within doctrines. There is no point in lamenting this: "we are such fools as mortals be," and this is the way we operate, part of our human nature. The only decent recourse is to bring things into the open, work for dialogue, retain the spirit of critique, and remember Blake's dictum: "Opposition is true friendship."

Deep ecology The guiding principle of this diffuse but important doctrine is to continue the Copernican revolution of decentering "Man" by removing him (the gendered pronoun is apt) from lordship over nature. This is a daring, radical, and necessary move, and compatible with some chief ideas of this study, especially the gendered bifurcation of nature, the concept of capitalism as the regime of the Ego, and the notion of intrinsic value. The chief point of tension, which needs to be worked out much more fully than can be done here, concerns the question of human nature itself.

No doubt an attitude of domination over other species plays an essential role in our ecological woes. But deep ecology has also to take into account that as a species we are fundamentally part of nature, and that our "nature" is to express nature's transformative power. At its far, anti-humanist edge, deep ecology can give the distinct impression that all of this is bad, and that the best thing for humans to do is to go back to a paleolithic existence in the wilderness, or live like the Unabomber, who used sophisticated technology to try to destroy industrial civilization and bring about the mass disappearance of humanity. By denying humanity's creative potentials, deep ecology is denying nature itself. Deep ecology needs to develop, then, an internal set of relations that will adequately give us a role *within* nature. This entails concern for what we might call, "fellow feeling," the affection of humans for each other as well as the rest of nature. A good case can be made that a deep regard for others, emerging, among other things, through the phenomena of justice, caring, and, indeed, love, is the saving character of our nature.[31]

The malignant side of deep ecology can appear in the preservation and enhancement of wilderness, in the course of which one can also erase the people who have lived there from time immemorial, so much a part of nature that they had no separate word for it, and certainly no word for wilderness. In the turbulent climate of contemporary ecopolitics, this is complicated by the needs of the US State Department and the World Bank to shore up their shaky legitimacy. In order to counter criticisms of their role in the ecological crisis, these institutions will make aid packages conditional on preserving wild areas – which then have added value as sites for ecotourism, a favored way of recycling the economic surplus. So a kind of bastardized deep ecology can be realized within the strategy of advanced capitalist elites, for whom nature is what looks good on calendars, as humanity loses its value.

In the decade 1986–96, more than 3 million people were displaced by development and conservation projects. This policy did not begin with deep ecology, but with the nineteenth-century conservation movement. In the United States this was very much tied up with getting rid of Indians. Our enjoyment of the great national park system, for instance, needs to be tempered with the recollection that 300 Shoshones were killed in the development of Yosemite, and that this was by no means an isolated case. Deep ecology, border politics, the genocide of indigenous peoples, and ecotourism, can all be rendered, then, part of the same package. This trap is loaded because of the pressing population crisis, which makes it easy to rationalize exclusion. The trait is by no means confined to deep ecology, but haunts the environmental movement at large, which has not covered itself with glory on questions such as immigration, often allying with reactionaries in a deluded and cryptically racist quest to keep our borders "clean." Certain exponents of deep ecology have disgraced themselves and the movement yet further by suggesting that pandemics such as AIDS are nature's, i.e. "Gaia's," way of

189

ridding itself of the pestilential species, *Homo sapiens*. So far as I know, they never apply the same reasoning to themselves or family members when they get sick.[32]

It follows that, in practice, deep ecology has to stay clear of this association and prove its *bona fides* as an ecophilosophy by incorporating the critique of domination over humanity, which leads necessarily to the critique of capitalism and the question of how to surpass capitalism. In fact, there is such a current with the ecophilosophy, chiefly represented by Arne Naess, the Norwegian philosopher who more or less sired the project. Naess has written of a potential rapprochement with socialism, saying that "it is still clear that some of the most valuable workers for ecological goals come from the socialist camps."[33] This has a lot to do with his origin within a European context where anticommunism and neoliberal ideology have not stifled the political intelligence with hatred of socialism. In North America, very few people influenced by deep ecology bother to read Naess, or would attend to statements such as the above.[34]

A substantial current of the deep-ecological position has meanwhile been assumed by the philosophically and/or spiritually minded, who tend to keep a comfortable distance from the messy world of struggle.[35] Some of these folk may be virtuous, but this implies no special connection with the critique of capitalism or the emancipation of labor. These are the kind of folks who tend to fall in line behind the fatuous pronouncement that green politics is "neither left nor right, but ahead" – a mere slogan which begs the question of what being "ahead" constitutes (see below), while forgetting that in the real world, that which does not confront the system becomes its instrument. In any case, the deep ecology ecophilosophy is far too loose to form itself into a coherent movement, and almost by definition excludes the formation of parties or any organized assertion of power. Indeed, what kind of a society can be formulated out of so negative and flaccid a doctrine as would hold: "Our first principle [with respect to resource conservation] is to encourage agencies, legislators, property owners and managers to consider flowing with rather than forcing natural process. Second, in facing practical situations we favor working within the minority tradition, in the local community, especially the bioregion."[36] Which brings us to an offshoot, centered in this very notion.

Bioregionalism The appeal of this doctrine, which connects some of the principles of community economics with the back-to-the-land movement, is obvious. Bioregionalism represents a specifically ecological rendition of the contemporary movement toward the breakup of nation-states. Where separatists typically define themselves in terms of distinct nations subsumed within the larger political entity, bioregionalists take this a step further, grounding – literally – themselves in the ecological preconditions of nationhood, that of the *place* shared by a people. This is not merely location, but the concrete ecological workings of a part of the earth: the flows of watersheds, the lay of the hills, the kinds of soils, the biota that inhabit a bioregion, all regarded as the organic substrate of a community built on human scale and dedicated to living gently on the earth and not over it. It would seem that the bioregion is the essential ground within which the principles of sustainability and its reliance on ecological technology and economics may be applied.

Certainly, an emphasis on place in any realized ecophilosophy is essential. It would be impossible to construct any adequate notion of an integral ecosystem without such a ground. It might be added that as someone who has chosen to live in the Catskill Mountains and Hudson Valley of New York State, and who has had good relationships with people in the back-to-the-land movement, I personally speak with affection for this point of view. Nevertheless, the attempt to extend it to bioregionalism as a ecophilosophy is to be challenged and rejected, because the idea is incapable of guiding social transformation.

Some of these difficulties may be seen in an essay by the bioregionalist Kirkpatrick Sale, who is led to posit a regime of *self-sufficiency* for the bioregion. A consistent bioregionalist has to do so in order to establish his view as an ecophilosophy.

What comes, however, with the "territory" is the need to define boundaries. Of this, Sale has the following to say:

> Ultimately, the task of determining the appropriate bioregional boundaries – and how seriously to take them – will always be left up to the inhabitants of the area. One can see this fairly clearly in the case of the Indian peoples who first settled the North American continent. Because they lived off the land, they distributed themselves to a remarkable degree along the lines of what we now recognize as bioregions.[37]

There are three significant problems with this statement.

First, what is an "area"? The term is vague in itself, but cannot remain that way if boundaries of the bioregion need to be decided, as must be the case if there is to be a "self" to be self-sufficient about. But who is to decide who lives where? Can this conceivably be done without conflict, given the differential suitability of different regions for productive development? And who is to resolve the anticipated conflicts, which will involve major expropriation? The land where I live is part of the watershed for New York City. Are the members of the Catskill Mountain Bioregion to declare that the city can go dry, and are they prepared to take up arms to preserve the integrity of the bioregion?

Second, the Indian peoples lived bioregionally because only about 1–2 million of them inhabited the now-United States at the time of the European invasion. Today's vastly greater population exists not in simple relation to place but in an interdependent grid. Remember, too, that the Indians fell into bitter warfare as their territory became destabilized by the European intrusion.

Third, and most important by far, the Indian's bioregional life-world was predicated on holding land in common, in other words, it was the original communism. The genocidal wars with the invaders had a great deal to do with the latter's capitalism that required the alienation of land as property, something the Indians would rather die than submit to (which is pretty much what happened). Capitalism has definitely not changed in this respect; and no coherent project of bioregionalism can survive if productive land remains a commodity, to be owned by absentees, hoarded, rented out, concentrated in fewer and fewer hands, and generally exploited. Sale is fully aware of the plight of the Indians, but ignores the implications of transforming capitalism. He writes that bioregional institution building "can be safely left to people who live there, providing only that they have undertaken the job of honing their bioregional sensibilities and making acute their bioregional consciousness" (478) – a pretty gross understatement of what history shows to be the need to transform society in a "communist" direction, without which a people simply cannot democratically control their bioregion. And if they rose up to take such control, how much imagination does it take to see what would be the response of the capitalist state?

Even if these problems could miraculously be ironed out, retaining Sale's autarkic concept of a bioregion would be impossible. He calls for self-sufficient regions, each developing the energy of its peculiar ecology – "wind in the Great Plains; water in New England; wood in the Northwest" (482). But how on earth are these resources to be made sufficient? I would be surprised to learn that the rivers of New England could supply more than a tenth of its energy needs; and as for wood in the Northwest (where there is more hydropower, though again not enough), how will Sale answer to the environmentalists – or the economists, or any sane person – if, say, Seattle is converted to forest-destroying and smoke-spewing wood-burning stoves? Of course, an ecological society would have greatly enhanced energy efficiency and reduced needs, but there is something slap-dash in these prescriptions, which seem deduced from a naturalized ideology rather than grounded in reality.

"Self-sufficiency," adds Sale, "before I am badly misunderstood, is not the same thing as isolation, nor does it preclude all kinds of trade at all times. It does not require connections with the outside, but within strict limits – the connections must be nondependent, nonmonetary and noninjurious – it allows them" (483). We should not misunderstand badly, or at all, but the understanding is hard. No required connections between bio-regions? Suppose your daughter lives in the next one (or, worse, the one beyond that) and you want to visit. Can you phone her, and whom do you pay for the purpose? Are there to be no roads, or rail systems, or airplane travel for the purpose? Are people only to walk between bioregions on trails through the brush, as the other means would require some monetary intercourse … ?

We need take this no further. Any effort to build society on the basis of strict bioregionalism dissolves in a flood of contra-dictions. What is missing are those measures which have to be taken so that the whole of society is transformed. Bioregionalism can be no more than an important ancilla to the building of an ecological society.

Ecofeminism Ecofeminism is a powerful ecophilosophy groun-ded by joining the two great struggles for women's liberation and ecological justice. However, it remains uncertain as a social move-ment. As ecophilosophy it theorizes the theme we have drawn as the gendered bifurcation of nature. This began with the control over women's bodies and labor, and is at the root of patriarchy and class. Over time, splits between classes, between genders, and between "Man" and nature, have undergone distinct paths of development and intertwine into complex patterns. They enter the history of capitalism at its foundations – in the reduction of nature to inert resources; in the valorization of cold abstraction and the identification of this masculine trait with what is truly human; and in the superexploitation of women, beginning with unwaged domestic labor, and extending to cheapened wage labor in the periphery and fodder for the sex industries. In the strange brew that is capitalist culture, money becomes the hieroglyph for the phallus, the signifier of power, and the laurel of competition – and the race is on.

It follows that capitalist domination always entails gender domination, and that the enmity to nature we are tracking is inte-grally related to its gendered bifurcation. Therefore, any path out of capitalism must also be ecofeminist. Ecofeminism should also

194

be anticapitalist, as capital and its state hold the reins of power by means of which women and ecologies are degraded. A substantial body of ecofeminist theory and practice meets this condition and is foundational to the project envisioned here.[38] But not all who call themselves ecofeminists, as with feminism proper, are anticapitalist. Some ecofeminists (using certain aspects of deep ecology and bioregionalism) take a kind of refuge in an unmediated relationship to nature, that is, they *essentialize* women's closeness to nature and build from there, submerging history into nature in the process. The "eternal feminine" results: archetypally maternal, close to the earth, and, in its further reaches, the source of goddess-based spiritualities and feminist separatism.[39]

Because essentialism takes its object outside of history, it can at best achieve a weak, imitative reconnection of what had been split-off. The holding and provisioning functions assigned to a historically degraded feminity cannot be recovered for the transformation of capitalist/patriarchal society. Essentialist feminisms, whether eco- or not, remain therefore essentially bourgeois in orientation. Their place is in the comforts of the New Age Growth Center, rather than on the barricades of struggle. These divisions keep ecofeminism from becoming a coherent social movement.

Social ecology This doctrine, the last ecophilosophy to be considered, builds on the central insight that ecological problems have to be seen as social problems, and specifically as the outcome of hierarchies. In contrast to deep ecology, bioregionalism, and essentialist ecofeminism, social ecology is intrinsically political; it begins with social critique, and follows this through to the envisioning of a political transformation.

Social Ecology may be traced to the activity of an individual, the late Murray Bookchin (d. 2006), whose signal contribution was to draw ecocentrism into the anarchist tradition. Bookchin was not originally an anarchist, but turned to it after disaffection with the communist movement in which he had been raised, and under the influence of the New Left of the 1960s. Bookchin became one of the pioneers in recognizing the impending ecological crisis and in seeing its radical implications. As an anarchist-communitarian he subsumed the struggle for ecological rationality into the notion of emancipation, which became represented as the notion of overcoming hierarchy, and eventually took form as a vision of liberated communities.

All this is resonant with many of the ideas argued in the present work. Why, then, is this not a book within the social-ecology tradition? The reason, as I see it, is partly theoretical, partly a function of how political movements have worked themselves out. The theoretical distinction has to do with the fact that for social ecology, hierarchy is regarded in itself, both as a kind of original sin and as the efficient cause of the ecological crisis. The particular path traced in the present work, which begins with gender domination, moves to class, and then, eventually, to capital, is eschewed in favor of a blanket condemnation of any human relationship in which person *a* has authority over person *b*. I cannot, however, see hierarchy as in itself generating the pathology of the ecological crisis. After all, there are rational forms of authority like the teacher–student relationship, which are grounded in the very human-natural fact that our young are born helpless into the world, and need the transmission of culture if they are to become human. This function is inherent to culture itself, which, unlike instincts, must be continually relearned and, in the process, changes. What makes a hierarchy require overthrowing is acquiring the character of *domination*, where this signifies an expropriation of human power for the purposes of self-aggrandizement, in contrast to those relationships of differential authority that are reciprocal and mutual (so that the student can look forward to becoming a teacher herself some day). What this means in practice is that hierarchies and authorities have to be concretely examined to see whether they are *just* or not; and this in turn requires that they be assessed in terms of the specific alienations of human creative power that occur in different historical settings. For this purpose the notions of gender and class, which connect real individuals to history and nature, are very apt, as is the idea of production as the defining characteristic of human nature.

These rather abstract points are given substance in terms of the actual political contours of an ecophilosophy such as social ecology. Social ecology continues the anarchist project, whose principal point of action has been the defense of community and the attack on state power.[40] Anarchism incorporates spontaneity and direct action along with communitarian values, and developed in the nineteenth century as an alternative to Marxian socialism. Since the revelations of twentieth-century socialism's potential for centralism, bureaucracy, and authoritarianism, and its subsequent collapse (to be discussed in the next chapter), anarchism has gained a renewed hold on the left. An influential strand has appeared in the post-Seattle emergence of new movements against globalization, in whose demonstrations it has taken a leading role.[41] This current emphasizes direct action, which is a necessary component to any radical ecopolitics, but not a sufficient one, as it leaves unspoken the question of building an ecological society beyond capital.

Social ecology is less concerned as a movement with direct action than with an appropriation of the communitarian values inherent to anarchism. These have also become integral to the various green movements, within which anarchism, and specifically its social-ecological form, have played a vital role. But the rejection of socialist and Marxian ways of approaching the ecological crisis sacrifices too much. In addressing the abuses of socialism, it tends to neglect trying to do what socialism did, namely, really take on the capitalist world system, in all its massive obdurateness and penetration of life-worlds. Anarchists and social ecologists generally profess to be anti-capitalist, but they tend to not analyze capitalism to its root in the domination and exploitation of labor. Similarly, they correctly emphasize the need to overcome the domination sedimented into the state; but they overlook the fact (chiefly from hostility to Marxism, I fear) that the prime function of the state is to secure the class system, indeed, that the two structures, class and state, are each

197

absolutely dependent on the other, so that we cannot address the one without the other. Thus if the state is a primary problem, so is the class system, and avoiding confrontation with this latter – which means in practice, avoiding giving central importance to the emancipation of labor – tends to vitiate the anarchist reading of things, and loses concreteness.

Having said this much, it remains to be emphasized that these difficulties do not in my view amount to an antagonistic contradiction between the positions of social ecology, or, indeed, of any anarchist formation, and those argued here. Whatever begins with radical rejection of the given order, combines it with the affirmation of freedom for all creatures,[42] and takes upon itself a humility that recognizes the shortcomings of all movements in relation to the task before us, is positioned to contend with the ecological crisis. Within these boundaries the active contestation of ideas goes forward. In truth, we are all groping toward a transformative vision deeper and wider than any yet subsumed under the labels of past struggles. One enemy we should all be able to agree upon is sectarianism, simply because such an attitude forecloses, indeed, denies, the depth of the problem.

To some degree these problems were embodied by Murray Bookchin himself. Charismatic as well as brilliant, but also unrelentingly dogmatic and vituperatively sectarian, Bookchin both created social ecology and led it into a *cul de sac*. There were structural reasons for this that extended far beyond any individual failing. When Bookchin first announced social ecology, indeed, when the environmental movements both radical and liberal got going, we were on the cusp between the affluent and expansive Fordist capitalism of 1945–70, and the neoliberal era that rages today. Bookchin launched social ecology with *Post-Scarcity Anarchism* in 1970, and both the title and the date of that work are revealing. The extent of the ecological crisis had not been felt, which enabled a relatively easy sense of utopianism. Neither the collapse of Soviet communism nor globalization had set capital so firmly as the brutal overlord of the world. Today things are dreadfully clearer; and even if full awareness has not yet taken hold, the emerging direction of "what has to be done" is sweeping all the ecophilosophies toward a new radical synthesis.[43]

I should think that one of the signal effects of the ecological crisis is that, by penetrating life-worlds to so monstrous a degree, capital has now undercut, indeed, obliterated the ground of opposition that fuelled the great debates between socialism and anarchism from the middle of the nineteenth century to the fall of the USSR. These are now historically irrelevant and can only be sustained by inertia, egoism and mental cowardice. Defense of lived space and of the Commons is now on an equivalent footing with the exploitation of labor. The Second Contradiction of capital, as developed by James O'Connor, has formalized this, and places the struggle for the integrity of nature and humanity on the same footing. This profound shift has redrawn the map of struggle. It is safe to say that we have only begun to take its measure.

Democracy, populism and fascism

"Democracy" is the favorite way of organizing humankind of everyone to the left of the late General Pinochet and the Olympic Organizing Committee. No word is dearer to the ideologues of the regime, who were given to hail "our side" as the democracies in the holy war against communism, and set up institutions like the National Endowment for Democracy to superintend the transition of developing countries into the camp of the West. Countries like Indonesia and Guatemala in the time of the Generals were hailed as democracies (sometimes qualified as "fledgling"), as has been Nicaragua in the post-Sandinista years, despite an appalling loss of freedom and participation. And every spasm of capital's global reach, for example, the Free Trade Agreement of the Americas, is legitimated with the promise that it will cement the rule of democracy in the Western hemisphere. This democracy is a regime where elites rule on behalf of capital using an electoral mechanism that affords some legitimacy, while permitting a limited degree of lower-class participation (in part to renew the talent base of the elites) along with a check on rampant corruption. The model arose deep within the history of capitalism, inasmuch as only technically free citizens could sell their labor power on its markets. Such freedom, as we have seen, has had always to be contained, whence democracy in its bourgeois form has been intrinsically constrictive on the lower classes while offering a means to power open to men of property.

If we regard the ideology of democracy with more than a little skepticism, however, it is only to fight for the true meaning of the notion, since the perpetual struggle for freedom that it encapsulates is nothing less than our coming into full species powers – which is to say, the power of men and women *beyond* the bourgeois notion of property. The struggle for substantive as against ideological democracy is therefore the necessary precondition for overcoming the ecological crisis, simply because this requires achieving a just society.

The fulfillment of democracy is not getting more people to vote, though such an outcome would be more democratic than what we have today. Nor is it giving voters better parties to vote for. Though, this, too, is a point on the road, it is limited by the fact that within the confinements of the given state, the power expressed in the polling booths is by definition stunted. If popular agitation built a more powerful electoral foundation, say, by achieving proportional representation so that smaller parties could meaningfully participate, then we could say that democratic power had been advanced, because power had to some further extent built its own base – but we would not rest at that level, either. By the same reasoning, worker ownership of corporations would be a relative democratization; yet so long as the firm has to play by the rules of the capitalist market, it remains self-defeating.

Because the compass of democracy points to the mobilization of our species power, full democracy will not happen without the overcoming of capitalism. Yet such a demand scarcely appears on today's parched political landscape. What we generally see are stunted derivatives, as in the vague identification of people of good will as "progressive." The term is highly dubious, as progress also means eliminating tradition and the integrity of the Commons. In any event, the question is begged: progressing toward what? Toward a virtuous citizenry placing checks on corporate power, who then stand about until startled by the next head of the hydra? Toward the gratification of an alternative "lifestyle" caught up in capital's consumerist regime? Or does it progress beyond the limits of the given? Our progressivism fails not because of its inability to spell out what the "beyond" may be, but through its indifference to the question, because of which it settles into the ecodestructive system on the ground.

Progressivism today is largely defined as *populism.* As the word suggests, for populism, the political agent is the "People," considered as one gigantic person rising up and becoming the subject of its own history. Populism is a compelling political construction with an immediate appeal. It fills each individual who accepts its terms with the power of historical agency, and, because it personalizes history, offers a cogent narrative. If the People is afflicted, then another kind of person, the personification of arbitrary and corrupt power, is doing the afflicting. A morality play is invoked. There is an injustice, a villain, and a hero-in-waiting: the People, set to rise up and smite its oppressor, or at the very least, to demand fairness. The model resonates across a great range of circumstances and historical moments. It animated peasant rebellions in the Middle Ages, the *sans-culottes* in the French Revolution, Luddites and Chartists in nineteenth-century England, and in the later nineteenth century, in America, took the name of populism itself and became a substantial force. Populist movements in America have made notable contributions wherever corrupt and alienating economic power has oppressed large blocs of people – farmers in the Plains and the South, small businessmen victimized by banks, urban workers afflicted by layoffs. Populist movements were behind William Jennings Bryan and his "Cross of Gold" agitation, and they have periodically resurfaced until the present, when the evils of globalization, striking home across a great variety of settings, have provoked resistance. The Greens are proud to be progressive populists, and the heterogeneous character of their demands, ranging from environmental protection to prison reform, changes in drug policy, and community economics, are readily assimilable to the populist narrative. In Ralph Nader they gained a recognized champion of populism, a man who has fought to redress the grievances of ordinary citizens and consumers victimized by corporate greed.

But populism's "People" does not exist except as a rallying point, beyond which it tends to fragment. After all, not all people are oppressed, for the oppressors are human beings, too. Nor do the oppressed exist as a homogeneous mass, for oppression has constructed significant lines of division. Would that these could be erased with a slogan! Yes, workers and small businessmen can go to a rally and feel united; even, let us imagine, blacks and whites, and Latinos and Asians can do so – or, taking it to another level of particularity, blacks of African-American extraction and of Caribbean extraction, or farmers or consumers, or wherever the fault lines have been laid down. But this does not make them a "People" once the event is over, nor will they become so until the hard and patient work has been done to find the lines of division and build counter-institutions to overcome the class and state structures that institutionalize oppression. Populism can itself be no more than a point of entry into the building of movements that address the structures that fragment a people. Unless it is surpassed, everyone will go home to his or her particular problem and things will go no further.

Or things may go badly. Populism, by personalizing oppression, can become a mythology whose evocative power welds together a divided people into a unified body: such is its evocative power. But there are serious pitfalls. For one, the populist myth encourages the idea that there was a kind of "golden age" before the Bad Oppressor entered the scene and made life miserable for the People. These days the corporation, especially because it achieved spurious personhood thanks to a nineteenth-century interpretation of the 14th Amendment, is exceptionally well situated for the role of villain. It is an easy matter to proceed from this to construct the myth that somehow we were in good hands before 1868, when corporate greed entered the world – and that this blissful condition will be restored if only corporate power can be checked. No matter that the notion of a golden pre-corporate age is not true; the idea is convenient to the legend of a happy era of small capitals sought by the neo-Smithians, and so a wishful illusion is perpetrated.[44]

There is a more ominous flaw to populism's mythos. Populism that remains merely itself is bound to fail because it cannot address the realities of power. What happens then to the myth? The answer, unhappily too often, is that its personalization turns malignant and persecutory. Sinister conspiracies are alleged to explain the persistence of corporate and financial power; or, in another turn of the screw, the blame is shifted onto alien others, of different color or ethnicity. This is the stuff of racism, which in actual history has been intertwined with populisms gone bad. Rural populism of the turn of the twentieth century failed when its militancy lost the thread of socialism; with this, it became virulently racist against blacks.[45] Progressive populists are reluctant to associate their cause with Father Coughlin; but the demagogic priest who dominated the airwaves of the 1930s was an authentic populist who took hold of massive rage against capitalism, turned it into a mythologized crusade against banks and then, when he lost the contest for power, turned rightward into anti-semitism and fascism; indeed, the dynamics of anti-semitism have often been rooted in populist mechanisms, with the Jew brought into the picture to unify the masses and deflect their antagonism from class enemies.[46] Today, these kinds of racist exclusion become especially likely in the context of conflicts over immigration afflicting both the United States and Europe.

The result reawakens the great nightmare of the last century: fascism, most of all, in its Nazi form. The special relevance of this painful association arises from the fact that Nazism was both a populism and a self-professedly ecological movement.[47] It goes without saying that the Nazis were never a "progressive" movement; quite the contrary. Emerging in the wake of a ferocious crisis of accumulation, they did criticize big business and call themselves National Socialists, because socialism had prestige in those days. But the Nazi project was a kind of populism precisely directed against actual socialism, which they countered with an organic ideology that sought a mythicized union of the Germanic people, workers included, with the soil. It was an ecology of merging, which became an ecology of splitting. This kind of unification is all too reminiscent of the nature mysticism still fashionable in certain ecological circles, especially the deep-ecological reduction of human beings to the status of just another species in the "web of life." Biological reduction fosters racist thought, which is, intellectually speaking, a demented effort to find subspeciation within humankind. Everyone serious about matters ecological should familiarize themselves with the say-ings of Hitler, or of Heinrich Himmler, leader of the SS, about the "decent" attitude of Germans toward animals, whence the master-race should be trusted with the "human animals" under its care, such as Slavs – trusted, too, to remove the verminous ani-mals like Jews, Gypsies, and homosexuals.[48] This is a degenerate ecophilosophy, beyond doubt, but an ecophilosophy nonetheless, and calls attention to the fact that the degeneration is inherent to whatever denies the value of the specifically human within (and not over) the manifold of nature.

No one should be so naïve as to believe that this way of think-ing is a matter only for historians to study. It is most doubtful that progressive populism will turn rightward; its fate lies more in absorption back into the capitalist mainstream. But there are other sources of a malignant ecofascism. A grim far-right pres-ence often recurs within green movements under the umbrella of falsely unified ecological thought. Considerable evidence of this has already appeared in England and Northern Europe, even in the great Seattle protests of 1999, when contingents of anti-semitic skinheads made an appearance. We should recall, too, that organicist thinkers like Rudolph Bahro betrayed an affinity for Nazi ideology; and that a founding German green and author of the bestselling 1975 work, *A Planet is Plundered*, Herbert Gruhl, did likewise. Indeed, Gruhl left the party to found an alternative because it had "given up its concern for ecology in favor of a leftist ideology of emancipation." Gruhl, it is well to recall, was the originator of the awful phrase, noted above, that greens are "neither left nor right but ahead."[49]

Neo-fascist ecological thought comes in many varieties, the common feature of which is to take some aspect of the ecological crisis and, under the guise of being "neither left nor right, but ahead," move in fact rightward. The instigation is usually population pressure and conflicts over immigration, the context of which are persistently uneven stretches of prosperity (as between the former East Germany and the remainder, or between Southern California and Baja, Mexico), and more basically, the breakdown of large swathes of the world under the chaotic conditions of capital. Presently, ecofascism is limited to a small number of elite intellectuals, just as street-fighting fascists are confined to small groups of radically disaffected youth. But there should be no underestimation of the potential of these movements given the potentials for much worse ecocatastrophes, especially when mixed in with the ominous growth of religious fundamentalism, a protofascist development we cannot discuss here.

With whatever admixture of ideologies, fascism is a potential breakdown pattern of capitalism. To say, "it can't happen here," is to misread the explosive tensions built into the capitalist system. All it takes is a certain degree of crisis, and fascism may be imposed, as a revolution from above, to install an authoritarian regime in order to preserve the main workings of the system. Regressive ideologies and racism are then introduced as ways of re-establishing legitimacy and displacing conflict. So much was learned in the last century; what we are poised to learn in this one are the fascist potentials in a capitalist system facing crisis of an ecological kind, especially one involving mass migration, as is increasingly the case and which will really take off once rising seas place many coastal areas under water. There are any number of scenarios, including looming pandemics on a world scale – consider only the gruesome unlikeliness of mad cow disease and its possible sequelae.[50]

The actual path of the unfolding crisis is not simply a matter of collapsing ecosystems, but, as in the débâcle of Katrina, the ongoing interaction of this with political responses. The possibilities are numerous, and need not be speculated upon here. What we need to bear in mind, however, is that although fascism may be introduced violently from above to save the system of accumulation, it necessarily introduces more problems than it solves. A fascist order will be more ecodestructive than the liberal one it replaces – because it is further from the democratic realization of human power that is the essential condition for ecological rationality, and because, as a manifestation of this, it builds unbearable and explosive tensions into society. The installation of ecofascism on a grand scale may in fact be the trigger that sets into motion the cascading avalanche that will bring an end to nature's peculiar experiment with a species on whom was bestowed the power to consciously direct evolution.

It is a fate we can choose to defy, because of this very power. But if we succeed in doing so, it can only be through a creative transformation of our existence. Populism and social ecology, green politics, community economics, ecofeminism, bioregionalism, cooperatives – the entire mass of ideologies and movements, coming from below, overlapping, interpenetrating and set going as progressive responses to the crisis – have been tried. They have discovered much, and taught us much, but nothing so much as the need to go further. It is time to see if this can be given the name of ecosocialism.

9 | Prefiguration

The Bruderhof

There are, in the eastern United States as well as the Dakotas, adjacent Canada and England, communities of Christian followers of Jakob Hutter (d. 1536), founder of the pacifist branch of the Anabaptists. This offshoot of the Radical Reformation, having endured the persecutions attendant upon their kind, found their way to the New World, where they built agricultural communes and prospered. In the twentieth century, a similar branch arose in Germany under the leadership of Eberhard and Emmy Arnold, first as a Christian pacifist collective, then as a Hutterite intentional community. Persecuted by the Nazis, they fled to Paraguay and built an agricultural commune. In the 1950s they came to the United States, where, under the name of "Bruderhof," they settled in Rifton, a town in New York's Hudson River Valley. By now, the Bruderhof (a Hutterite term for "community of brethren") had separated from the original Hutterites, who found them too much in the world. The worldliness of the Bruderhof included a shift from agricultural to industrial production, with an associated embrace of technology. They entered the business of making high-value learning aids for schools and disability centers. While the commodities so produced never captured more than a small share of this market, the realized profit was considerable and enabled the community to grow. Once a Bruderhof community reaches a certain size, say between 300 and 400, it "hives," dividing and forming a new unit elsewhere. In this way, there are now six Bruderhofs in the United States and two more in England, linked by dedicated phone lines, so that all eight communities can be placed in instant contact with each other simply by picking up a receiver and pressing a button. They have their own publishing house as well, Plough Books, through which their ideas can be disseminated; and I am also told that they possess a small fleet of aircraft, bought with the profits from their business.[1]

There are a number of interesting things to be said about the Bruderhof – whom, it should be added, I have visited on a number of occasions, and worked with on several projects: first, the Bruderhof thrive in the capitalist market. They make fine and useful objects, using sophisticated machinery, computers, and a functioning distribution and sales network, including catalogues, trucks, etc. In short, they are successfully integrated into the economy.

Second, Bruderhof are radically non-capitalist. The "value" added onto and extracted from their learning aids derives from the capitalist market at large. Surplus-value from the point of production does not figure into this picture. No value is added from their own labor, for the plain reason that the Bruderhof are communists. In the enterprises from which their money is made, they are all paid the same amount: nothing. Nor is there any hierarchy within the factory; there is division of labor, of course, but no boss. The plant managers have no particular authority beyond their differentiated task. A visitor to the plant is greeted with a starkly different scene from that which obtains in the standard capitalist workplace. Workers self-direct, come and go at different hours, punch no time-clocks. Time is not bound, nor is work dominated by considerations of productivity. Octogenarians and seven-year-old children work side by side as they please, sharing in the labor. There is no contradiction between this relatively indifferent productivity and the profitability of their factories, because the Bruderhof are not driven to accumulate and increase market share, but are content with sufficient incremental profit to meet their needs, which is made possible by the technology at their disposal. Work is driven by the desire to make fine objects and the larger ends to which it is put.

Third, being communists, the Bruderhof hold "all things in common." Beyond a few minor personal possessions, they have no individual property – no cars, no DVD players, no designer jeans, no subscriptions to *Self* and *Connoisseur* magazines. The community takes care of all their needs with its collective profits: communal meals, education, and healthcare, for there are schools on the premises for the young, and Bruderhof physicians to care for most problems. What has to be done outside, such as tuition for advanced study[2] – say, of their doctors – is likewise paid for by the revenues of their factories. By the same token, the material needs of the Bruderhof are considerably lighter than the typical American, both because they share in most things – including the ownership of a few motor vehicles for going here and there – and because everything about their world radically denies the culture of consumerism. Thus the ecological load imposed by Bruderhof is substantially less than that of the population at large, and if we could somehow figure out a way to get all the people of the industrialized nations to live so lightly on the earth, there would be no crisis of anywhere near the present scale to worry about.

If the Bruderhof are any example, we can affirm that neither industrialization nor technology can be the efficient causes of the ecological crisis. They are immersed in both and consume lightly, nor show any compulsion to grow. The reason is the social organization of labor, which under these communistic conditions causes the withering of capital's rage to accumulate.

But these findings open up new questions. What are the conditions, both inner and outer, that enable so radical a shift to occur? What does this imply for markets in an ecologically sane, that is, *ecocentric*, society? And what does this say about socialism? Can we, in fact, get all the people to live this way? Should we?

As for the first question, there is no mystery. The Bruderhof are deeply Christian, which they interpret as Christian-communist. The "holding all things in common" does not derive from Karl Marx, but from the biblical record of the first Christians, Acts 2:44–5: "And all that believed were together, and had all things common; And sold their possessions and goods, and parted them to all men, as every man had need." No matter that it has been perennially betrayed, the notion of communism remains foundational for Christianity. It has a long and intricate history,

Prefiguration

within which Marx himself (who included in his best-known definition of communism, the phrase, "to each according to need")
belongs.[3] The Bruderhof are simply being orthodox when they
affirm communism. However, it needs to be added that they take
this quite a distance. For they do not only practice Christian
communism, but preach it with a vengeance, and this makes
them of special interest to us.

There is probably no more militant group on the left today
than these descendants of the Radical Reformation. They have
gone on pilgrimages against the death penalty, have sent their
children in solidarity to blockaded Cuba and Iraq, and have
become spiritual counselors to Mumia Abu-Jamal. The theme
of these activisms is always to counter a persecution, as Jesus
was persecuted, and as they themselves have been. That is the
Christian Logos playing itself out in historical actuality, creating a new history to which their communism integrally belongs.
Communism for the Bruderhof is not an economic or a political
doctrine but one aspect of a universalizing spiritual force. The
community does not tell others to be communists because they
believe in its economic or even social superiority, but because being communist is part of the "good news" they wish to spread as
Christians. It is an integral element of a spiritual totality. They do
not want people to be communists for the sake of communism;
they want them to be as Jesus, for which end communism is an
essential practice.

We would say, then, that the Bruderhof have found a way
to offset the capitalist market by inserting a spiritual moment
into their worldly practice. Markets, the economists tell us, are
powerful signalling systems, generating the prices that serve to
tie together all economic agents. But this assumes that all agents
are equivalently tuned to prices and monetary values and that
they all obey the same logic and reason – or, in terms of our
discussion, that they are not Bruderhof. For when the market
into which all economic actors are inserted issues the signal,
"maximize profit and market share!", these economic actors do
not hear the command, as they are marching to a different drum,

and their practical faculties no longer resonate to the force field of capital. They simply do not "value" their business that much. I have been told by Bruderhof that if it ever came down to a choice – if, for example, their political activity required that they all go to jail, or if the pursuit of their enterprise became too contradictory for whatever reason – then they would give up the business gladly. I am sure this is true. For Bruderhof, the meaning of productivity, and the labor arrangements necessary for this to be maximized, are only dimly lit points on the screen of a world-view where faith shines more brightly. The Bruderhof are an *intentional* community, and intentions, properly understood, can be material forces.

It must be that an important reason cooperatives, organic farms, etc., succumb to capital's force field is the lack of an offsetting belief-system which enables them to renounce profit-ability. But this needs to be taken to another plane, if only to avoid the conclusion that our coops need to convert to radical Christianity in order to enter the promised land of ecosocialism. Such is clearly not the case, first, because an ecosocialist society must be fully democratic, and not the province of any religious interpretation; and, more specifically, because the Bruderhof are not actually ecocentric in their orientation. They neither espouse particularly ecological concerns, nor is their practice compatible with ecocentrism, especially in the sphere of gender, where a highly patriarchal structure clashes fundamentally with the values of ecological transformation.[4] Although the spiritual dimension of things is to play a very fundamental role in the process, ecosocialism cannot be religious, not least because religion is a kind of binding of spirit that tends to foreclose the opening to ecological transformation.

But that is not the main point here, which is that the Bruderhof go further than the ordinary cooperative in resisting the force field of the capitalist market because they are an "intentional" community. Therefore the generation of some kind of collective "intention" that can withstand the power of capital's force field will be necessary for creating an ecosocialist society; and it must

Prefiguration

be the "moral equivalent" of the Bruderhof's all-encompassing belief. When the Bruderhof resisted the blandishments of the market, they were saying that the commodities they made meant something radically different from what bourgeois society would impose. Instead of the set of signals generated by the market, Bruderhof respond to a whole set of qualitative relations inserted into the meaning of the commodity. Further, these meanings were part of a reconfiguration of their *needs*. This is another way of stating what the *use-value* of the commodity became to them, for use-value is a universe of meanings pertaining to the satisfaction of needs and the wants that manifest needs. This applies not just to the commodities the Bruderhof make, but also to the productive relations in which they engage in order to make them – inasmuch as costs of production are themselves prices of commodities: the machines, the energy to run the machines, the inputs of materials, and, most important, the labor expended in making their "goods." For the Bruderhof, the entirety of their production is subsumed into a schema of use-value directed toward providing the means of going forth as Christ. That, in a word, is their "intention."

Intentions are deployments of values, about which a brief amplification would be in order. Use-values stand at the juncture of a more original form of value and the kinds of value inherent to an economy. This original, or *intrinsic* value, may be thought of as the primary appropriation of the world for each person, in two senses: it is the way we first come to appreciate things and relationships in childhood; and it is, throughout life, the value given to reality irrespective of what we do to reality. In terms of reality-as-nature, intrinsic value is a kind of ablation of our productive power; that is, we intrinsically value the nature that we have done nothing to, that will always stand and beckon, that is our primordium and cosmos – not for sale, and not to be made into a commodity, rather, the "suchness" of nature, its intrinsic being, both sensuously immediate and eternally beyond our ken and grasp. It is the sense of the world conveyed in words like "wonder," "awe," or simply the quiet appreciation of the day without respect for what can be made out of it – including, of course, the making of money. Intrinsic values apply to the spiritual side of things, and also to what is playful, and are manifestations of an attitude we might call an "active receptivity" toward nature.

Use-values represent the form of value relevant to the application of labor to nature, or production, whether this be done for pure utility or as an exchangeable commodity. Use-values signify a more "transformatively active" relation to nature, the kind of transformation being different in the case of utility and exchange. Clearly, use-value is necessary for human life; and one might venture to say that a realized, ecologically integral life can be carried out through a rich interplay of use-value-as-utility with intrinsic value, in other words, through a combined transformative and receptive relation to nature.

Commodity production expands human capability but, by introducing the germ of exchange, also becomes the serpent in the edenic arrangement noted above.[5] With this shift, nature shifts from being "for-itself" (which implies being for us insofar as we are part of nature) to a state of objectification within the framework of an economy. The matter does not stop here, but depends upon the way that economy and the society within which it is embedded deploys the different kinds of value. Since use-value now implies the presence of an exchange-value, it will be in a relationship with that exchange-value. Exchange-value, like use-value, entails a mental registration. Though it does not exist as such in nature, it exists in the mind of a natural creature, where, like any idea, it can have various valences and intensities. Thus, some people are very attached to exchange-value, so that one could say that they "value exchange-value." Indeed, exchange-value can have use-value – for is not money the usefulness of exchange? Use-values also stand between intrinsic values and exchange-value, and express varying degrees of estrangement from nature. Certain use-values are in a position of differentiation, wherein they are close to, and seek to restore intrinsic values; while others are alien, or, as we say, split from intrinsic value, as in the use-value of money.

Ecological politics can be translated into a framework of values. The Bruderhof care very little for exchange-value, opting instead for a radically Christian intrinsic value. The economy has its laws; but whether those laws are obeyed depends on the subjective balance within individuals, which in turn depends upon their social relations. This can be sketched as a kind of coefficient between the two kinds of economic value. If we call use-value, uv, and exchange-value, xv, then the coefficient, uv/xv, expresses in a rough sort of way the balance of forces disposing toward acceptance and rejection of the capitalist force field. I say, rough, not because these elements are indeterminate, but because they are qualitative and profoundly political. They exist not as something we can measure and put on a graph, but as collective practices and sets of meanings, which have been struggled over and command in varying degrees the loyalties of people. When we say more, or less, with respect to use- and exchange-values, we mean it in the sense of "more fully realized." From this angle, capitalism comprises that society which sees to it that xv>>uv, so that people internalize the signals of the market and obey them as gospel; and furthermore, that the use-values of commodities are configured to the needs of exchange- and surplus-value, and not to those of nature's intrinsic value, nor to that of a fulfilled human nature, whence we get sports utility vehicles, caffeinated soft drinks, roundup-ready soy beans, Huey helicopters, submission to globalization – and linked to this the loss of contact with nature and its reduction to mere matter and energy.

The "usefulness" of this kind of formulation derives from its potential to pry off the heavy stone laid over the possibilities of transforming capital, thereby opening the field to a wider and more differentiated range of action. Under normal capitalist conditions, exchange-value prevails and use-values are subordinated and degraded, both as they stand and as they are constantly multiplied to serve endless, wasteful, and destructive commodities. Observe how "used cars" are now called "pre-owned cars." Consider the indifference with which people throw things out once they are "used": the specter of styrofoam cups (even at gatherings of ecologically active groups); the shelves of Toys R Us groaning with plastic items awaiting their batteries and the swift transfer to the dump. Like the passage from the straight razor endlessly sharpened to the baggie full of throwaway razors, life itself has become disposable. My grandfather repaired watches, one of hundreds, perhaps thousands, of his kind in New York City. Now his successors are as rare as snow leopards, and they work on items of conspicuous consumption while I wonder whether to throw away the Casio and buy another because the strap has broken. What is cost effective? This has become the "to be or not to be" question of capitalism; and in the search for surplus value it drives sensuously creative labor out of the market and replaces hand-craft with automated technical prowess.

In a liberated and ecologically sane world, use-values would take on a character independent of exchange-value, not to rule but to serve the needs of human nature and nature. They would, in other words, be shifted in the direction of intrinsic value. There is no necessary reason why this could not happen – although it cannot happen without a social transformation which expands democracy, allows the great range of human powers to be expressed and consolidated, and incorporates the great, countervailing intentions necessary to nullify capital's force field. Were there enough ecocentric militants about, organized according to coherent praxes that went beyond voluntarism to link the one with another across a great international theater of action, well then, the capitalist order could be surpassed. It would not stand one day if enough of the people said no!, in thunder, to it. Of course there is an enormous hedge here: if *enough* people decide, including soldiers and police, who are people, too, and indeed, workers.

Ecosocialism now reveals itself as a struggle for use-value – and through a realized use-value, for intrinsic value. This means it is a struggle for the qualitative side of things: not just the hours worked and the pay per hour and benefits, but the control over work and its product, and of what is beyond mere necessity – a

Prefiguration

control that eventuates in the creation and integration of new ecosystems, and also incorporates subjectivity, beauty, pleasure, and the spiritual. These demands were part of the labor tradition, as workers asked for not just bread but roses, too. We would take it to the limit of its implications: the ecosocialist demand is not just for the material things (bread) on one side, and the aesthetic things (roses) on the other. It regards both bread and roses from the same perspective of enhanced and realized use-values – or, better yet, as *post-economic* intrinsic values: bread and the making of bread to become aspects of a singular ecosystemic process into which a universe of meaning is condensed – for what has more resonance than the "staff of life"? And roses are not external pretty things; they, too, have to be grown by labor. They, too, have a universe of meaning, closed to the eye dulled by exchange, a universe of terror and beauty to the eye opened:

> Oh Rose thou art sick.
> The invisible worm,
> That flies in the night
> In the howling storm:
> Has found out thy bed
> Of crimson joy:
> And his dark secret love
> Does thy life destroy.[6]

Socialism

If we wish to restore the intrinsic value of nature in this sad world, we have to break down capital, and the power of its exchange-value, thereby freeing use-values and opening up the differentiation with intrinsic value. But the consistent demand for the liberation of use-value from the clutches of exchange leads inexorably to that one use-value into which is condensed the core of capital: labor-power. This is the sticking point, and it makes no sense at all to evade it.

Ecosocialism is more than socialism as traditionally known, but it is definitely socialism as well. Capital is the efficient cause of the crisis afflicting ecologies, but the *sine qua non* of capital, the one feature that defines its dynamic above all others, is the commodification of labor power and its reduction to abstract social labor for sale on the market. If one prefers another line of explanation for the ecological crisis, so be it, and this consideration does not hold. But if capital is truly the enemy of nature, then we do not overcome it absent the liberation of labor. This demand, which is the core of socialism, eco- or otherwise, comes down to the following:

Undoing the separation of the producers from the means of production. And this means a basic change in property relations so that the earth, viewed as the source of all use-values and all ecosystems, is appropriated by the "associated producers." Otherwise there is no overcoming of separation. With the overcoming of separation, the use-value of labor ceases being subordinated to exchange-value: labor would be freed from the chains of capital and human power would become freed from false addictive needs and able to resume its potentials. We would attain a *freely associated labor.*

There is much more to ecosocialism than this, but we need to dwell on the fundamental theme, as its implications are significantly different from the standard complex of green politics. Greens in the United States, for example, have "ten key values," each meritorious. Yet none raises this demand, except derivatively; and in practical fact, almost all greens would reject it in favor of a populist position.[7] We have already pointed out that this leaves capital in the driver's seat, with all that implies. Now the goal of socialism itself needs to be confronted, and, first of all, the taboo that has descended upon its name, at least in the United States.

I think I would be a rich man if given a dollar for every time someone has helpfully pointed out that it's not good form to use the word, socialism, in political discourse, unless, of course, one wants to rouse the audience against an enemy. People, I have been told on countless occasions, turn off at the sound of that word, with its triple association of economic failure, political

217

Prefiguration

repression, and environmental blight. Ecosocialism, it is said, will never get to first base so long as it remains associated with the disgraced socialist tradition.

It is important to deal with these objections head-on, and neither finesse them by trying to think of another word for the same thing,[8] nor dismiss them by pointing to the anticommunist blight on the political intelligence. For the fact is, the nations who called themselves "socialist" in the past century did display all three of those defects; and the fact also remains that as a result of the epochal collapse of the Soviet system, along with the tremendous setbacks in other societies that either called themselves socialist or had the name given to them, the morale of the socialist cause has taken one blow after another, and has pretty well declined to the vanishing point over the past decade. There are a number of questions to be tackled here; chiefly, whether the societies in question were actually socialist, why their failings took place, and whether a fully realized socialist society would fall into the same abyss.

As for the first of these, one must unequivocally say that "actually existing socialism" never passed over the threshold of restoring to the producers control over the means of production. In other words, it did not live up to the stirring words of the *Communist Manifesto*, that the goal is for society to become "an association in which the free development of each is the condition for the free development of all."[9] It is essential that we not confuse the customary definition of socialism, that it consists of *public ownership* of the means of production, with the true definition, that it consist of a *free association of producers*. The latter implies the former, no doubt, but the converse is definitely not necessarily so. A free association implies the fullest extension of democracy, with a public sphere and public ownership that is genuinely collective and in which each person makes a difference. But the word "public" is tricky, and can signify another kind of alienation, namely, that of the state, or the party, or the leader, or whomever gets substituted for the producers and owns and/or controls the means of production in their stead. It is this latter turn of events that became the fate of socialisms past.

The notion of a free association of producers is indisputably the keystone of Marx's conception of socialism. It can be demonstrated as much as one likes from a study of Marx's life and work – just as it can be demonstrated to have not been the case for the "actually existing socialisms," chiefly the USSR and its satellites in Eastern Europe, or China, or Vietnam, North Korea, and, with varying degrees of exactitude, for the socialisms of Latin America, Cuba, and Nicaragua.[10] These latter all relied on some kind of alienating substitute "public," generally speaking, the Party-State, as the active force directing the revolution. There is as little doubt about the two sides of this proposition – of what Marx actually intended, and of what actually happened in socialism – as about the phases of the moon, and yet the error of identifying these failed experiments with Marx's concept of socialism still persists.

We need to ask why they all seemed to fail this way and whether this general failing was not in itself an indictment of the core socialist notion; and, consequently, whether there is any chance of building a socialism along the lines of a free association of producers, and with ecological rationality. Several characteristics stand out among those societies that made, and failed to realize, socialist revolutions. First of all, they were all in peripheral and dependent status among the capitalist powers. This meant that they started with two strikes against them: they were economically weak to begin with and unable to meet even the basic needs of their people; and they had to face the hostility of the stronger adversary from the moment of the inception of revolutionary power. To these may be added the third strike that put these ventures out so far as the realization of socialism is concerned: they all, each and every one, lacked democratic traditions and the institutions of civil society that fostered such traditions.

In the gestation of a revolution, there is first the pre-revolutionary period, with a buildup of tension, a delegitimation of the established authority, and the growth of a revolutionizing movement. Next comes the revolutionary moment as such, aiming at seizure of state power, with greater or lesser degrees of violence and the introduction of contradictions that have to be handled further on. Finally, the transformation of society begins; this is the revolution proper, an inevitably extended period of struggle. On day one after the moment of triumph, all that has been achieved is a new state apparatus: no small accomplishment given the importance of the state as an instrument of coercion and direction, yet with no necessary effect on society itself. To be more exact, any effect depends upon the character of the revolutionary movement, a fact of great importance for us. To the extent that the movement is conspiratorial, or cut off from the development of society, its triumph will find society an inert mass requiring leadership from above; to the extent that broad strata of the population participate in the revolutionary process, so that it becomes a kind of gigantic school, so will the triumph become the acceleration of an organic (in the terms employed here, ecosystemically integral) development in which the democratic potentials of socialism can be released.

The actually existing socialisms came to exist by virtue of the corruption and weakness of their *ancien régimes*, often accelerated by war – or, as in the case of the Soviet satellites, because of the proximity of these regimes to a powerful center of influence. Thus, the first two stages of the revolution were, however bloody and contested, open for the winning. But in all cases, the third and essential stage of social transformation was foreclosed by an ensemble of forces that, however distinct from country to country, shared a common inaptitude for the democratizing motion of socialism.

In Russia, where there was virtually no democratic heritage, the Czarist police forced anti-democratic, conspiratorial patterns on the Bolsheviks, who took power – despite their name, which means "majority" – as a small minority. The revolution fell into their lap thanks to the First World War, which also, however, further crippled society. Then, in a counterrevolution of immense savagery, greatly abetted by Western intervention and invasion, the extraordinary needs of "war communism" carried on in a situation of maximum chaos, put the seal of authoritarianism on the process. Lenin and Trotsky resorted to terror as an instrument and specifically blocked the free development of labor, shutting down the workers' councils, or "Soviets," and crippling the unions. At the same time, they espoused the emulation of capitalist efficiency and productivism as a means of survival. Is it any wonder, then, that socialism failed to take hold – or that the stage was set for Stalin's barbarism?[11]

In China, where again there was effectively zero democratic heritage, a much more extended period of internal development of the movement took place prior to the triumph. However, this was inordinately marked by warfare. Massacres of the Communist Party in 1927 set the stage for more than twenty years of guerrilla war, a militarization that deepened with the Japanese invasion and the Long March. Alongside this, bitter memories of humiliation and penetration by imperialism in this most ancient – and once pre-eminent – society created a burning desire to catch up with the capitalists. The extensive militarization, the persistence of warlord tradition, the ongoing struggles with Russia and the United States, coupled with the imperial status granted to Mao Ze Dong, set the stage for chaos. Combined with the impulsive grandiosity of the latter, the result became the horrors of the Great Leap Forward, with its associated famine, and the Cultural Revolution. Despite certain remarkable and brilliant advances, especially in the countryside, is it any wonder, again, that socialism failed to take hold – or that the stage was set for Deng Xiao Peng's capitalist road?[12]

Similar considerations held for Vietnam, hardened by generations of colonialism, US invasion, and postwar punitiveness by the superpower. In Cuba, yoked with centuries of dependency, the limiting factors took the shape of being scissored between superpowers; for Nicaragua, it was an even greater underdevelopment, and an incomplete revolution with a sudden dénouement that left great chunks of the bourgeoisie intact, while exposing the revolution to the vengeance of Big Brother to the North; for the Eastern Europeans, it was revolution imposed from above and the constant shadow of Stalinist Russia; in case after case, the elementary conditions for socialist development in the period after revolutionary victory were either not present or crushed.

This should not be interpreted as a blanket rejection of the accomplishments of these regimes; for socialism is not a switch one turns on and off, and part-way toward a socialist ethos is still some way forward. The people of the former USSR, presently facing social disintegration on a scale unparalleled for a nation not invaded in war, have just cause to look back with pride on the full employment and solidarity of the Soviet era, as well as their heroics against Nazism. First-hand experience with Cuba and Nicaragua has convinced me, as it has many others, that what was being germinated there remains of inestimable value to the future of humanity, if value be measured in terms of dignity and generosity instead of money.[13] The Nicaraguan revolution had to be slaughtered, according to Oxfam, because it posed the threat of a "good example" to other nations in the United States' sphere of influence. As for Cuba, all of its empty shelves do not nullify the fact that it offers resources of education and healthcare that would make most of the people of the South believe they were in heaven were they to wake up there one day. Nor should it be forgotten that Cuba is the first, and still the only, country to have adopted organic agriculture on a national scale – no doubt out of harsh necessity thanks to the US blockade and Soviet collapse, but nonetheless feasible because there was no agribusiness there to stand in the way of rational planning.[14]

Still, part-way toward socialism is not far enough; not only were these models not exportable, but they were primed to self-destruct. They resembled less a breakthrough than a rubber band stretched to the point of recoil. The vectors pulling actually existing socialism back included the social and cultural forces sedimented into the psyche by generations of patriarchy and autocracy. However, these would never have had effect without the failure of the productive system to transcend the *ancien régime*, and, specifically, to overcome capitalism. The actually existing socialisms did not, of course, reproduce the capitalist structures of the West. Instead, they rearranged capital to introduce other engines of accumulation, notably using the state and political means rather than economic incentives as in traditional capitalism. This ended up by proving that old-fashioned markets work better than centralized state control for purposes of accumulation. One may be forgiven for not hailing this as the greatest of discoveries. The "bottom line" – if we may borrow appropriately here from capital's lexicon – remained accumulation; and the presupposition of accumulation remained, as ever, the hierarchical division of labor and the extraction of surplus value through exploitation. There can be no mystery as to why this fatal contradiction forced the state under actually existing socialism to be specially coercive and non-democratic, nor why a new type of bureaucratic ruling class arose by virtue of control over the state apparatus – nor why the workers secretly, and eventually openly, longed for good old-fashioned liberal capitalism, whose wage mechanism creates more opportunities, whose state can afford to provide certain limited democratic rights, and where the more fluid productive system churns out a much greater amount of higher-quality goods. After all, if one is going to live under capitalism, one might as well do it properly.[15]

The basic contradictions of the state capitalism that was called actually existing socialism had complex ecological effects, although the end result was worse than that under market capitalism. To be more exact, its effects were intensively worse, and extensively less so, owing to poorer overall productivity. These were, it should be repeated, end results; on the way to that end, the actually existing socialisms did grapple with the ecological question in an interesting way. It is scarcely appreciated, for example, that in the first decade of the Soviet system, a great deal of attention was paid to conservation, and an effort was made to integrate production with natural laws and limits. This impulse was grounded in a pre-revolutionary environmental movement, and a tradition of radical innovation that accompanied the early years of Bolshevism and included a great deal of concern about ecology. It was nourished by radical innovators like Aleksandr Bogdanov, whose *Proletkul't* movement attempted to open Russian culture to democratic impulses; and supported to a degree by none other than Lenin, who, as Arran Gare writes, "interpreted Marxism in such a way as to acknowledge the limitations of the environment, [and] of the existence of dynamics within nature with which humanity must accord."[16]

There were, however, countervailing forces at work in all the major figures of Bolshevism, and in the doctrine itself. Despite his ecological insights, Lenin harshly attacked Bogdanov in his 1908 *Materialism and Emperio-Criticism* for an alleged "idealism." To this, Lenin opposed a sharply dualistic materialism, rather similar to the Cartesian separation of matter and consciousness, and perfectly tooled, like Cartesianism, to the active working over of dead, dull matter by the human hand.[17] A function of this was to overcome the national "backwardness" and sloth, that dreamy, vodka-soaked, impractical immersion in Mother Russia which had haunted its intelligentsia,[18] and in so doing, to move full speed ahead into industrialization and modernity. From this angle, Russia's modern history is dominated by a messianic ambition and ambivalence toward the West. Bolshevism incorporated features of both. A ferocious drive to catch up with the West shaped its world-view from the start, and was accelerated by the severe crisis of the early years. The tendency was especially pronounced in Lenin's brilliant associate, Leon Trotsky, architect and commander of the Red Army during the counterrevolution, and a cosmopolite and modernizer, *par excellence*. Though a resolute atheist, Trotsky's worship of technology was of messianic proportions. This was expressed in a rhapsodic paean to Communist Man after the Soviet triumph, in which Trotsky allowed himself to fantasize about a future of rearranged rivers and mountains, in which the human body itself would be reshaped into that of a Superman who conquers death, the great entropic leveller. In the Soviet utopia, a heroic Bolshevism redeems fallen humanity.[19]

The gruesome outcome is well known, but bears brief reflection. After Stalin's accession to power in 1927, persistent economic stagnation triggered a second revolution, now from above. Whatever democratic impulses had endured through the early period of the Bolshevik regime were jettisoned, and the entire might of Soviet society was concentrated on building the forces of production for all-out accumulation. The result was utter top-down control, maximum subordination of human beings to the production process, the surplus being taken by the state, willingness to let millions die for the larger purpose, the deification of the ruler and the party-state to mobilize messianic forms of legitimacy, profound cynicism and mendacity, and last but certainly not least, a reign of terror to eliminate the remnants of opposition. In this regime, Trotsky's musings were given an official imprimatur even as he himself was driven out and eventually murdered. "Within a few years all the maps of the USSR will have to be revised," wrote one Stalinist planner, while another opined that the conservation of nature for its own sake "reeks of ancient cults of nature's deification," and a third proclaimed the goal of "a profound rearrangement of the entire living world ... All living nature will live, thrive and die at none other than the will of man and according to his plans." Still another called for eliminating all references to "plant communities" in biology books. In other words, as Stalinism developed, the very notion of ecology came under attack, in addition to ecologies.[20] This was the framework which spawned Lysenko's official doctrine that acquired characteristics can be inherited, and that did in fact set about to rearrange the Russian map, diverting rivers, creating cities overnight, building colossal hydroelectric plants, and so transforming the land that what took three hundred years under capitalism was accomplished in one generation.

Were Stalin's monstrosity still with us, it would win the gold medal for enmity to nature – and indeed there was an element of outright hostility to nature in Stalinism beyond what obtains under market capitalism, even after Stalin died and the regime had ceased using terror. That Stalinism did not survive owes something, moreover, to its radically anti-ecocentric character.

225

Prefiguration

Choked with pollution, beset with declining agricultural yields and haunted by nightmares like the virtual disappearance of the Aral Sea, the Soviet system lacked internal correctives and was hurled down into a chasm of ecocatastrophe. In good measure, this lack of adaptability lay in a rigid, self-perpetuating bureaucratic regime fixedly programed on the goal of accumulation. As inefficiences proliferated and the internal market withered for lack of consumable goods, accumulation became increasingly difficult. A chief response to this crisis was a heightened exploitation of nature. Ecological concerns kept being shelved, a vicious cycle set in, and, abetted by US policy, collapse was only a matter of time.

Our Marx

How does one assess this in relation to the ecological potentials of socialism? To some, the answer is straightforward: because the USSR was fundamentally non-socialist, there can be no relation. The Soviets, it is said, broke with socialism from the moment they put the clamps on labor and started the emulation of capital. Given the way of the world, the rest was fore-ordained: gigantism, bureaucratic state capitalism, the stifling of democracy – all contributed to a radically anti-ecocentric regime that would have likely executed Marx had he shown up in Moscow in 1935. From this angle, the extreme enmity toward nature that marked Stalinism is an example of how a noble ideal, once perverted, can turn into its opposite, as Satan, once the favored son of God, became God's greatest enemy.

But this is too simple; it smacks of consolation, not a facing of reality. For the truth is that almost the entire socialist tradition, including those branches of it unburdened by Stalinism, has largely been unable to appropriate an ecocentric attitude. There have been a few important individual exceptions, like Rosa Luxemburg and William Morris, and a strong recent effort to correct things, but these hopeful signs do not relieve us of the necessity of accounting for what has been on the whole a significant lapse. Despite all the recognition of the fact that there is a global crisis of nature for which capital is primarily responsible, the fact remains that minding nature still tends to strike the typical socialist as an afterthought, both in the sense that nature does not come immediately to the socialist mind, as well as that the caring for nature is something added onto existing socialist doctrine rather than integral to it. An integral appreciation of nature's intrinsic value is not at the existential heart of socialism, nor does nature command a passion comparable to that reserved for the emancipation of labor. This is accompanied by a somewhat naïve faith in the ecocentric capacities of a working class defined by generations of capitalist production. To the characteristically socialist way of thinking, labor, once freed from the prison-house of capital, will unproblematically proceed to rearrange production in an ecologically sane way.

Here is an example from *Against the Market*, by David McNally, an otherwise estimable work that argues for a full socialism grounded in the emancipation of labor. After showing convincingly how the "socialist economy does possess an inbuilt drive to increase the efficiency of production: the impetus to maximize free, disposable time," McNally continues with the observation that just as capital increases people's needs but "restricts their opportunities to realize them," so will socialism liberate "this *positive side of capital's self-expansion* from the alienation and exploitation associated with it." He elaborates: "Three things follow from this. First, the reduction of necessary social labour *cannot be at the expense of the range of human satisfactions*. On the contrary, the productivity gains brought about by the development of the forces of production would in all probability be distributed in two ways ... : by *increasing the social output to raise consumption levels* ... and, after that, by reducing necessary social labour." The second and third principles are that this reduction in social labor "could not be at the expense of the conditions of work itself" nor of "the natural and social environment outside the workplace."[21]

This finesses a serious contradiction between raising consumption levels and protecting "the natural ... environment outside the workplace." Are workers – not just in the industrial West, but also in China, India, Indonesia, etc., as required by the internationalist ethos of socialism – to have more cars, even ecologically better cars, without further deterioration of ecosystems? Questions like this scarcely arise in socialist discourse, which however much it may surpass capital morally and economically, has significant trouble going beyond capital's fatal addiction to growth.

McNally claims there is a *positive side of capital's self-expansion* which can be liberated. But this is ecologically quite dubious. One expects gases to self-expand. But humans, being organisms in ecosystems, can only *self*-expand to the detriment of the ecosystem, and/or as a sign of its degeneration, the way algal blooms signify that a pond is disintegrating ecosystemically. As alienation and exploitation are overcome, therefore, we would not expect human life to expand, but rather to *develop* ever more subtle, interrelated, mutually recognizing, beautiful, and spiritually fulfilled ways of being. We should not seek to become larger within socialism, but more *realized*. Bach did not quantitatively expand music, making it louder and more insistent like forms of techno-rock music that mirror capitalist relations; he rather saw more deeply into its possibilities and realized them. So would it be expected for an ecocentric society, where the ideal of growth as such simply needs to be scrapped. *Sufficiency* makes more sense, building a world where nobody is hungry or cold or lacks healthcare or succor in old age. This can be done at a fraction of the current world output, and would create the ground for ecological realization.

Sufficiency is a better term than the ecological buzzword, sustainability, as the latter leaves ambiguous the question of whether what is to be sustained is the existing system or not. But in either case, humanity needs to greatly reduce its load on planetary ecosystems. The customary response of environmentalism is to think of restraining consumption. But such a focus is repressive, requiring some combination of market forces, as by making gasoline more expensive to discourage purchase of gas guzzlers, and eventually cars themselves; along with coercion, as by rationing or exacting legal sanctions like prison. Measures of this sort may be necessary in the quasi-emergency defined by global warming, but they are never desirable, and get us no closer to an ecological socialism that would build on the liberation of labor sought by "first-epoch" socialism and seek the restoration of use and intrinsic value by liberated producers.

Actual socialism was ill-formed by history for this task. Forged at the moment of industrialization, its transformative impulse tended to remain within the terms of the industrialized domination of nature. Thus it continued to manifest the technological optimism of the industrial world-view, and its associated logic of productivism – all of which feed into the mania for growth. The belief in unlimited technical progress has been beaten back in certain quarters by a host of disasters, from nuclear waste to resistant bacteria, but these setbacks barely touch the core of socialist optimism, that its historical mission is to perfect the industrial system and not overcome it. The productivist logic is grounded in a view of nature that regards the natural world as an "environment," and from the standpoint of its utility as a force of production. It is at that point that socialism all-too-often shares with capitalism a reduction of nature to resources – and, coordinatively, a sluggishness in recognizing ourselves in nature and nature in ourselves. When McNally says that socialism "cannot be at the expense of the range of human satisfaction," then, he is failing to recognize that these satisfactions can be problematic with respect to nature because they have been historically shaped by the domination of nature; and more, that the industrial tools and techniques that pass into the hands of the workers after the revolution are also a sediment of that history. Therefore, unless the socialist revolution also undoes the domination of nature, which is to say, becomes ecosocialist, its satisfactions – and the needs and use-values in which they are grounded – are going to tend to reproduce the past. Simply overcoming the power of exchange-value can be no more than a necessary condition for this. From another angle, there can be no ecosocialist environmentalism as such, since to the ecological world-view the notion of nature as an environment outside us will wither away.

Recognition of ourselves in nature and nature in ourselves, in other words, subjective as well as objective participation in ecosystems, is the essential condition for overcoming the domination of nature, and its pathologies of instrumental production and addictive consumption. For an example, we may turn to Rosa Luxemburg, mentioned above as one of the few socialists who showed what might be called an authentically "ecocentric way of being." I mean this existentially, for Luxemburg was not ecologically oriented in her views of what socialism ought to be (unlike William Morris, whose thought was consciously ecocentric, albeit without using that term).[22] But what she did evince – and this is connected with her gender – was the capacity to express a fellow-feeling for non-human creatures which is quite exceptional in the Marxist tradition. Witnessing the beating of a buffalo from her prison where she was kept while protesting the war, Luxemburg wrote the following in a letter:

> the one that was bleeding, all the while looked ahead with an expression on its black face and its soft black eyes like that of a weeping child who has been severely punished and who does not know why, what for, who does not know how to escape the torment and the brutality ... I stood facing the animal and it looked at me: tears were running from my eyes – they were *his* tears. One cannot quiver any more painfully over one's dearest brother's sorrow than I quivered in my impotence over this silent anguish ... Oh! My poor buffalo! My poor beloved brother! We both stand here so powerless and spiritless and are united only in pain, in powerlessness and in longing.[23]

Such an ethos in itself does not ecosocialism make – that would require what Luxemburg did not do, namely, elaborate a consciously ecocentric line in her socialist practice. Nor does it imply a fundamentalist position on animal rights, which forgets that all creatures, however they may be recognized, are still differentiated and that we make use of other creatures within our human nature. Nor does this imply a deep-ecological affirmation of "wilderness" that splits the wild away from the human and would just as soon dispense with the latter; nor, to go yet further down the track of nihilism, would it consist of the kind of deep-ecological attack on industrialism infamously associated with Theodore Kaczynski, the Unabomber. To overcome the limits of actually existing socialism requires, rather, a synthesis in which humanity is restored to ecosystemic differentiation with nature. To follow the example of Luxemburg, it would connect existential fellow-feeling with a sense of justice, and build from there. In other words, the option of traditional socialism for the travails of labor needs to be matched by, and dialectically interwoven with, an equivalent existential option for nature. The wounds of one must be felt with the same passion for justice as those of the other. Our very being needs to be turned toward nature, not as an afterthought nor as an instrumental necessity for production, but as a sensuously lived reality. And this needs to be grounded in specifically ecocentric relations of production lest it become a purely voluntaristic slogan.

As for Karl Marx himself, we find a bewildering array of opinions concerning his ecological *bona fides*. From one side there is a fairly robust tradition alleging that Marx essentially shared the enmity toward nature evinced by the Bolsheviks, or at the least set them on their profoundly anti-ecological path. In this view, which may be termed the "Promethean" interpretation, the founder of historical materialism is tasked with enough elements of the domination of nature to justify the often-made identification with the god who gave humankind fire, and whose temerity was punished by Zeus by being chained to a rock, where he suffered the assaults of an eagle on his liver. The substance of the indictment holds Marx to have been an advocate of technological determinism, of productivism, of the ideology of progress, and of hostility to rural life and primitivism – in sum, as an unreconstructed apostle of the Enlightenment in its rankest industrial form.[24]

An opposing point of view, recently argued by Marxists such

as John Bellamy Foster and Paul Burkett, energetically contests the thesis, and holds that Marx, far from being Promethean, was a main originator of the ecological world-view. Building their argument from Marx's materialist foundations, his scientific affinity with Darwin, and his conception of the "metabolic rift" between humanity and nature, Foster and Burkett consider the original Marxian canon as the true and sufficient guide to save nature from capitalism.[25]

To enter the substance of this debate would distract us from the thread of the present argument. But we may say the following: that it is foolish to reduce the subtlety of so profoundly dialectical a thinker to any label or singular interpretation. A close reading will show Marx to be no Promethean.[26] But he was no god of any kind, either, only the best interpreter humanity has ever had of its own historical emerging; and this great virtue sprang from the integration of a passion for justice with intellectual power and dialectical gift. However superior it might be, Marx's thought, being a human product, remains time-bound and incomplete. For this reason it becomes most realized when most free, or to use his own expression, "ruthlessly critical of everything existing."[27] This would include, needless to say, being critical of itself. Therefore, Marxism today can have no greater goal than the criticism of Marx in the light of that history to which he had not been exposed, namely, of the ecological crisis.

Here it needs to be observed that, however Marx may not have been Promethean, there remains in his work a foreshortening of the intrinsic value of nature. Yes, humanity is part of nature for Marx; but it is the active part, the part which makes things happen, while nature becomes what is affected by human activity. Except for a few entrancing anticipations, chiefly in the *Manuscripts* of 1844, nature to Marx appears directly as use-value, and not as what use-value leaves behind, namely, recognition of nature in and for itself.[28] In Marx, nature is, so to speak, subjected to labor from the start. This side of things may be inferred from his conception of labor, which involves an essentially *active* relationship to a kind of natural substratum.

Now there are two ways of not being active. There is *passivity*, with its implication of inertia; and it is from this condition that Marx sought to free the alienated realities of labor under the domination of capital. But there is also *receptivity*, which is not passive and inert at all, but another kind of activity; and it is this side of things that Marx – and by and large, the socialist tradition – failed to see. When Rosa Luxemburg felt for the buffalo, she was being receptive to its anguish. There was recognition there, which meant a taking in of the buffalo's being, and its reawakening inside her. Is this the female position? Well, yes, so long as we keep in mind, first, that it is a potential available to all humans; and, second, that it is the constructed and relegated female position, at once the source of women's strength and the measure of their downfall in male-dominated society.

Full receptivity is of both identity and difference. The world is taken in, but never fused with the self. This is a knack of language, which represents the given, but as imaginative signifier that never stays still. To recapture the receptive moment in labor, therefore, requires an active opening of being. This does not simply absorb the world and register it subjectively. It opens being to the world as prelude to the transformation of the world; and it links the making of poems and songs to the making of solar ovens. It is a *ful-filling*, which is both essential to the freeing of labor and to the ecological transforming of labor, so that labor may transform nature in an ecologically integral way. The opening of the self to the world engages the sensuous imagination and our full being. Absent the receptive moment in labor, the self is closed, impacted inside itself, and isolated from others and from nature.

We return to the anti-ecocentric moment enshrined by capital: the way of the Ego. This is the secret to the riddle of growth and the mania of consumption. These twin compulsions of the reigning order are expressions of an impeded motion between inner and outer world. Occluded and incapable of a full life, human being compulsively turns to grinding out commodities without end, and, just as compulsively, to consuming them. The insertion of exchange-value is that invisible barrier caging in the capitalist Ego, a film of abstraction reinforced with the titanic power of the capitalist state and cultural apparatus. That is why these must be taken down, and why labor must be really, truly freed. But it becomes free in order to transform production eco-centrically. The recovery of intrinsic value proceeds through a struggle for use-value, a struggle in which the goal is embedded in the path.

Ecocentric production

Nature does not produce anything. Rather, it evolves new forms that interact with each other in ensembles we call ecosystems, which become the loci of further evolution. As it turned out on earth, this led to a creature who introduced production into nature, and then economies, class economies, and capitalism which, spreading cancerously, generates our ecological crisis. Production is therefore nature's formativity as expressed through human nature.

What distinguishes production from natural evolution lies in the dimension of consciousness as shaped by language and social organization. Human beings work with a mental image of nature; we represent the section of nature before us – itself virtually always modified by previous labor – then act upon it to transform it according to an envisioned end. In every instance, some prearranged configuration of nature-as-transformed-by-labor is imaginatively appropriated, then rendered according to a plan. Production is therefore inherently temporalizing and incorporates the future; that is why we call it pro-duction, to make with a view ahead.

Humans do not choose whether to produce, but there are numberless ways of producing. Capital is one such organization of production that violates ecosystemic integrity through the interposition of exchange-value as an instrument of exploitation. Each such moment is a cutting of the specific interconnectedness that defines an integral ecosystem. The hope of socialism is to overcome exploitation and bring down the regime of exchange-value. Ecosocialism develops this further through the realization of use-values and the appropriation of intrinsic value. From the angle of production, this means building ecosystemic integrity. As an integral is a whole, ecological production has as its over-riding condition the creation of wholeness.[29] Ecosystems are not to be regarded in the way of commodities, as countable and isolable things. They are, rather, mutually constitutive, interacting with and transforming each other. That is why the notion of an "environment" sits ill with an ecological world-view. There is no "outside" in nature, where all beings inhabit and co-determine each other, and where subtle force fields interpenetrate reality and can be registered in consciousness. Similarly, producing ecosystemic integrity connects form through all dimensions, temporal as well as spatial. Past being is integral to present being regarded ecologically – in contrast to capital's fetish of the new. And there is no being intrinsically alien to ecocentric production, except capital itself, the creator of alienated labor, strangers and false boundary lines. A considerable number of interwoven patterns are involved here, some of which are presumed to be more prominent than others in the concrete instance.

1. The *process* of ecocentric production is aligned with the product; thus, the making of a thing becomes part of the thing made. Since the end of production is satisfaction and pleasure, as in a finely made meal or garment, pleasure would obtain for the cooking of the meal or the designing and making of the garment. These processual pleasures are generally reserved for hobbies under capitalism; in a society organized around ecocentric production, they would comprise the fabric of everyday life.

2. For this to happen, labor has to be freely chosen and developed, in other words, with a fully realized use-value as against its reduction to labor-power. At first and for some time, this is a matter of shifting the coefficient, uv/xv, in the direction of the numerator in order to build anticapitalist intentions. Since use- and exchange-value are not immediately comparable, this involves the dialectical "negation of the negation": exchange is negated through a withdrawal from capitalist values, in which

235

context, realization of use-value ensues, further delegitimizing capital and furthering the rupture. The "Food Not Bombs" projects in cities like San Francisco and New York have been examples of this; and the fact that this seemingly innocent activity has brought down severe repression upon itself is a sign of just how subversive the notion is.[30]

3. Mutual recognition is required for the process as well as the product, such being the condition of ecosystemic integrity. The most important implication of this is that it rules out hierarchical and exploitative relations of labor, and fosters democratization at all levels of production, and, *mutatis mutandis*, all of society.

4. Production stays within the entropic relations of natural evolution, in which the inputs of ambient solar radiation are able to subserve the creation of order. Because the "closed" system within which the Second Law applies is the earth + surrounding cosmos, nature provides a certain space for creating lower entropy from the binding of solar energy – a space, however, that requires distinct limits if it is to be sustained. It is precisely the aim of ecocentric production to incorporate limits into functioning ecosystems, in stark contrast to capital. Therefore, it goes without saying that ecocentric production makes use of all modes of conservation and renewable energy. An additional implication of living within the entropic law is that direct human labor would replace, so far as possible, the consumption of the low-entropy of past aeons sedimented into fossil fuels, the release of which markedly increases entropy to destabilizing levels. But the "so far as possible" is defined through the active interposition of human agency into nature. Instead of living passively and, indeed, parasitically from the negentropy stored in fossil fuels, humanity now will live more directly and receptively embedded in nature; thus more sensuously, too, with an overcoming of the ancient division of labor between head and hand and an enhancement of craft. From another angle, the fulfilling of a use-value/ecosystem is accompanied, at the level of the subject, by a quantum of satisfaction, joy and aesthetic realization. All this is summed up in the notion of "virtue,"[31] and it comprises

the coming together of dialectical ensembles within a free human being.

5. "Limits to growth" are to be predicated on a reorientation of human need made possible by enhanced receptivity. Clearly, highly developed production need not be dependent on destabilizing inputs of energy. Singing songs is certainly productive, and creating them, even more so. Even interpreting dreams is productive, because it introduces a new subjective configuration into the human ecosystem. So the way time is passed becomes integrally related to the form of production, and what is perceived as necessary. By regarding limits to growth in terms of altered needs, we still address the question of "sustainability." But we treat it non-technocratically and in connection with the basic organization of labor and the question of satisfaction, in other words, from a qualitative standpoint.

6. Such considerations apply to the question of technology, once it is no longer seen as a "technical" problem, subjugated to considerations of profit and efficiency. The making and using of technology in ecocentric production is directed, rather, toward the making of ecosystems and participation within ecosystems. The enhancement of use-values and the corresponding restructuring of needs becomes now the social regulator of technology rather than, as under capital, the conversion of time into surplus value and money. We would expect considerable areas of technological overlapping between capitalist and ecocentric production. One would, for instance, use sophisticated medical imaging in each case, and this one application implies the whole edifice of informational and electronic science. But it makes a world of difference if a technology is incorporated into medical profiteering, or used to care for the organismic aspect of a human ecosystem. Capital would have technology isolated from the manifold of social relations of which it is but an element. But ecocentric production includes theory as well, and has as its deepest consideration the fullest range of interconnections. Therefore to begin seeing a machine or a technique as fully participant in the life of ecosystems is to begin removing it from

exchange and restoring a realized use-value. This is what is called familiarly in ecological discourse an "appropriate technology," and indeed it is, as technology enabling us to appropriate nature in human ways.

7. If we take the notion of human ecosystems seriously, we are led to fully incorporate consciousness into them. Fullness here implies the development of the receptive mode of being. It entails a consciousness of nature as such, according to the principle that the interconnections of a human ecosystem include subjective recognition as an element – not alongside of, but integrally related to physical connections.[32] An organic farm is not simply a collection of organisms; it is those organisms interrelated in a universe of meaningful recognition through the farmer. This does not make the farmer a lord over the farm, or the gardener mistress of the garden. It means that the farm, and the garden – and the whole universe to which they connect, are integral to the human self who produces through them. A relative of mine could catch fish with his bare hands. This feat required a contact with the fish that went beyond the coarsely physical, along with a kind of mutual recognition between human and animal. Such recognition could, if it were realized in production, extend to the entire universe as a fully active and alive consciousness.

The relative in question was male, and the function of recognition is as open to individual men as to women. Nevertheless, the systematic development of an ecological consciousness across our civilization depends on overcoming the barriers between humanity and nature, which, as we have seen, requires overcoming the dualism imposed by woman=nature/man=reason; and for this, patriarchy itself needs to be overcome. I am certain that at least 95 percent of readers would identify Rosa Luxemburg's account of seeing herself in the suffering buffalo as the work of a woman, without knowing the gender of its author in advance. Men are simply not socialized to feel that way; while women are by and large socialized to limit themselves to feeling this way. That a woman such as Luxemburg would escape the constraints of intellectual suppression placed upon her gender is not an astounding finding, needless to say. But under the dominant gender system such occurrences, no matter how frequent, remain individual exceptions to a dualism that must be overcome if we are to survive.

To build ecocentric production, then, means restoring the eco-systemic capacity for interrelatedness and mutual recognition; most elementally, to restore nature as a source of wonder and be open to nature. The grandeur of the untrammelled world is an essential aspect of this, but not its whole. Wilderness, recall, is a constructed category with its own use-value, while actual nature, whether experienced in the Grand Canyon or in the intaking of a breath, is always directly "at hand," even if scarcely realized. A man can visit the Grand Canyon and remain preoccupied by his stock quotes; another sees a tree, as Blake put it, as only a green thing in the way. But trees still abound, and each is a wonder, as is a blade of grass, or a paramecium.[33] To be open to nature means being receptive to ecosystemic being without the fear of annihilation that is the legacy of the male Ego. The masculine construction of being interprets receptivity as the castrated con-dition of the female. Receptivity is read as passivity, with the symbolic threat of being swallowed up by the world-mother. Gaia is a Medusa or a Harpy to the Ego. The terror induces severe death anxiety with associated mental repression, distancing, reduction of nature, and counter-aggression, along with com-pulsive production and consumption: in this way human nature is *restricted* to tearing nature apart and aggressively rebuilding it at ever-greater distances. The ensemble enables separation and is the core attitude of the domination of nature as it surfaces into productivism with a fierce energy, an attitude which has so permeated the capitalist (and state capitalist) mentality as to be read as an axiom.

The larger, and practical, virtue embedded here is an expan-sion of the immemorial role assigned to women, that of providing and caring for life. The profound rationality inherent to this role is both downgraded and split-off in gendered bifurcation of nature.

239

Prefiguration

Overcoming this gives to production a specifically ecocentric form. The functions of receiving, provisioning, and holding, once sequestered in a lower social level, now prevail, and, in so doing, move to become the regulating principles of production. Eco-centric production, therefore, goes beyond the virtues of formal distributive equality to women, or their access to previously male preserves like strenuous athletics. It also negates the lowliness of what had been sequestered as "woman's work," and transforms this, while realizing use-values associated with it.[34]

If past being is integral to present being in ecocentric produc-tion, so will future being. An important political principle now emerges – one that applies to the production of use-values for the sustenance of life, and also to the production of ways beyond capital. The potential for the given to contain the lineaments of what is to be may be called *prefiguration*. It is intrinsic to ecocentric production, rendering the *provisioning* of ecofeminism as the *previsioning* of a utopian moment, right in the midst of the exigencies of the present.

The prefigurative praxes that are to overcome capital in an ecosocialist way are at once very remote and exactly at hand. They are remote insofar as the entire regime of capital stands in the way of their realization; and they are at hand insofar as a moment toward the future exists embedded in every point of the social organism where a need arises. Many instances are bound to wither – it is, after all, very difficult to imagine any ecosocialist inspiration arising from a trip to Wal-Mart beyond rage at the given order; others will propagate, but not very far, like hauling recyclable junk mail to the dump; still others will propagate, perhaps even to a transformative extent, but take a wrong turn, like that of fascism; finally, there will arise those that move in an ecosocialist way. It goes without saying that in the real world there can be no neat categorization capable of covering all possibilities. If everything has a prefigurative potential, then prefiguration will be scattered over the entire, disorderly surface of the world. This fact generates another principle of ecosocialist politics: it is, besides being prefigurative and building upon the transformative potentials of found configurations of events, also *interstitial*, in that its agency can be found almost anywhere, according to the unfolding and play of contradictions.

This is a blessing, because it signifies that there is no privileged agent of ecosocialist transformation, but it also imposes a great responsibility. For as they now exist, instances of ecocentric production are both scattered and mainly entrapped like irritants in the pores of capital. The task is to free them and connect them, so that their inherent potential may be realized. We cannot rest in this until ecocentric production has become an ecocentric *mode* of production. When this happens, for which an extensive struggle must be anticipated, the power to regulate society will be in ecosocialist hands.

10 | Ecosocialism

If we imagine that decrees are all that is needed to get away from competition, we shall never get away from it. And if we go so far as to propose to abolish competition while retaining wages, we shall be proposing nonsense by royal decree. But nations do not proceed by royal decree. Before framing such ordinances, they must at least have changed from top to bottom the conditions of their industrial and political existance, and consequently their whole manner of being.[1]

The general model of ecosocialist transformation

Revolutions become feasible when a people decides that their present social arrangements are intolerable, when they believe that they can achieve a better alternative, and when the balance of forces between them and that of the system is tipped in their favor. None of these conditions is close to being met at present for the ecosocialist revolution, which would seem to make the exercise upon which we are about to embark, academic. But the present is one thing, and the future another. If the argument that capital is incorrigibly ecodestructive and expansive proves to be true, then it is only a question of time before the issues raised here will achieve explosive urgency. Indeed, precisely this has begun to happen since the first edition of *The Enemy of Nature* appeared in 2002, in the rapidly surging anxiety about, and interest in contending with global warming, a phenomenon certain to grow more agitated with each passing year, and which necessarily brings to the fore the problem of capitalism, and hence the solution represented by ecosocialism. It is most definitely high time, therefore, to take up the question of ecosocialism as a living process – to consider what its vision of society may be and what kind of path can be made toward it.

We call ecosocialism that society in which production is carried out by freely associated labor and with consciously ecocentric means and ends. When such production takes hold across the society as a whole, we are able to call it a *mode* of production; thus ecosocialism will be a society whose mode of production is ecocentric. This does not mean that no other forms of production coexist. Indeed, certain markets, and therefore commodities, are bound to continue within ecosocialist society for the foreseeable future. However, the coordinated agencies of society – state, civil society, culture, religion, etc. – are centered about ecocentric production; and this centering also hems in markets and keeps them functioning according to ecocentric ethics rather than profiteering. Use-value and quality are valorized over exchange-value and quantity, and the economy is now embedded within society rather than, as under capitalism, standing over society.[2]

Humans do not only produce things; they also produce themselves. Capitalism, as a society dominated by an alienating economy of exploitation, creates the addictive character types whose unfulfilled lives fuel its cancerous overconsumption. The freely associated labor of ecosocialism, by contrast, is sensuous, deeply gratifying and non-repressive. The very foundation of need itself is transformed so that the presently intolerable "footprint" of the affluent capitalist societies may be lifted from the ecosphere.[3] This is the only rational way of approaching the stark problem of the North's overconsumption that haunts the ecological question.

A society made by freely associated people can have no blueprint laid down in advance. But the character of the labor which is its foundation will mark the result. Since freely associated labor implies face-to-face interaction, the logic of ecocentric production leads to a fine-grained, site-specific kind of cellular base to society, linked with loosely configured coordinative bodies regulating trade, communications, provision of justice, and arbitration, as well as those functions that are simply better done centrally, such as specialized medical centers, research institutes, universities, concert halls, and so forth. The logic will be one of

243

a dialectic between parts and whole, each of which requires the other; and although there will necessarily be tension between the various levels, as there must be in any dialectical process, the presence of freely associated labor as the ground of society keeps the intrusiveness of the state at bay. There is an autonomy and self-reliance to freely associated labor that will not be pushed around by massified and totalizing institutions.

Will ecosocialist society be trouble-free? Of course not; nothing human is. Twenty-five years in the study of psychoanalysis amidst seventy years of observing life in the world has stripped me of all sentimental illusions about human nature. But I know, too, that we are creatures of manifold possibility, and that what conduces to the goodness of will within the human condition is the free association of labor. It is this that allows life to be expressed, and gives us dignity. What makes a person strong is the capacity to give, to reach out, to be engaged in the flux of life – and also to for-give, both oneself and others. These are all functions of freely associated labor. They allow us to overcome our madnesses, including the desire for revenge. They can all be given ecocentric values and are embodied in policies such as the prohibition of capital punishment, the insistence upon radical democracy and respect for the rights of all creatures, including, to be sure, human beings. The whole notion of human rights derives from freely associated labor, which is ultimately the expression of our true being.

The notion of ecosocialism is a kind of wager that freely associated labor will generate ecocentric ends; and that the latter will imply, indeed demand, freely associated labor. Hence the two streams of an ecosocialist process are mutually generative; they develop and propagate themselves in a process whose imaginative envisioning we have called "prefigurative." What prefiguration sees before us is an *integral human ecosystem*; this forms itself into larger unities – "solidarities," to use a basic term drawn from the labor movement, and these prefigure labor's free realization. Thus ecosocialist formations coalesce in nature's great formativity and drive toward that "another world which is possible" which the

World Social Forum movement has intuited as the suppressed dream of humanity.

The "another world" is at present no more than a dim possibility, and one would have to say, not even likely, given the mass of violent institutions, crippled human beings, and ruined ecosystems encountered in the reign of capital. But to worry about that is a luxury that cannot be afforded. It saps the will to act, to fight for the only world worth fighting for. No doubt, we are capable of suppressing ourselves through what Blake called "mind-forged manacles": after all, a monstrosity such as capitalism does not arise simply through coercion or indoctrination. Even though it is not in human nature as such, it most certainly expresses a potential within human nature. But though we suffer from a permanent liability toward delusion and self-destruction, this remains paired with an affirmative, integrative power which is the birthright of every person thrown into the world.

Toward an integral Commons

The general motion toward ecosocialism is this: that as the contradictions of society unfold, cracks in the system appear, moments of rupture when the possibility of new configuration arises. Then the integrative power that is the prefiguration of freely associated labor confronts this opening, along with the semi-inert, ecosystematically torpid, dimly conscious, frayed and fragmented ensemble of elements thrown forward from the past, and seeks to transform them. It infuses the fragmented ensemble with consciousness and form, and gives it a degree of ecosystemic being.

In these ensembles, the "past" is not something to be thrown aside; it is also a living repository of tradition, memories of lost or abandoned dreams, remnants from the whole prehistory of a people, and indeed, of humankind. This is the juncture in which nature appears. To the human being, nature and the past are different aspects of the same thing; they are what is prior to the production that defines the present moment, and therefore can enter into the transforming of production. And since *pro*duction

245

is the forward-looking making of things, in these conjuctures, past, present, and future are brought together. In this, there are creative possibilities, as ecocentric labor is applied to the ensemble, and sees in its fragments the lineaments of a latent wholeness; it is visionary, and recognizes an emergent form; it sees history embedded within nature, and nature infusing history with intrinsic value. This is how ecocentric labor acts prefiguratively and, a process of recognition, makes an integral human ecosystem out of a semi-inert ensemble – an ecosystem that stays connected to nature, intrinsically primed to widen and deepen its range of connections, an ecosystem that prefigures ecosocialism itself.

Prefiguration is not the shallow postmodernism that mines the past for the advertising and entertainment industries, nor is it the fascist rendering of the past into myths of legitimacy for patriarchal authority. It is a continual process of rediscovery, a restoration of dignity to what "has been" to find what is "not-yet." First-epoch socialism, with the exception of William Morris, failed to grasp this principle. The same may be said for the shallow "progressivism" in which much of the contemporary left is mired. In its indifference and even contempt for the past it reveals nothing so much as embeddedness in capitalism.

The task for ecosocialism is to work consciously with ensembles as they have been thrown forth and to see in them the germ of integral ecosystems to come. Now we need a better word here than "ensembles," which is too abstract and non-specific. There is such a term, which abounds in present-day ecological politics, and admits of a great variety of interpretations. We have used it before in this study; and now need to give it ecosocialist content. The word is *Commons*. The notion is redolent with history and betrayal; consider only its freezing into an arm of the bourgeois state as "The House of Commons," or its corruption into that classic of neoliberal pseudoscience, Garrett Hardin's "The Tragedy of the Commons" (which among its many defects never bothered to define what a Commons was).[4] Or its relationship to "commune" (as in the Paris Commune of 1871 – see below) and "communism." Or its usage in such opaque constructions as the Global Commons, and so on.

One prevailing theme of the Commons is that it is "enclosed" by the march of the formal, class-bound economy. This has a twofold meaning: that the people of the Commons, that is, the primary producers of society, are forcibly separated from their means of production; and that the rulers are made richer by the enclosing. In other words, closing the Commons means both the robbery and the alienation of the original people, as part of the creation of private property; it is the precondition for the "primitive accumulation" of capital, and is continually reproduced in capital's invasions. Note, too, that enclosure made commoners into "free" laborers, free to go to the city, free to live in appalling poverty and filth, free to become proletarians and sub-proletarians in the rising regime of capital, a process that still obtains throughout capital's ecumene. From another angle, an enclosed Commons, like the commodity itself, is subjected to a kind of splitting from the whole of things. Enclosure furthers the metaphoric sense of an ecosystemic ensemble cut off from the whole and subject to splitting and degeneration.[5]

Let us take this sense of things, then, and use the term, Commons, as a sign of a kind of struggle, a moment of disruption from a relatively organic past threatened by a present organized about property and commodification, yet illuminated by the possibility of an ecosocialist future. On the ground, the struggle will be between those who would enclose the Commons and those who would reclaim it. The former speak today in the name of capital; the latter meanwhile struggle for the integrity of the eco-system comprised by the Commons and its human community. In other words, the Commons is not a physical place but a kind of event that is happening in a human ecosystem and in which the integrity of that ecosystem is at stake.

Now we are able to specify the motion of ecosocialist politics more concretely. It consists of locating the emergence of a Commons, and intervening to favor the victory of ecocentric forces. A great range of struggle can be seen in this light: the efforts of communities to de-commodify the conditions of life, such as water, or to resist the intrusion of polluting industry (in other words, movements toward "environmental justice"); the building of autonomous zones of production, in other words, relatively outside of capital; the struggle of labor to unionize (for what is a "union" but the ecocentric coming together of those caught up in capitalist production, with the sign of its flourishing that archetypal notion of ecocentricity – *solidarity*); the politics of non-violent struggle against globalization or militarization, with its *affinity groups*, also paradigmatic of ecocentric organizing. Each in its way is a battle for a kind of Commons, a piece of human ecosystem, more integral, more formed, more realized. Each points us toward ecosocialism.

Patterns of ecosocialist mobilization

The return of the Paris Commune For two months in the spring of 1871, the people of Paris ruled the French capital, striking fear and consternation into the hearts of ruling classes everywhere and standing forth as a perennial inspiration for radical left-ists, whether socialist or anarchist.[6] The Commune arose out of complicated machinations in the course of the French defeat by Prussia; and what it signified was the ability of ordinary citizens to organize themselves and exert power in a directly democratic and non-violent way – albeit configured by a constant threat of murderous destruction, which eventually became a bloody reality once the forces of the state rallied and projected their "legitimate" violence – memories of which haunt Père Lachaise cemetery in Paris, where, near the graves of Proust, Oscar Wilde and Chopin, one can find the plain brick wall against which the Communards stood as they faced the firing squad.

The Commune drew on extensive exposure of the working people of Paris to socialist and anarchist influence. Its great legacy was to demonstrate the power of freely associated labor.[7] It was neither the first nor the last effort of "common" people to run their society, however, only the most famous. In its name as well as substance it looked back to medieval methods of self-organization, and, beyond that, in the deep recesses of time, to the original classless societies. Since 1871 something of the sort has been repeated on innumerable occasions all over the world, both in revolutionary contexts and also as the rising of semi-autonomous communities in the interstices of various existing states.

Under conditions of ecological crisis, various ruptures are bound to appear within the late-capitalist world accompanied by some disintegration in the state. In these lacunae, or to use the derisive term applied to countries like Somalia or Haiti, "failed states," we can see the same kind of processes as eventuated in the Paris Commune itself, namely, a relative absencing of state authority and within the newly opened space an opportunity for the emergence of a form of the Commons with more or less freely associated labor and ecocentric intention. We briefly list four instances, to give an idea of the range of possibilities.

1. The catastrophe visited upon the city of New Orleans in the wake of Hurricane Katrina has already been discussed. This was truly a kind of instance of a failed state, whose downfall had been prepared by various disintegrations brought about by capitalism and racism over many years and brought to a head in the second Bush administration. In the immediate aftermath of the storm a great wave of volunteers, college students, community activists, Greens, and other people of good will gathered in the city and, working with and often under the leadership of the battered inhabitants, began to rebuild civil society outside the baleful influence of the degenerate capitalist state. A considerable, even inspiring, amount of good was done in the course of this, a portion of which still stands as of this writing. However, the efforts failed to propagate into the prototype of a new society like Paris of 1871; and, as we have observed, a year and a half later the great city is in some ways more miserable than ever.

There was no one cause for this doleful result, but a cacophony of many: the scale of the shock to the material underpinning of the city (something that did not obtain for Paris during the Commune); the rapid return of capital to exploit the destruction for

249

purposes of ethnic cleansing and building of new, higher-value real estate while using the city now as a theme park image of itself for the benefit of the tourist trade (this would be equivalent to the return of the French army to Paris one week after the Commune got started); the tremendous damage wrought over time by racism, poverty, systemic crime, and disintegrated communal life (again, something foreign to nineteenth-century European cities rooted in pre-capitalist communality); finally, the lack of a coherent political culture of the sort that gave solidarity to the Paris of 1871. What New Orleans strove for in the aftermath of Katrina was the reconstruction of a Commons; but what it lacked was the real foundation for such an endeavor. A prefigurative process therefore could not take hold and ecocentric community could not propagate. And so the venture collapsed. It became an exercise in voluntarism, often heroic, almost always admirable, yet unable to stand against the disintegration of New Orleans.

2. In the wake of the triumph of the African National Congress and its allies over South African apartheid, the newly minted democratic state of 1994 embarked on a brilliant process of reconciliation with its racist past, guided by a constitution that was the most advanced in the world. But at the same time the new regime signed on, hook, line, and sinker, to the project of global neoliberalism, became a regional subimperial power, and took the IMF for its guiding spirit. The predictable happened: class divisions widened, splitting the blacks from each other; and great numbers of the masses fell into the abyss of capital reserves for those who do not contribute to the production of surplus value. Meanwhile, the upper reaches of South African society have been able to live lives of First World elegance, comfort, and charm. Having triumphed over the scourge of apartheid, millions of South Africans felt a uselessness and despair that rivalled and in some ways exceeded the ravages of apartheid days.[8] The results, in terms of crime (where South Africa is considered the world leader, with a rate some eight time the average), and one of the very worst AIDS pandemics on the planet, are what could have been expected.

In this case, the failed state did not collapse or withdraw so much as create a subclass for which it had no use. What is remarkable, however, is that a subset of this same underclass has behaved differently, opting to re-create Commons in the most unlikely of environments – the shack towns in which they have been forced to live. One such group, the Kennedy Road community in Durban, has the further misfortune to live adjacent to one of the largest toxic waste dumps in Africa. And yet live they do, and have organized themselves into a modern simulacrum of the Commune.

"*Abahlali baseMjondolo*" means "the people who live in the shacks," in Zulu; and that is what they call themselves.[9] In the case of this creation of the Commons, several threads have been woven into the fabric of a rather vital community. First, there are traditions on which they draw – the tradition of anti-apartheid struggle, and, before that, the tradition of Zulu self-determination; second, there is a fortuitous relationship with an institute at the nearby University of KwaZulu Natal, the Centre for Civil Society (CCS), a multi-ethnic and eclectic body of radicals whose prime goal is to give support to projects like this; finally, there is the tradition of struggle in Durban itself, where Gandhi originated Satyagraha, where powerful trades unions build class-consciousness among workers, and where the World Conference on Racism was held in 2001.

The combination of these elements keeps the community alive and in constant agitation directed against the South African state. This latter, having betrayed the hopes of 1994, puts the squeeze to conditions of life such as water, sewers, and electricity and shows every sign of wanting to drive the shack towns out entirely. The situation is complicated by all kinds of internal conflicts within the shack community and with CCS itself, as well as with other ethnic groups, such as the nearby Indian community. It is hard to predict a positive outcome for this project, for the simple reason that there is so little in the way of productive activity that can sustain *Abahlali baseMjondolo*; indeed, their chief workplace is the waste site itself, and many defend fiercely the right to employment there. Yet a community that can march about under a banner called, "The University of Abahlali baseMjondolo," and attends the conferences of the CCS, periodically livening up the heavy Marxist discourse with poetry, chants, and dancing, gives testimony to that fiery, elusive but essential ecosocialist category, the human spirit.

3. Ecosocialism will be international or it will be nothing. And when its history is written, a starting point will be noted as January 1, 1994 – the day that NAFTA went into effect and the EZLN replied with revolution of the oppressed in Chiapas, Mexico.

The EZLN has been the most prefiguratively successful example of a reclaimed Commons in the image of the Paris Commune. It is on rural ground, comprising over a thousand communities organized into thirty-two autonomous municipalities, all within the boundaries of Mexico yet not a part of the state. It is now thirteen years since the EZLN, after eleven years of prior *sub rosa* organizing, came out of the rain forest to shock the world. This longevity, which has recently radiated its effect to the neighboring province of Oaxaca and uses advanced modes of communication to retain its lines of contact with internationalists everywhere, is proof positive that autonomous zones of resistance can arise within capitalist nations, albeit in special circumstances that are not reproducible everywhere. But that is just the point: no conditions are reproducible everywhere. Therefore, the builders of ecosocialist alternatives will have to learn how to be site-specific. And like the Zapatistas, they will have to organize patiently to build their political culture and its productive relations.

The EZLN has been called the first "postmodern" rebellion, but this term merely describes its refusal to play by the rules of previous dogmas. Where postmodernism in the metropolis describes a kind of ransacking of tradition and a deliberate courting of the chaotic, the Zapatista movement, as ecosocialism, creates positive content through definite ways of creating freely associated labor and definite ways of pursuing ecocentric goals. These are not conjured out of air, but arise through a deliberate appropriation and transforming of tradition. One of its core features has been to overcome the gendered bifurcation of nature by reaching into the pre-patriarchal past to valorize female forms of production. This has been one of the core features of Zapatismo, which has transformed the lives of women to a greater degree than anything comparable in the politics of either North or South.

As for ecocentrism in Chiapas, let me quote from a fundraising letter seeking support for schools – nine having been built in 2006, and four more sought for 2007:

> This letter is being written in the midst of an almost impossibly ambitious state-wide agro-ecology/health educational tour where mental fences are falling and hope growing during inspiring discussions spoken in Tsotsil, Tseltal, Cho, Zoque (with a smattering of Spanish) about human dignity, democracy, and saving the planet. Healthy little Neem trees are bridging borders across the state and Zapatista corn is being tested for GMO contamination by indigenous agro-ecology activists. After months of planning and preparation this environmentally focused educational journey is a truly inspiring and deeply rewarding experience.

The EZLN provides the first model of revolutionary ecosocialism on a bioregional scale.[10] Despite constant harassment by an army vastly superior in firepower, the Zapatistas retain a kind of ecosystemic integrity. They form a society within a state yet without a state, productively united in resistance. What Marx said of the Paris Commune, that it lived the idea of the "dictatorship of the proletariat," could be said, therefore, of the Zapatista path to ecosocialism, with the wider lesson that there can be no single path valid for all peoples. The peasants of Chiapas, after all, are not, by any definition, proletarians. But peasants, proletarians, informal workers, housewives in the North, etc., are all producers in one degree of antagonistic relationship or another to the global system of accumulation, and all are now brought together by ecological crisis. This is not to say that all these instances recognize their common mission against the "Great Satan." Such is scarcely the case at present; indeed, frequent misunderstandings and bootless antagonisms emerge, and will have to be overcome in the name of solidarity.

4. The last example is different in that it does not involve reaction to immediate oppression. It is rather an example of an ecosocialist initiative done, so to speak, for its own sake, using as its state-free space a terrain neither abandoned by nor wrested from the state, but where the state never bothered to go in the first place because the land was so barren. Thus it defines another dimension of communal arising.

Gaviotas is an intentional community built in a remote zone of Colombia's highlands. Here, beginning in 1971, one of the harshest environments on earth has been transformed by freely associated labor using ecologically rational technology. On what was once a blighted and arid plain, the soil toxic with naturally occurring aluminum, today stands a reforestation project larger than all the rest of Colombia's forestry projects combined, some 6 million trees, a source of resin and musical instruments. These and other commodities are produced outside of capitalist circuits, and without a capitalist state – in other words, with enhanced use-values and reduced exchange-value – on an island of non-capitalist and ecocentric production which could become part of an archipelago of prefigured ecosocialism.[11]

It is worth noting that Gaviotas, a town arising *de novo* in the middle of nowhere, uses the past to appropriate emancipatory tradition, not, however, from Colombia but from Paraguay, whose eighteenth-century Indian communities, organized by Jesuits, underwent more than a century of autonomous development until empire claimed the territory. One connection is the making of musical instruments, a form of production that sits lightly upon the earth. As Paolo Lugari, the visionary founder of the Gaviotas community, said of the Paraguayan world: "Everyone ... was taught to sing or to play a musical instrument. Music was the loom that wove the community together. Music was in schools, at meals, even at work. Musicians accompanied laborers right into the corn and *yerba mate* fields. They'd take turns, some playing, some harvesting. It was a society that lived in constant harmony – literally. It's what we intend to do, right here in this forest."[12]

What the Paraguayans did reminds of the happy interrelation

of play, song, and construction in the life of children, as, for example, at a good nursery school. If we think of this comparison as disparaging adult work settings, then we have missed a central point of ecosocialism. For children and adults alike have an inherent, spontaneously emerging need to sing, dance, and play. This enters directly into ecosocialist production, whether its use-values are restored from capital's degradation or created *de novo*. The machinery of capitalist production does not only bind the body temporally; it also expresses the life-denying character of male domination, which enforces repression, stifles the flowing of life-forces, and has cursed production with pain since the expulsion from Eden. The overcoming of male domination also restores to production its intrinsic pleasure. There will be plenty of hard work to do; but hard work freely chosen and collectively carried out is a great joy. It is this gratification that replaces the curse of *having* that dominates capitalism with a society organized around *being*, that can live lightly upon the earth. Because the expressiveness of music or poetry is intrinsically unattached to things but emerges from within the human being, it moves from subject to object and enters the ground of ecocentrically realized practice.

Zones of ecocentric production Gaviotas is a productive collectivity along the lines of the Paris Commune in that it is an ecosocialist society built outside the state. But a multitude of productive collectives arise within the pores of capitalism. All can prefigure ecosocialism according to their anti-capitalist intentions, the free association of the labor that makes them go around, and their ecocentrism. Some begin with the earth, such as community gardens or other initiatives in community-based agriculture like farmers' coops. Others move within spaces of avanced technology.

As an example of the latter type, consider the alternative media community, situated at the Archimedean point of capitalist legitimation and control. Here, prefigurations of the new society in the form of "indymedia" centers have arisen over the last decade, initially as collectives of radical media activists in the cities visited by anti-globalization protests. Often the independent centers stayed on after the waves of street protests receded; meanwhile, others autonomously arose using the same model. Their way having been prepared by a generation of media activists, the centers manifest a flexible and open structure, a democratic rendering of the use-values of new technologies like the internet, and a continual involvement in wider struggle against the regime of accumulation and empire.[13] They grow and gather into national and international collectives, forming nodes on a web unified by anti-capitalist vision. The same force that binds together the movement for democratic media also tends to keep it ecosystemic, i.e. democratically communitarian, and, to that degree, unwilling to compromise with the powers that be. In this way the spontaneously developing collective evolves into a *community of resistance*, one defined by praxis rather than place. It would be better, perhaps, to say that their place is everywhere, prefiguring the global scope of ecosocialism, and, in contrast to the plan of traditional green theory, cosmopolitan to the core.[14]

In these communities, labor has become relatively freely associated. However, actual ecosocialism requires that the entire international division of labor be overcome, including that of proletarians, or wage laborers, and this is a problem the difficulty of which can scarcely be overestimated. Capital's domination of labor is predicated on separating workers from the means of production, and also from each other. This is the foundation of its triumph, and has become sedimented into the labor movement itself, which, being dependent upon jobs within existing capitalist workplaces, often shares with capital resistance to environmental protection, while being divided nationally or regionally, North and South having many separate agendas. In the process many labor organizations have become sclerotically bureaucratized and mere fossils of their transformative selves.

This is an urgent problem for the "red" branches of the red–green movement engaged in prefiguring ecosocialism, in particular, the numerous offshoots of first-epoch socialist formations.

One at times hears complaints from this quarter that the argument advanced in this work undercuts the "privileged" role to be played by the international proletariat in socialist revolution. Well, yes, it is true that the imminence of planetary eco-collapse reconfigures the project of resistance to capital. That is simply manifestation of the need for Marxists to keep in touch with a changing reality. However, the ecological crisis certainly does not mean that the effort to counter capital in those workplaces where surplus value is produced should slacken – indeed, it is unthinkable that an ecosocialist society can be built that ignores the reality of proletarian labor and the need to incorporate this great body of humanity into the new way of production. But the fact remains that effective organizing of labor needs to take into account the radically new conditions of the ecological crisis. In other words, red socialists need to incorporate the ways of ecocentrism into their theory and practice, and reach out to wage laborers with an enhanced consciousness of "what is to be done"; this implies as well, "what is not to be done," which is to say, continuing on the suicidal path of industrial capitalism and endless, cancerous growth.

Autonomous zones of production are not privileged over struggles in capital's "dark satanic mills," except for having the good luck of being able to offer more direct routes to ecosocialism, while traditional organizing of labor must engage in a more complicated process of re-education of workers and institutional demolition along with building a new world.[15] But this can be seen as a form of privilege, in that the offshoots of first-epoch socialism must be, so to speak, "special forces" able to undertake so difficult a project. In any case, there is no hereditary privilege in the effort to overcome capital just as there are no blueprints for the ecosocialist society. If the advocates of the primacy of traditional class struggle as the engine of history wish to prove their point, the way lies open to them. Nobody within the ecosocialist movement can or should stop them from doing so.

As to the compatibility of actually existing socialism for ecosocialism, bear in mind that in those parts of the world where a degree of authentic socialism has taken hold, prefigurative paths to ecosocialism have also appeared. We have already mentioned Cuba's introduction of ecocentric agriculture on a national scale; and should add that in "Bolivarian" Venezuela under the Chávez government, considerable attention is being given to ecocentric development.[16] It is too soon to predict the outcome. All that need be said here is that, in contrast to the "Paris Commune" model of autonomous development where state control has broken down and renewed state violence is the ever-present threat, under this latter circumstance, a strong, more or less intact, socialistically-oriented state[17] plays a leading role in the process. Here the threat is that it eventually becomes too strong and stifles the emergence of freely associated labor, causing the movement toward ecosocialism to stall.

Taking on the whole

Global warming is not the only aspect of the ecological crisis to have reached planetary proportions, nor is it the only one with the potential to actually destroy the human species. But it definitely has the most power to seize the world's imagination. This is because of global warming's literally spectacular quality, the way it manifestly affects other aspects of the crisis – for what on earth can evade the influence of climate? – and last, and certainly not least, for the way in which global warming puts the entire history, and the prehistory as well, of industrial capitalism into the dock. Here the leading culprits are in full view: the whole petro-apparatus, from the pushers of "automobilia" to the imperial apparatus that wages endless war to keep the carbon[18] flowing from the ground, where it belongs, to the atmosphere, where it will destroy us. In a word: a moment for the global realization of ecosocialism has arrived.

That the struggle about global warming is also a class struggle and therefore to be overcome through ecosocialism is, needless to add, suppressed in normal discourse. Here all eyes are on the legions of technocrats and their effort, undoubtedly important, to figure out just how global warming might unfold, and how to mitigate its effects, that is, how to get carbon out of the atmosphere and keep lethal doses of greenhouse gases from entering. But the heart of the problem is not technical; with all due respect to Al Gore, there is a *really inconvenient truth that cannot be dealt with technologically* in the struggle against global warming.[19] As the authoritative Intergovernmental Panel on Climate Change (IPCC) put it in its final report of May 2007, the worthy measures needed to bring down the carbon level in the atmosphere can be seriously disrupted by "vested interests" who will fight efforts at capping carbon.[20]

No amount of greenwash can obscure who those interests are. For even if the oil firms also make solar panels, and no matter that the automobile industry will exploit market demands for cars with better fuel economy, the giant corporations who profit from hydrocarbons still have hundreds of billions in fixed capital invested in keeping the carbon flowing, and they are no more able to set that aside for long-term benefit to the world than you or I are able to willfully stop breathing for ten minutes in a higher cause. The brain stem will not permit a voluntary diminution in oxygen metabolism; and the survival mechanisms of capital dictate the same with respect to interruptions in accumulation. To underscore: the vested interests act as capitalists and not as human beings – and it is as capitalists that they have to be fought. And the battle against petro-capital needs to be waged throughout the whole domain of capital, which is to say, globally: through the state, by intervening where the state needs to act, and in such a way that shifts the balance of forces away from capital; and in civil society, to build countervailing institutions of resistance and alternative production, institutions that prefigure the ecosocialism to come.

The struggle is differentiated into Northern and Southern campaigns, notions that refer not so much to fixed geography as to the distinction between capital in the metropolis and the periphery, where most resources are extracted from nature.[21] In the North we see emergence of campaigns such as:[22]

- initiatives to build public works whose impact is reduction of dependence upon petroleum, for example, light rail networks; this is not a technological fix, as the technology is already well known; it is a struggle for the state, a political struggle; similar struggles would be toward demanding of the state that it regulate fuel efficiency more strenuously; or stop airport expansion; or get rid of subsidies for fossil fuel extraction, superhighway construction, pipelines, rebates for SUVs, and so on;

- replace these with subsidies for renewable energy development; inducing the development and purchase of high-efficiency autos such as hybrids; methods of efficiency enhancement; promotion of local community initiatives to conserve energy, etc. Ideally, these subsidies should be drawn from heavy taxation of oil superprofits (it clears the mind to realize that the five leading oil companies "earned" $375 billion in profits in 2006);

- force the state to provide subsidies to workers laid off by the moving away from the carbon economy – a key consideration in overcoming the hostility of traditional labor organizations to environmentalism;

- the above are demands upon the state; there is also need for direct struggles to preserve the integrity of relatively intact ecosystems, such as old growth forests, against the "Clean Development Mechanisms" (CDMs) of the Kyoto regime;

- litigation to force corporations, especially energy corporations, to bear the costs of these transitions.

None of these is in itself more than a reformist gesture to democratize the state and bring the corporate sector under control. Taken as a whole in the present context, however, they comprise a profound shift in orientation. Further, they slow the accumulation of atmospheric carbon and gain time for more radical measures, for example, nationalization, to take hold.

In the South, meanwhile, struggle is of the "environmental justice" type, comprising more or less direct defense of the

Commons against intrusion by capital and its many calamitous effects. Actions such as those below dramatize this fact and build precious solidarity:

- the threat by Indians in Bolivia and Ecuador to commit mass suicide if big oil (including Occidental Petroleum, a company partly held by Al Gore's family) invades their territory;
- legal action against Chevron by Ecuadoran Indians to try and recoup damages for the terrible pollution and harm done to their lives;
- similar challenges by Inuit from the North Slope in Alaska;
- bans on petro-extraction won by the people of Costa Rica;
- protests by people of the Niger River delta, ranging from militant nudity by women to armed guerrilla movements, all operating under the outrageous assumption that the wealth under the ground should be under the control of the people who live on the ground;[23]
- and, finally, further linking North and South and placing the struggle against petro-capital on an ecosocialist path, the anti-war and anti-imperialism movements.

Two major strategic themes can move activists along the path. They are both animated by the need to see the demands of carbon reduction as constituting a goal that can only be met by resolutely radical action. If, as the best opinion holds, it will be necessary to reduce world carbon emissions by 60 percent and those of industrial society by 90 percent by the year 2030 if we are to evade the fatal scenario of "runaway global warming," that is, where positive feedback loops supervene and the situation is out of control, then it is compelling to recognize that such a goal cannot be met in the context of industrial capitalism, and its compulsion to expand chaotically, nor can it simply be seen as bourgeois commentators would have it, as a technical question. It is rather a clarion call to move rapidly toward a kind of society where the capitalist system is radically brought down so that it cannot block this course of action. In a word, the crisis of global warming is capital's *Götterdämmerung*; it is the moment when the profound maxim of Rosa Luxemburg, that we live in an age defined by the choice between "socialism and barbarism," has come to be, except that history has now defined this in terms of "ecosocialism and ecocatastrophe." Concretely, this implies the following:

First, a unified perspective against the regime of the Kyoto Protocols and its likely successors, which define the newly minted markets for trading emission credits along with the CDMs in which Northern corporations employ various gimmicks in the South to offset continuing emissions. The emissions markets are get-rich-quick schemes; while the CDMs are exercises in neo-colonialism that further enclose the Commons, destroy indigenous lifeworlds and drive people into the mega-slums of the South. All aspects of Kyoto, to repeat, are primed to not work, being indeterminable and endlessly subject to manipulation and fraud, precisely because Kyoto signifies turning the administration of climate change over to the very corporate powers who created the problem in the first place.[24]

As Kyoto is discredited, the possibility of a socialist alternative emerges, and, with it, the second theme enters. The deciding matter is the question of sustainability. Capitalism is unsustainable as a total system, not simply because it overproduces, but because the whole world it makes is incompatible with ecological balance. As we have seen, capital generates a society of addiction, as an overweening ego reproduces itself along the fault lines of destabilized ecosystems. As a result, an immense degree of self-deception and denial is built into the debate on climate, which tends to minimize the degree of damage to come, along with the degree of change necessary to build a world that no longer spews intolerable amounts of carbon into the air.[25] Hence the craving for the technological fix that will enable continuing lives of reckless consumerism within the cocoon provided by capital. Trusting blindly in its innovative powers, people defend themselves against the "really inconvenient truth," that capitalism led us into this nightmare and does not have the least clue as to how to free us from it.

Everything hinges on whether detachment from capital can take place. Ruthless critiques of its ecodestructivity and nihilism – as in the instance of anti-Kyoto campaigns – are necessary but insufficient in themselves unless coupled with a credible hope that ecosocialism provides a real alternative, with its combination of freely associated labor and ecocentric practice signifying liberation from the tyranny of possession. The "wager" described at the beginning of this discussion, in other words, needs to be put into practice in the concrete effort to prove humanity capable of rising above the bondage placed by capital on our powers, and the nightmare of runaway global warming this portends.

For this to happen, all the various campaigns mentioned above will have to be extended further and be interrelated, and increasingly grounded in the production of non-industrial values and regimes of energy alternatives to the hydrocarbon economy. We can imagine this occurring focally, in one country, or in an archipelago of liberated ecosocialist zones, like a net of Chiapases, and propagating along various axes until the planet is ecosocialist. Under conditions of global warming, with many unpredictable calamities to come and the ever-present looming of right-wing and even fascistic measures to hold the system together, a very rough and bumpy ride is certain. How many will perish, what will be the map at the other end? All this is anyone's guess . . . and an occasion for some further speculation as to how to proceed.

The ecosocialist party and its victory

Two models of party-building dominated the last century: the parliamentary parties of the bourgeois democracies and the "vanguard" Leninist party of the Bolshevik tradition. Neither model belongs to the ecosocialist project, which cannot be voted into power, and dies stillborn if internal democracy is not made integral to its growth. Leninist parties succeeded in installing first-epoch socialism chiefly because they were configured to the largely pre-capitalist societies in which their revolutions succeeded. Those capitalisms vanquished by first-epoch socialism were either imperial offshoots of metropolitan capital, or backward regimes grafted upon a largely pre-capitalist society. They encompassed neither the internal penetration nor the external global reach of capital's present order, both of which radically change the revolutionary project.

Modern capitalism legitimates itself by invoking "democratic values." This is spurious, as we have seen, but however unfulfilled, it remains a real promise that rests upon a definite foundation. By fragmenting life-worlds and traditional hierarchies, capital sets humanity loose into an unfree freedom of formal liberty and stunted development. The uneasy balance is kept going in capitalist institutions, which bind it for purposes of accumulation. To go beyond capital, one begins, then, with the betrayed promise of freedom and builds from there. It follows that the means of transformation have to be as free as the ends. That is why vanguardism, where the party is separate from as well as ahead of the people, is a non-starter. Only a freely evolving praxis of participation can mobilize the imagination and bring together the innumerable points at which anticapitalist struggle originates. And only a "party-like" formation, which postulates a goal common to all struggles without constraining them from above, can organize this into "solidarity solidified" and press toward power. Thus the party is formed from its own dialectic; it is a "holding together" both objectively and subjectively – the former being the provision of material conditions, the latter being the attunement to intersubjective and relational nuance, all subsumed into the practical notion that dialectic is a matter of artfulness and subtlety – and the lived fabric of ecosystemic being.

Though open to individuals, the ecosocialist party should be grounded in communities of resistance/production. Delegation from such communities will supply the cadre of party activists as such, and the assembly that is its strategic and deliberative body. The party is to be internally funded through contributions by members, structured in such a way that no alienating force can take financial control. The delegates and such adminstrative bodies as may arise within this structure are to rotate on a regular basis and to be subject to recall. Further, the deliberations of the assembly, indeed all the activities of the party except certain tactical questions (for example, the details of a direct action), are to be open and transparent. Let the world see clearly what the ecosocialist party stands for – if this is worthwhile, it will only draw in more participants; if not, one needs to find out sooner rather than later.

As a general rule, parties calling themselves socialist have remained largely unable to transform their political thinking in an ecocentric direction. By contrast, the various green parties have been defined as an ecocentric movement to begin with. Experience has shown, at least in the United States, that by defining themselves as a progressive populism within the framework of bourgeois democracy, Greens are congealing as a kind of intermediate formation that stops considerably short of what is needed for transformation. Green activists continue to make valuable contributions; but their parties lack a prefigurative vision surpassing the given society. As a result, green parties tend to lapse into narrow reformism and anarchic bickering. And when they have achieved some state power, as in Europe, Greens, with some notable exceptions, have tended to prove loyal to capital, giving it a shield of ecological responsibility.[26]

One sign of the limits of green politics as presently practiced has been a severe inability to reach out to communities of non-European origin. Frequently chastized for their lily-white make-up, Greens regularly inveigh against the problem and resolve to do better. Yet little changes. The reason cuts to the core of the green dilemma: the parochial values intrinsic to localism. Unless the notion of community is advanced in a universalizing way, it loses transformative power and, despite good intentions, drifts toward ethnocentricity. Therefore the Greens' vacillation on questions such as immigration and prison reform, and their general inability to appeal, at least in the United States, with more than token gestures to blacks and Latinos, is no oversight. From this perspective, a politics against and beyond capital needs to be as firmly rooted in overcoming racism as it is in environmental mending. The two themes intersect directly in the "environmental justice" movement, grounded in the defense against capitalist penetration and pollution by communities of color, and often led by women, hence ecofeminist as well as ecosocialist and drawn into the campaign against petro-capital.[27]

But the chief defect of green politics, in the United States and, to a degree, elsewhere, has been an inability to recognize what capitalism is and means. This defect deprives them of a view of the whole of society, and cripples their interventions. Hence green parties need to be anti-capitalist (as obtains in the UK among a goodly fraction of Greens), even as red parties need to incorporate ecocentricity. Combined, the "red–green alliance" can set forth to build ecosocialism.

If such a political formation arose, combining all the tendencies developed to now, including the fidelity to building a global movement toward a new carbon economy, it could generate a dialectic that can rapidly accelerate the motion toward ecosocialism. There will be tens of thousands of local and regional experiments and practices which would respond to its call, and come together to join strategies. These tendencies would join with communities of activation to make this possible, and their power would be accordingly magnified by it.

There is no point in predicting a scenario according to which this will expand, beyond the core condition that it occur in context of capital's inability to regulate the ecological crisis, and the unifying perspective given by the struggle against petro-capital and to overcome climate change. At some time within this span, the communities arising from the process may be imagined to grow to a point of relative autonomy such that they can begin providing material support for activists, with bases of operation and, in the case of those considerable number of communities producing food, wool, hemp, solar technology, etc., the actual means of subsistence for people engaged in revolutionary struggle.

Now, it may be imagined, the movement of events is self-sustaining, rapid, and dramatic. Communities of place and of praxis increasingly coalesce to form miniature societies; and these enter into relations with others both inside and outside the national boundary. Capital may be expected to respond with heightened efforts at repression. A heroic phase begins, with much sacrifice. The global might of the capital system now encounters a set of factors it has never dealt with before.

- The forces against it are both numerous and dispersed.
- They operate with changed needs, and on the basis of a mode of production capable of sustaining itself with small inputs, alternative energy and labor-intensive technologies; and they have secure bases and "safe houses" in intentional communities of resistance, now extending across national boundaries.
- Their many allies in the interstices of the mainstream society are capable of forming support groups and "underground railroads."
- As with all successful forms of revolutionary protest, the oppositional forces are capable of shutting down normal production through strikes, boycotts, and mass actions.
- The forces of capital have lost confidence, and are further undermined by support for social transformation within the alternative parties and their various niches in the state. This extends to armies and police. When the first of these lay down their arms and join the revolution, the turning point is reached.
- The behavior of the revolutionaries is spiritually superior; and the examples they set are given credibility and persuasiveness by the brute facts of the crisis and the gathering realization that what is at stake here is not so much the redistribution of wealth as the sustenance of life itself.

Thus it could be that, in an increasingly hectic period, millions of people take to the streets, and join together in solidarity – with each other, with the communities of resistance, and with their comrades in other nations – bringing normal social activity to a halt, petitioning the state, refusing to take "no" for an answer, and driving capital into ever smaller pens. With defections mounting

267

and the irreducible fact all around that the people are demanding a new beginning in order to save the planetary ecology, the state apparatus passes into new hands, the expropriators are expropriated, the 500-year regime of capital falls, and the building of a new world can begin.[28]

A usufructuary of the earth

From the standpoint of a higher economic form of society, private ownership of the globe by single individuals will appear quite as absurd as private ownership of one man by another. Even a whole society, a nation, or even all simultaneously existing societies taken together, are not the owners of the globe. They are only its possessors, its usufructuaries, and, like *boni patres familias*, they must hand it down to succeeding generations in an improved condition.[29]

Thus Karl Marx, in the third volume of *Capital*. The notion of usufruct is an ancient one, with roots going back to the Code of Hammurabi, though the word itself arises in Roman law, where it applied to ambiguities between masters and slaves with respect to property. It appears again in Islamic law, and in the legal arrangements of the Aztecs and the Napoleonic Code – indeed, wherever the notion of property reveals its inherent contradictions. Interestingly, the Latin word condenses the two meanings of *use* – as in use-value; and *enjoyment* – as in the *fruitful* pleasure expressed in freely associated labor. As commonly understood today, a usufructuary relationship is where one uses, enjoys – and through that, improves – another's property, as, for instance, community groups would use, enjoy and improve an abandoned city lot by turning it into a garden.

Because we are human to the degree that we creatively engage nature, the self is defined through its extensions into the material world. We become who we are by *appropriating* nature, transforming, and incorporating it, and it is within this frame that the notion of property logically arises – to be set against that property which is the result of *expropriation*, and which forms the scaffolding of class dominative society. In any case, a person with no possessions whatsoever is no individual at all, as s/he has neither radiations of the self nor particular grounding in nature. It follows that in an ecologically realized society everyone will have rights of ownership – a place of one's own, decorated according to taste, personal possessions, such as books, clothing, objects of beauty, likewise – and of special significance, rights of use, and ownership over those means of production necessary to express the creativity of human nature. This latter most definitely includes the body – whence the reproductive rights of women are logically secured, along with the rights of free sexual expression.

The notion of property becomes contradictory because each individual person emerges in a tissue of social relations, and, in John Donne's words, is never an island. Each self is therefore a part of all other selves, and property is inexorably tied into a dialectic with others. This may be imagined as a set of nested circles. At the center is the self, and here ownership exists in relatively absolute terms, beginning with the body, intrinsically the property of each person. As the circles extend, issues of sharing arise from early childhood on, each potentially resolvable according to the principle that the full self is enhanced more by giving than taking. For realized being is generous. The more lightly do material possessions weigh upon the self, the more fully can one give, and the richer one becomes.

The domain of use-value will be the site of contestation. To restore use-value means to take things concretely and sensuously, as befits an authentic relation of ownership – but by the same gesture, lightly, since things are enjoyed for themselves and not as buttresses for a shaky ego or occasions for profiteering. Under capital, as Marx famously saw, what is produced is fetishized by the shroud of exchange-value – made remote and magical. In the fetishized world, nothing is ever really owned, since everything can be exchanged, taken away, and abstracted. This stimulates the thirst for possessions that rages under capitalist rule. The unappeasable craving for things – and money to get things – is the necessary underpinning of accumulation and the subjective dynamic of the ecological crisis. We have seen that the circuits of capitalist society are defined by *having* – and excluding others from having – until society becomes a collection of gated communities inhabited by lonely egos, each split from all and the atomized selves split from nature.[30]

Ecosocialist society is defined by *being*, achieved by giving oneself to others and restoring a receptive relation to nature. Ecosystemic integrity is to be restored across all the nested circles of human participation – the family, the community, the nation, the international community, or, with a leap across the humanity/nature membrane, the planet, and beyond it, the universe. For capital, property rights of the individual Ego are sacrosanct, and become solidified into class structures, whence they succeed in dispossessing masses of people from their inherent ownership of the means to produce creatively. This is only the legal aspect of a regime of fetishized relations. Within ecosocialism, the bounds of the individual ego are surpassed as use-value overcomes exchange-value and opens a way for the realization of intrinsic value.

In the new society, the right of an individual to freely appropriate the means of self-expression is paramount. Society is structured to give this primacy by differentiating ownership between individual and collectivity. Although each person – and each family as the extension of personhood into reproduction – has an inalienable right to good housing, the ownership as such of the housing and the land upon which it stands is collective, and granted by the collectivity. In this way, there arise distinct limits on the amount of property individuals can control, both from the standpoint of domestic usage as well as that of the control over productive resources. No person is to be allowed to arrogate such resources, therefore, as would permit the alienation of means of production from another. There will be no such arrangement as now obtains, where well over a billion absolutely landless people, along with several billion more who must sell themselves on the market because they are effectively without control over more than the slenderest threads of property, confront a tiny fraction who own virtually all the wealth-producing world and the means of violence to enforce this. Extending further out along the nested circles, we find that those things essential for social production are to be shared by all and not owned by the few.

The extension proceeds, as Marx realizes, to the planetary level, and devolves downward from there to govern the particular laws of ecosocialist society. Taken all in all, the earth we inhabit should be regarded, not as our collective property but as a wondrous matrix from which we emerge and to which we return. Perhaps it will be easier to dislodge the ruling class from their cancerous ownership if we remind ourselves that this is not done to transfer ownership to "the people" or some surrogate. Indeed, ownership of the planet is a pathetic illusion. It is plain *hubris* to think that the earth, or nature, can be owned – and stupid to boot, as though one can own that which gives us being, and whose becoming we express. The notion of standing over and against the earth in order to own it is at the core of the domination of nature. A usufructuary is all we can claim with regard to the earth. But this demands that our species proves its worth by using, enjoying, and improving the globe that is our home. From that reigning principle can be derived those individual regulations that are to subserve the metabolism between humanity and nature called ecosocialism. No class ownership of the means of production stands at one pole; absolute ownership of one's self at the other – for the self is the earth emerging into consciousness at this one point of individuality; while the institutions of ecosocialist society exist to set going the ways of using, enjoying, and improving our common firmament.

The society that emerges from the storm of the revolution will at first be only marginally capable of fulfilling this project. Its highest priority is to set things going in a truly ecosocialist direction and its first goal is to secure the "free association of producers." Each term here needs to be respected. The association is *free* because in it people self-determine; hence society must make means of production accessible to all. It is a free *association* because life is collective; therefore the relevant political unit is a collectivity drawn together by mutual productive activity. And it is of *producers*, which is to be taken in the human–natural sense and not economistically. This means that the whole making of the human world is to be taken into account rather than just that which contributes or controls exchange-value. Since a core goal of ecosocialism is the diminution of exchange-value's domain, it valorizes forms of productive activity to the degree that these foster ecosystemic integrity, whether this be the raising of beautiful children, the growing of organic gardens, the playing of excellent string quartets, the cleaning of streets, the making of composting toilets, or the invention of new technologies for turning solar energy into fuel cells.

To secure the association, we need ways of preventing the emergence of alienating agencies. Private ownership of means of production has been shown to be the chief of these under capital, but the Soviets showed that the state can just as well fill this role. And since the gain of state power by the revolution is essential for redirecting society, so must the revolution give high priority to building ways of dissolving that power and preventing the state from turning into a monster over society. A key principle is the internal development of true democracy, the absence of which crippled all previous socialisms. That is why alternative party-building in the pre-revolutionary period is an essential – not to win state power in the here and now, which is out of the question, but to democratize the state insofar as possible, and to train people in the ways of self-governance so that when the revolution is made they will be in a position to sustain democratic development. Another essential principle is the enfranchisement of productive communities, enabling power to flow from the producers – or, since everyone produces and has multiple productive affiliations, from those collectivities that best express their free association and the enhancement of ecosystemic integrity.

A fourfold division of society confronts the ecosocialist revolution. First are those who have engaged in revolutionary practice, either as political agents and/or as members of communities of resistance. Second are those who did not participate actively yet whose productive activity is directly compatible with ecological production – the housewives, nurses, schoolteachers, librarians, technicians, independent farmers, etc., along with the very old, the very young, the ill, and those on welfare or otherwise marginalized (including many of those in prison). Third are those whose pre-revolutionary practice was given over to capital – the bourgeoisie, proper; along with those legions involved in work more or less worthless from an ecosocialist standpoint – the PR men, the car salesmen, the ad executives, the supermodels, the cast of *The Apprentice* and like shows, financiers, security guards, wealth psychologists, and so on. Finally, we find arrayed between the second and third categories, the great body of workers whose activity added surplus value to capitalist commodities, whether as industrial proletarians, field hands, truckdrivers, and so forth. Many of these latter worked in polluting, ecologically destructive settings; others in industries that have little or no place in an ecologically rational society, for example, weapons factories or those making diet sodas. All will have to be provided for and retrained if society is to be rebuilt.

Clearly, it will be no easy matter to reallocate productive activity among so vast an assemblage. The following broad principles may be useful.

1. An interim assembly of delegates from the revolutionary communities of resistance constitutes itself as an agency to handle the redistribution of social roles and assets, to make sure that all are provided for out of common stocks, and to exert such force as is necessary to reorganize society. The assembly will convene in widespread locations and send delegations to regional, state, national, and international bodies. Each level will have an executive council with rotating leadership, recallable by votes from the level below.

2. Productive communities (and now they may be authentically called "cooperatives"), whether of place or praxis, form the political as well as economic unit of society. The priority of

those groups who made the revolution will be to organize others and create paths for the rapid assimilation of other workers to the network of productive communities. This includes all able-bodied people, the ex-perpetrators of capital as well, who – with a few egregiously criminal exceptions – will be allowed to participate in building an ecosocialist world.

3. During the transition, incomes will be guaranteed, using the reserves now in the possession of the revolution. This is combined with transforming other sites considered outside the value-producing economy of capital, for example, child care, into productive communities, thereby giving reproductive labor a status equivalent to productive labor. At first the old money will be used, though given new conditions of value, namely, according to use and the degree to which ecosystem integrity is developed and advanced by any particular production. Thus, determination of ecocentric value becomes the ultimate standard, rather than abstract labor time.[31] Although no one in ecosocialist society shall do without, actual remuneration, and, more importantly, approval and sense of worth and dignity, comes with the fulfillment of use-values. This is what is meant by Marx's famous maxim, "from each according to abilities, to each according to need."

4. In each locality, one such community would directly administer the area of jurisdiction. For example, town government would be considered a collective whose product is the provision of ecologically sound governance – and also an assembly elected by all the inhabitants of that area. Each area, therefore, may have several assemblies – one for adminstration, another for wider spheres of governance.

5. Each productive community participates fully as soon as it demonstrates its fidelity to ecosocialist principles. And as it joins, it plays a political role in its local assembly, sending delegates and votes to the next level.

6. Two vitally important functions will devolve onto the more central assemblies. The first will be to monitor the degree that communities under its jurisdiction are contributing to ecosys-

temic integrity; and to give a kind of weight to communities according to their contribution. This supervisory body potentially has considerable power, limited, however, by the fact that it serves at the behest of the productive communities themselves.

7. The second function pertains to the general coordination of activities, the provision of society-wide services like rail systems, the allocation of resources, the reinvestment of the social product, and the harmonization of relations between regions at all levels, including the international. But this we leave for the future, confident that those who have won through to an ecosocialist world will have the strength and wisdom to solve its problems. As ever, the key lies in the degree to which democracy, now realized as freely associated labor, has become a living presence in society, which it imbues with the intrinsic value owed to nature and its wayward human children.

Ecosocialism

Afterword

A book that makes as many claims as *The Enemy of Nature* deserves rounding off with an Afterword. But I must confess I found this no easy task. Over and over again I would begin writing this section, then leave off, unsatisfied. The problem was one of tone, finding the proper register to finish off so weighty a subject without seeming heavy. Yet the heaviness would keep returning, until in frustration I thought of dropping the whole passage.

I then recalled something a student had once asked, to the effect of how one could keep from despairing while studying such awful things as the ecological crisis and the ghastly power held by capital over our existence. I had said something perfunctory at the time, but the question continued to flit in and out of my mind, and, as it did, took on a somewhat different value. For the fact was, I did not despair; for whatever reason, I actually found myself in good spirits as I studied the crisis further and devised the ideas that have gone into this work. It didn't make sense at first, given how dreadful is the predicament in which we find ourselves – but there did seem to be a logic to it. And then I thought back to the opening sentence of my Preface, in which I had written of people becoming frozen in their tracks by the dawning realization of capital's radical ecodestructiveness, and it occurred to me that the best tack which my Afterword could take would be to address this dilemma, and try to show in however halting a way that there were grounds for actually being of good cheer within the perspective argued here.

The thesis that drives this work, that capital is both eco-destructive and unreformable, is either true or false. If it is false, then I have been wrong and the apologists for capital right. But their correctness would require a great sea-change in capital, a historic adaptation and overcoming of all its evil tendencies.

This will be great and good news. For capital will now, having overcome its ecological ordeal, be a better system entirely. It will stand forth not as the enemy, but as nature's friend. Capable of regulating itself, it will be a true friend to humanity as well. The rising tide will lift all boats, and poverty, exploitation and oppression will be things belonging to the dim prehistory of our species. We will have entered a truly golden age.

So there will be plenty to cheer about if *The Enemy of Nature* turns out to be wrong. But what if I am right, and the choice is either to end capital's reign or face the destruction of our world? Now things seem to be grimmer and more complicated as we turn to face our enemy. But is this really so? What has been proposed here is a line of reasoning to help us come to grips with a great crisis. Whether or not one adopts it – whether or not this book was written in the first place – capital's ecodestruction will take place. All that has been striven for here is to face things squarely – to alter the perception of an impending disaster, to meet it actively instead of passively submitting to the terms of understanding dealt out by the dominant system. And surely it is better to actively comprehend rather than numbly submit to the logic of one's destroyer. Is it not liberating to realize that the mighty capitalist system is at heart a trick played upon us? The delegitimation of its principle of exchange, the revelation of how human possibilities are stunted under its regime – all this opens a path to the intrinsic beauty of the world and lets us join with others of like mind.

If capital is a delusion, then private ownership of the globe is part of that delusion. And once we realize as much, the principle of usufruct will come to apply. Now this tells us to improve and enjoy that which is another's, though it happens to be our home. Why should we wait until after the revolution before doing so? Indeed, the revolution has already begun once this is appreciated – and if the principle of usufruct tells us that we should enjoy the earth, should we not also enjoy freeing the earth from bondage?

The great themes of the ecological crisis do not alter our existential position, which remains framed by the fact that each of us is allotted a limited time on the earth and, within it, the opportunity of living as best we can. But it does shape what that best might be, and here, it seems, the great virtue of addressing the crisis appears. For what other generation has been given the change to transform the relationship between humanity and nature, and to heal so ancient a wound? What a fantastic challenge! All creatures must end, and all species. Even the earth, and time and space will vanish. But our creatural destiny is to have a degree of choice over our end. We should not allow the exit to occur under the cold, cruel hand of capital; it is an ending unworthy of the beauty of the world.

> All Human Forms identified even Tree Metal Earth & Stone; all
> Human Forms identified, living going forth & returning wearied
> Into the Planetary lives of Years Months Days & Hours reposing
> And then Awakening into his Bosom in the Life of Immortality.

(William Blake, *Jerusalem*)

Notes

1 Introduction

1 Meadows et al. 1972.

2 Much of this is taken from Donella Meadows, "Earth Day Plus Thirty, As Seen by the Earth," distributed on the internet. Meadows, tragically recently deceased, is also a co-author of Meadows et al. 1992, a follow-up study to *The Limits to Growth* (Meadows et al. 1972) which argued hopefully – but mistakenly – that, of all the major environmental crises, ozone depletion is the only one for which concerted international effort has been successful. In 2006 Al Gore made a similar claim about the wonderful power of collective state effort to bring about ozone reduction in his *An Inconvenient Truth* (Gore 2006); however, in October of that year NASA reported that the Antarctic hole was the biggest ever, covering 11 million square miles. This is best accounted for by the runaway effects of global production overriding the prudence of regulation.

3 Personal communication, Daniel Faber. This is the highest for the ten-year period during which such measurements have been taken (these being, according to Faber, almost certainly too low, as the information is based on voluntary reports by corporations).

4 The footprint "measures humanity's demand on the biosphere in terms of the area of biologically productive land and sea required to provide the resources we use and to absorb our waste." To the extent this is positive, so is civilization (or any given country, or even person) "unsustainable," that is, using up the planet faster than the planet can regenerate. It became positive in the early 1980s – consistent with the argument here that sees the 1970s as the turning point of the crisis – and has increased every measurement since. Currently (last calculated, 2003) the figure is 25 percent as against 21 percent in 2001. Another way of looking at this is that it takes fifteen months for the earth to regenerate a year's usage. (WWF 2006). Needless to say, all of these kind of calculations are methodologically problematic. What emerges is not any particular figure, rather, a compellingly ominous tendency, no matter how one looks at them.

5 Slater 2007. Recall that the 1990 value of goods and services, i.e., economic product, was $39 trillion. Actually this figure stagnated in the 1990s, thanks to the collapse of the Soviet bloc. With Russia now flexing its oil wealth (thereby increasing the rate of

disaster), the global product began climbing precipitously again in the new millennium.

6 Meadows et al. 1992. The authors – no Marxists – conclude rather grimly: "[there is] a self-limiting constraint on population. Population will eventually level off, if industrial output per capita rises high enough. But the model contains no self-limiting constraint on capital. We see little 'real-world' evidence that the richest people or nations have lost interest in getting richer. Therefore we have assumed that capital-owners will continue to try to multiply their wealth idefinitely and that consumers will continue to be willing to increase their consumption" (118).

2 The ecological crisis

1 Brown 1999. See Wisner et al. 2005 for a comprehensive study of the interrelations between the various factors.

2 In the time framework of concern for present survival, or "sustainability." So long as we have green plants, eventually the excess carbon put into the atmosphere will find its way back into some kind of combustible form, but that event is many thousands of years away, and, in any case, long after the present ecological crisis will have played itself out.

3 A very considerable degree of influence, it must be said. Among the innumerable effects of global warming is an alteration of the range of disease vectors. Thus mosquitoes, and with them malaria, for example, are found higher on mountainsides. "All ecological disruptions [...] tip the balance between people and microbes in favor of microbes" (Platt 1996). See also Mihill 1996.

4 The beginnings as well as the ends of historical events are as a general rule impossible to pin down. Iraq – ancient Mesopotamia, or the Land Between the Two Rivers – is the present site of the most ancient civilization, and the first to undergo ecocatastrophe (the salination of irrigation systems in the second millennium BCE; see Ponting 1991), as well as the latest, thanks to the United States. After a long eclipse under the Ottoman Empire, Iraq had to endure, then overthrow, British colonialism after the First World War. During the reign of the bloodthirsty dictator Saddam Hussein, Iraq became a client state of the United States, which promoted his use of "weapons of mass destruction" against the Iranian revolution in a horrendous war. The United States turned against Saddam once his usefulness was over, and after he attacked Kuwait to try to recoup his wealth, set out to destroy him. This initiated American violence against Iraq in a war of genocidal and ecocidal proportions that has unfolded in three phases: that of the First Gulf War in 1991, the epoch of sanctions lasting until 2003, and the invasion since March of that year. The history

of Iraq since 1919 is unthinkable unless we take into account its huge petroleum reserves, second largest in the world and the easiest to extract.

5 Within the limits of this work, I can only offer the following in support of this argument: As to the basic decision about energy supplies, Vice-President Cheney, strategic director of the second Bush administration, set the theme as far back as 1999, when he was CEO of Halliburton. As the London *Independent* noted (January 7, 2007): "'Where is the oil going to come from to slake the world's ever-growing thirst?', asked Cheney, who then answered his own question: 'The Middle East, with two-thirds of the world's oil and the lowest cost, is still where the prize ultimately lies.'" This line of approach was continued directly into the Energy Task Force Cheney organized as soon as he took over the state after the theft of the 2000 election. Comprised almost entirely of "oiloligarchs," many from the criminal energy corporation, Enron, the Task Force issued its report in the spring of 2001, Cheney concluding that oil supplies were going to be flat over the next period no matter what the United States did (i.e., he accepted the reality of Peak Oil), whereas demand for hydrocarbon fuel necessarily had to keep rising – the necessity being that of the basic logic of capital (see Chapters 3 and 4). Hence the United States was going to have to become more

aggressive in securing energy supplies in the period ahead. See Kovel 2001b.

The invasion of Iraq was the main result, perhaps along with, as many have speculated, the deliberate exploitation of 9/11 as the "new Pearl Harbor" to legitimate the whole upsurge of pre-emptive aggression and the descent toward fascism. It is important to understand both the continuities and the degree of rupture with previous policy. The motion toward gangsterism and naked aggression was not uncontested within ruling circles. The big oil corporations did not go along with the reckless invasion, the economic apparatus of capital being more cautious than its militarized state. And there were serious disagreements with previous administrations, notably that of G. W. Bush's father. These have persisted right through the issuance in late 2006 of the Baker–Hamilton report, James Baker being Bush Sr's chief adviser. As we know, this was flatly rejected by the younger Bush. What turned the day toward the Bush Jr–Cheney cabal also had a lot to do with the recruitment of a group of intellectuals, the so-called Neoconservatives, highly Zionist and closely integrated with the State of Israel; these assumed a degree of control of state policy unprecedented in American history, and became the actual architects of the Iraq war. For a discussion, see Kovel 2007: Ch. 6. The actual depredation of Iraq and associated ecological costs are covered in Kovel 2005.

6 A particularly fine (and free) study is Lohmann 2006. As for the influential study by Al Gore, *An Inconvenient Truth* (2006), see Chapter 8 for discussion.

7 A definition of which might read: the inability to predict the end state of a system from its initial state.

8 As Bob Herbert wrote in the *New York Times* (January 15, 2007): "The police department here is a sour joke, and crime is out of control. More than 16 months after the storm, children roam the street with impunity during school hours. Debris still covers most of the city. Doctors, hospitals and mental health facilties are in woefully short supply. Thousands of residents are still living in trailers, and many more are stuck more or less permanently out of town."

9 Compare with the record of Cuba against hurricane damage (Levins 2005a and 2005b).

10 The ethnic cleansing is more than a direct result of the storm. In addition to the many thousands displaced by floods and still dispossessed, the catastrophe set into motion a complex chain of events between private developers and the various arms of government, including the mainly black government of the city. Thus the storm became the occasion for unleashing powers of private acquisition. As of late January 2007, 4,534 basically sound units of housing affordable to the poor are imminently slated for demolition, to be replaced by "luxury condominiums." In addition, privatization has seized the beleaguered educational and health systems of the city. See Quigly 2007.

11 See Davis 2006 for a study of how festering megacities are becoming the prime sites of ecological breakdown across the planet.

12 Earth is undergoing the greatest loss of species since the ending of the era of dinosaurs 70 million years ago. The rate, some ten thousand times the normal over recent millennia, is slated to double again by mid-century, chiefly driven by habitat destruction, though direct killing and pollution also play a role.

13 By fascist here we mean the mobilization of an authoritarian state ever more closely integrated with its corporate sector, and guided by archaic, mythic, and racist ideologies. See Chapter 8, where it will be argued that this is both highly likely and destined to worsen the crisis.

14 Even the more sober capitalists realize this. I have heard twice, in 2000, and again in 2006, predictions from the insurance industry – the one fraction of capital with the most to lose in the crisis – a prediction that by the year 2065, rising insurance claims will exceed the growth of the economy, thus bringing down the show.

3 Capital

1 Estimated deaths range from 2,000 to 20,000. This figure is drawn from Kurzman 1987: 130–3. For further summaries of evidence, see Montague 1996; also the website: www.corporatewatch.org/bhopal/.

2 Hanna 2006 et al. has the most recent summary of the damages and the resistance.

3 From Montague 1996: "After all the lawyers and Indian government officials had taken their fees and bribes, the average claimant received about $300, which, for most victims, was not enough to pay their medical bills."

4 The notion derives from Aristotle's *Metaphysics*, where the efficient cause is one of four elemental causes, the others being the formal essence (in Plato's meaning) of a thing, the ultimate material nature of that thing, and thirdly, the final cause, or goal, toward which a thing is headed. The efficient cause is, by contrast, the source of a thing's motion, which may or may not be external to the thing in question. Much of this exceedingly difficult text (actually a series of lecture notes) is given over to critique of Plato and other philosophers for not taking the efficient cause into account (Aristotle 1947: 238–96).

5 This passage, and most of the evidence in this section is drawn from Kurzman 1987. Kurzman, it may be added, approached his work as a journalist with no ax to grind, as revealed in a number of sympathetic passages about Carbide's executive leadership. However, the next item is taken from testimony given at the end of 1999, in the ongoing civil action suits in India.

6 Kurzman 1987: 25.

7 Montague 1996, citing Lepkowski 1994.

8 Shiva 1991. A great many people now reject the view of Carbide as to the merits of this transformation, which among other things has driven many rural Indians to choose pesticides as a means of suicide, usually because of their intolerable debts.

9 Morehouse 1993: 487. Quoted in Montague 1996.

10 These terms appear on the first page of Volume I of Marx's *Capital*, an indication of how important he thought them.

11 Drawn together in O'Connor 1998. The "First Contradiction" is that of the classical "realization crisis," where cutting workers' wages makes it more difficult for them to purchase the commodities they produce.

12 Marx 1973: 334. Martin Nicolaus, translator and editor, draws a conection between this passage and Hegel's *Science of Logic* (Hegel 1969).

13 Marx 1973: 335, italics in text.

14 In the first cycle, the simple circulation of commodities, C is a commodity sold for a given sum of money, M, which is then exchanged for another commodity of equivalent value, C'. In the

second cycle, which is of capital, a sum of money, M, is advanced into circulation to pay for a commodity, C, which is then sold for a different sum of money, M'. If M' is greater than M, the prime desideratum of the capitalist, we have M'–M, or ∆M, as the "surplus value." Marx uses the term, "value," as synonymous with exchange-value.

15 *Capital*, Vol. I (Marx 1967a: 252–3).

16 In an end-of-the-millennium survey by the BBC of who was the greatest man of the last 1,000 years, the Secretary General offered Adam Smith as his first choice. Can we imagine Dag Hammerskjold or U Thant doing the same? Annan, whose behavior during the Rwandan genocide should have at least gotten him sacked, was instead rewarded for his unquestioning loyalty to transnational capital. Happily, the British people voted Karl Marx the honor.

17 Courtesy of José Tapia, economist, University of Michigan, "More Inconvenient Truths. Tapia. Pdf."

18 Personal communication, José Tapia.

19 Here is the latest in a long series of shenanigans. The American Enterprise Institute, heavily funded and controlled by Exxon Mobil, has offered cash bribes and other emoluments to climate scientists to counter the unceasing findings of global climate agencies that sound the alarm about warming (Sample 2007).

20 Lohmann 2006 best summarizes the issues. For particular studies, see Bachram 2004 and Isla 2007. The ecocatastrophe is even to be celebrated by those whose life is oriented toward accumulation. In France, for example, the terrible storms of 1999 not only turned out to have little macroeconomic impact; they were said to be, according to Denis Kessler, president of the French Insurance Companies' Federation, "a rather good thing for GDP." This is because the damages caused by such events for a highly developed country are relatively low – no shanty-towns in France, plenty of emergency equipment, etc. – and exceeded in monetary value by the funds spent on repairs, which tends to renovate damaged property in a more modern manner. As Hervé Kempf commented: "It looks as though the world's economic decision-makers have decided to do nothing about climate change on the basis that if no change happens, we shall take advantage of a form of growth that continues to intensify the greenhouse effect; and if it does happen, we shall be able to protect ourselves from it – and it may even have a favourable effect on the global economy." Describing the loss in Hurricane Mitch of 20,000 people who perished because their shacks were hastily assembled on hillsides and in the path of mudslides, Kempf went on to say: "Venezuela's flood victims counted for little economically in

so far as the country's oil output remained unaffected" (Kempf 2000: 30).

4 Capitalism

1 Slatella 2000: D4.

2 The term derives from the phenomenological philosopher Edmund Husserl.

3 The elective was under the auspices of the Tropical Medicine faculty at Columbia University's medical school, which had formed a liaison with the Aluminum Company of America, proprietors of a large bauxite mine in the small town of Moengo. Suriname lies roughly 5° N of the Equator, and presents an essentially Amazonian ecology, with rivers discharging into the Caribbean Sea. In the remoter jungles lived a dwindling group of Caribe Indians, while closer to the sea, though still in dense rain forest, dwelt the "Bush-Negroes," descendants of escaped African slaves. It is to these latter that the observations apply.

4 See Kovel 1997a. McDonald's has formed marketing linkages with Coca-Cola, as well as other icons of globalized capitalist culture, such as the Olympic games.

5 Watson 1997; Jenkins 1997; Fiddes 1991.

6 Crossette 2000a; Gardner and Halweil 2000. According to Worldwatch, 1.2 billion are now overweight, matching the number of starving people. Another 2 billion comprise the "hidden hungry," with bad diets. Four hundred thousand liposuctions were performed in the United States in 1999, and 80 percent of malnourished children lived in countries that reported food surpluses. The situation since the first edition of this work has continued to worsen, to the point where childhood obesity, with its predisposition toward diabetes and many other health problems, has become a scandal.

7 Crossette 2000b. The UNICEF report is the first comprehensive survey of the phenomenon, and details violence, worst for the poorest, at every aspect of the life-cycle, from aborted female fetuses, the killing of female babies, underfeeding of girl children, lack of medical care, sexual abuse, and fatal beatings of grown women. This pervasive violence, which beyond doubt represents a major increase from the level of traditional society, comes from those closest to the violated women, and reflects the general breakup of intimate life in a world whose communal structure is destabilized by capital's penetration, and closely related manifestations like massive immigration. By contrast, in traditional societies, for example, those of the North American Indians, rape and the abuse of women were among the most severely punished and rarest of crimes. This was one reason why many settler women in the American colonies "defected" to the Indians.

8 Public Citizen 1996.

9 Engels 1987; Bowden 1996.

Bowden's extraordinary account focuses on the subculture of photographers and TV journalists who document the madness.

10 Nathan 1997.

11 Ordonez 2000.

12 "Nano" refers to the contraction of machines to the level of individual molecules, the word referring to 1/1000 of a "micron," i.e. a millionth of a millimeter, the scale of molecular processes. See Drexler 1986. Although the later phase of a technology may replace an earlier one, as the electronic calculator makes the mechanical slide rule obsolete, the overall effect is additive and combinative. Thus gigantic jet planes incorporate electronic technology without ceasing to be huge; or computers guide the development of molecular-scale technologies, then become incorporated into such technologies.

13 DeBord 1992.

14 Thompson 1967; White 1967.

15 Marx 1963: 41.

16 Kanter 1997, A22. The author, a professor of management at Harvard Business School, accurately observes that despite the then success of the economy, an "undercurrent of cynicism (along with fatigue from increased workloads)" is rife – in fact, 46 percent of employees of 1,000 large corporations feared layoffs in 1997 as compared with 31 percent in 1992. Meanwhile, the remaining workers suffer from yet another mental illness, "layoff survivor sickness," characterized by anger, depression, fear, guilt, risk aversion, distrust, vulnerability, powerlessness, and loss of motivation – accompanied by an increase in stress-related claims. This occurred in an economy widely deemed "as good as it gets."

17 Bass 2000. The only level of conflict reported in the article, based upon research done at Penn State University, was that the behavior stimulated sexual harassment by male customers, who mistook the robotic friendliness for a come-on. Otherwise internalization was quite successful. Note the mutilation of the Golden Rule: the worker wants to treat everybody as she herself is treated. So she treats them as a means to the end of accumulation, just as she is treated. But the only coherent interpretation of the moral law, as Kant realized, is to treat persons as ends in themselves, not as means, or things.

18 See Rogers 2005, for a discussion of garbage as such, the massive production of which is unique to a capitalism that lives to expand and turn over commodities at ever greater rates.

19 Williams 2000.

20 Harvey 1993.

21 The term is from Freund and Martin 1993.

22 Purdom 2000.

23 As bad as the situation in the United States may be, it is dwarfed by the traffic-generated nightmares of cities in the "newly industrializing countries." In

NICs, an even more unregulated capital induces scenarios like that in São Paulo, Brazil, where the rich have taken to using helicopters to avoid roads "hopelessly clogged with traffic" and subject to the "carjackings, kidnappings of executives and roadside robberies [that] have become part of the risks of everyday life for anyone perceived to have money." However hard it may be to enter the Kingdom of Heaven, it is easier for a rich man to buy a helicopter than for a poor man to buy a car in São Paulo – nor is parking much of a problem, as the gated communities where many rich people reside offer ideal settings for landing pads. The noisy monsters have predictably become status symbols ("Why settle for an armored BMW when you can afford a helicopter?" goes one slogan), as some 400 flit through the air and create an even more nightmarish environment for the average citizen (Romero 2000). Gated communities, with private police forces and the like, are a major accompaniment of the ecological crisis as it affects urban space in the age of automobilia. I recall reading that in the United States, nearly 30 percent live in such fragmenting enclaves.

24 Wald 1997; Turner 2000.

25 See the discussion in Chapter 1, where this point was raised.

26 Peet 2003 provides a useful summary.

27 The World Bank, set up along with the IMF at the 1944 Bretton Woods conference, was originally designed to help with postwar European reconstruction. It then shifted to the Third World, made major infrastructural loans (which included financing the plant at Bhopal) and became increasingly involved with "adjustment" of peripheral economies in order to integrate them better with the needs of global capital. The IMF, by contrast, was originally set up to maintain the standard of fixed interest rates established after the war. After 1971, when these rates began to float, it turned to making loans to troubled economies and clearing them for further capital investment by the Bank, hence, its involvement with the notorious Structural Adjustment Programs. As for the WTO, it emerged finally from its chrysalis in 1995 after its predecessor, the General Agreement on Trade and Tariffs, finished its preliminary organizing. There are, of course, many other facets to this machine, including the G8 summit of great economic powers, a host of special banks, UN participation, and so forth, but they needn't be taken up here.

28 The follies of the second Bush administration may be signalling a reorganization away from American hegemony. This is certainly a momentous change, but, with global capital up and running, does not alter the basic argument; however, it will pose many political challenges and opportunities.

29 George 1992.

30 Murphy 2000.

31 Pooley 2000, an article focusing on the case of Tanzania.

32 Stiglitz 2000, in which we find: "The IMF staff [...] frequently consists of third-rank students from first-rate universities. (Trust me: I've taught at Oxford University, MIT, Stanford University, Yale University, and Princeton University, and the IMF almost never succeeded in recruiting any of the best students.)" So that's what we need – as they put it in the Vietnam era, the "best and the brightest."

33 Bond 2004.

34 Kovel 2005.

35 Barlow 2000; Peet 2003.

36 De Brie estimates about one-third to one-half of this in drugs, the rest divided between computer piracy, counterfeiting, budgetary fraud, animal smuggling, white slaving, etc. In other words, a good estimate of simply the trans-border crime amounts to some 20 percent of world trade. Allowing that only half of that ends up as profit, and that a third of this is lost in money-laundering operations, the net realized annual profit from international crime stands at some $350 billion (de Brie 2000). See also, Bergman 2000.

37 *Multinational Monitor*, June 1997, p. 6. Summers's now-infamous remarks were made in an internal World Bank memo in 1991, when he was an underling economist for that institution.

The outrage was such that he became Secretary of the Treasury and President of Harvard – from which he was fired in 2005 for sexist remarks. Wolfensohn was responding to suggestions that the World Bank write off the debts owed to it by developing countries. Skilling was sentenced to twenty-four years and four months in a federal prison on October 23, 2006, for his role in the Enron fraud case. He was CEO of Enron from February to August 2001, thus almost certainly playing a major role in Dick Cheney's energy task force that laid out the scenario for United States hegemony over global energy supplies, including, to be sure, the invasion of Iraq.

38 Dobrzynski 1997.

39 Deogun 1997. Alas, poor Ivester, his dreams came to nought, and he was eventually sacked for not delivering on them.

40 Some works I have found valuable in tracking the various concrete forms taken by the crisis are: Athanasiou 1996; Karliner 1997; Beder 1997; Tokar 1997; Steingraber 1997; Fagin and Lavelle 1996; Colburn et al. 1996; Pring and Canan 1996; Rampton and Stauber 1997; Lappé et al. 1998; Shiva 1991; Gelbspan 1998; Gibbs, 1995; Ho 1998; Thornton 2000. More, of course, are being written all the time, especially about global warming and the energy crisis. These have been cited in their place.

5 On ecologies

1 See, for example, Goudie 1991. Alongside the manifest and immediate effects are others more pervasive and subtle, such as the spread of substances on currents of air and water to every spot on the earth. Thus, polar bears turn out to have huge concentrations – in fact, the highest anywhere – of pesticide residues sprayed thousands of miles away. Of course, we should keep a sense of proportion: only an infinitesimal portion of the substance of the universe has been altered by human activity. It's just that this speck of dust happens to define our existence.

2 The best single account of the history of ecological thought is Worster 1994.

3 As in Bateson 1972.

4 See, for example, Christian de Duve 1995. Working within an entirely materialist frame of reference, de Duve, a Nobel Laureate, insists that because of the large number of linked successive steps necessary for the emergence of life, this could not have been a freak or random event, rather, "the universe was – and presumably still is – pregnant with life" (9). See also Fortey 1997. Where de Duve builds from the atomic level to the ever-growing complexification of living form, Fortey presents a panoramic view of the whole march of evolution.

5 According to Paul Davies, we have some 10^{100} years to wait for this, a comfortable interval (Davies 1983). The relatively imminent cosmological catastrophe, which will surely wipe out the earth itself whether or not humans are still on it, is the scheduled turning of the sun into a red-giant star, whose dimensions will reach the orbit of this planet in a mere 5 billion (5×10^9) years – roughly the time the earth has been in existence. So we are halfway there.

6 As for the Second Law, the mathematical physicist Roger Penrose raises the question of its cosmological relationships in an extremely interesting contribution. The entropy principle defines time's arrow – i.e. it determines whether t or t' is the later for any closed system according to which one corresponds to greater entropy for that system. Penrose asks how this can be more than a circular definition, in which entropy increases with time, while time's arrow is defined as that direction in which entropy increases. "Something," he wonders, "*forced* the entropy to be low in the past [... W]e should not be surprised if, *given* a low-entropy state, the entropy turns out to be higher at a later time. What *should* surprise us is that entropy gets more and more ridiculously tiny the farther and farther we examine it in the past!" Penrose observes that we take in low entropy food in order to sustain the low entropy necessary for life. But "[w]here does this supply of low entropy come from?" Ultimately, as we know, from photosynthesis, the foundational way that life on

earth struggles for existence. But this is to say, that we draw low entropy from the sun (whether we eat plants that bind solar energy into living form or other creatures who eat the plants). "Contrary to a common impression," continues Penrose, "the earth (together with inhabitants) does *not* gain energy from the sun! What the earth does is to take energy in a low entropy form and then spew it *all* back into space, but in a high-entropy form [radiant heat, i.e. infra-red photons, replacing higher frequency visible photons]." Thus there are few photons of high energy coming in and relatively more of lower energy going out – an increase in entropy. Now, this is because "the sun is a *hot-spot in the sky*," in which energy is concentrated, and this in turn is because of the "gravitational contraction from what had been a previously uniform distribution of gas (mainly hydrogen)." The sun, like any star, heats from this contraction until thermonuclear reactions set in and keep it from contracting further and hence burning itself out. It follows that gravity is the ultimate source of the sun's energy – and through it, life on earth (and, to be sure, fossil fuels). Indeed, gravity is the ultimate cause of nuclear energy as well, the heavier isotopes of uranium, etc., arising in the gravi-tationally compressed interior of neutron stars – and of course it is the direct source of geothermal energy along with the energy of tides, the two other energy vari-ants of relevance to life on earth. Deep-sea hot vents are loci of forms of life not dependent upon photosynthesis, and, in certain views, may have been the cradle of life on earth. Tides, of course, are an active component of many important ecosystems, especially coral reefs. In sum, gravitational clumping determines the Second Law, through the initial spreading out of matter and energy through all space in the "Big Bang," and its secondary coming together through gravity. (In contrast to a thermally driven system, where uniformity is equivalent to higher entropy, a gravitation-ally driven system is at its most ordered, least probable state when uniform; hence the appearance of form as such may be more properly assigned to that phase of the development of nature in which non-gravitational modes of energy engage and interact with gravitational modes.) At this point the argument passes into the uncertainties of quantum gravity and ceases to be relevant to the present work. The point to be em-phasized is the ultimate linkage between cosmological forces and the great regulatory principles of life and terrestrial ecosystems, i.e. the fundamental unity of nature (Penrose 1990: 410–17, ch. 7 *pas-sim*; italics in original).

7 Fortey 1997: 65. Fortey points out that the great variety of strom-atolite forms which evolved over the next billion years, including

reefs, are essentially one creature extending hundreds of miles. The arrival of animals destabilized the stromatolitic mats, which had prepared the way for more complex forms by creating atmospheric oxygen. Now they only endure in special environments where nobody is there to eat them. The evolutionary biologist Lynn Margulis follows a similar, though much more daring, line of thought in her "endosymbiosis" theory. See Margulis 1998.

8 We set aside the question of the formal organization of cosmological nature. Here the levels of energy and the form taken by matter are so remote from that occurring on earth that the notion of ecology makes little sense. The term, after all, derives from the Greek *oikos*, or home. Strictly speaking, we would have to substitute another term for the "ecosystemic" extension into the cosmos.

9 The classic text is Schrödinger 1967. First written in 1944, before the discoveries of molecular biology, this is one of those inspired leaps that shows the power of a good theory to look ahead.

10 Lovelock 1979.

11 "Opposition unites. From what draws apart results the most beautiful harmony. All things take place by strife" (Fragment 46 in Nahm 1947: 91). Edward Hussey writes of Heraclitus: "the perpetual struggle of opposites and the justice that balances them

are indistinguishable and both equally present in every event" (Hussey 1972: 49). Within contemporary biology, heated debate occurs about the question of equilibrium and struggle. Chaos theory captures something of this flux, with its doctrine of "strange attractors," non-linear processes, and the capabilities of butterfly wings to set off typhoons. As the *Oxford Dictionary* puts it: "scientifically, chaos denotes the behavior of a system which is governed by deterministic laws but is so unpredictable so as to appear random, owing to its extreme sensitivity to initial conditions." Glieck 1987 provides a popular introduction. Botkin 1990 presents the impact of this on ecology as such. Missing from these theories are notions of dialectics, as developed below, in the next chapter, and in particular, a coherent relation to human ecologies. I am generally in support of the position argued by Richard Levins and Richard Lewontin (1985), especially the essay, "Evolution as Theory and Ideology" (9–64). Both the notion of progress and that of equilibrium are taken to task by these distinguished biologists.

12 See my *White Racism* (Kovel 1984), for a discussion of how the biologization of race-as-pseudospecies has come about, particularly with regard to white-over-black racism. These days, racial essentialism is still prevalent as a discourse, only now, well-rewarded savants write

long, thickly researched tomes in which the "Black Problem" is located in a cultural, rather than a biological, framework. But an essence by any name remains a reification frozen out of historical time. See, for example, Herrnstein and Murray 1996; Thernstrom and Thernstrom 1997.

13 To add a bit to this highly compressed account: the enlarged brain and upright posture necessary for freeing the hands comprise a kind of evolutionary contradiction, for the latter results in a rigid pelvis which has difficulty in allowing the former to be born. This was solved by allowing the brain to be born immature and having it undergo a considerable amount of development *ex utero*. This plays a central role in the replacement of instinct with cultural learning, and also in the peculiar importance of childhood to human beings. The need for protracted child care, in a slowly maturing creature who has to be carried about for a long time owing to the loss of clinging instincts (which persist only in vestigial form, as in the Babinski sign known to neonatologists) has had incalculable influence on our cultural inheritance, indeed, culture may be said to have arisen out of this conjuncture.

14 Hegel, Nietzsche, Freud, Lacan, and others – all matters beyond present scope – stand in the line of those who uncovered this relationship in Western thought; though it may also be said that the entirety of our spiritual traditions are built upon figuring it out.

15 A caveat: almost all of these points will be contested by those who point to the care given by elephants to their dead, or to the use of language by whales, and so forth. Lest there be misunderstanding, let me emphasize that species-chauvinism is not my intent. To establish an ensemble of human–natural traits is not to locate these in any particular species, but to say, rather, that any species with the power to adopt them can arrive at the ambivalent position of humans. If my dog recognizes me, that gives him a degree of human being; just as severely demented people have lost that attribute. But there is a specific putting together of these things that is distinctively human, and which other, perhaps more sensible, creatures do not share.

16 The architect, in contrast to the bee, "raises his structure in imagination before he erects it in reality. At the end of every labour-process, we get a result that already existed in the imagination of the labourer at its commencement" (Marx 1967a: 178).

17 For a discussion, see my *History and Spirit* (Kovel 1998b).

18 "Neither nature objectively nor nature subjectively is directly given in a form adequate to the *human* being. And as everything natural has to have its *beginning*, *man* too has his act of coming-to-be – *history* [...] History is the true natural history of man" (Marx

1978b: 116; italics in original).

19 For human society, this has been expressed in terms of sacrifice, with its many ramifications.

20 Quammen 1996.

21 Colburn 1996.

22 The brain-child of a Tasmanian, Bill Mollison, permaculture designs living environments using architectural principles and taking into account the whole range of global to local interrelations. In certain settings, e.g. South India, microclimatic changes have been induced that reverse generations of ecological degeneration. In others, substantial food production has been achieved in urban settings. See Mollison 1988. See also Whitefield 2004, as well as www.permaculture.co.uk/main2.html. It should be added that the permaculture movement evinces little awareness of the social issues raised in this study.

23 This discussion is principally drawn from Hecht and Cockburn 1990. Another important factor is the frequency of flooding that divides and in effect shuffles the landscapes. Thus there is no singular efficient cause here. As Hecht and Cockburn point out, people tended to follow the flooding and therefore to work synergistically with nature in the production of new areas for allopatric speciation.

24 Hecht and Cockburn 1990: 44. Timing is essential, as is planting before the blaze so that agricultural succession begins immediately after the fire,

followed by crops of other cyclical variety, so that a rich and complex ecosystem is rapidly restored. Proper attention is also paid to recycling ashes, etc., as well as the techniques of "cool burning," which controls pests but allows desired plants to flourish.

25 The ethnobotanist William Balée has shown that the Ka'apor Indians of northeast Brazil were able to name and use 94 percent of the plant species in a sample area of 2.5 acres. This is extreme. But most forest populations (not just aboriginal Indians) know and use about 50 percent of the plant species. Cited in Hecht and Cockburn 1990: 59.

26 Two authors who both explored and celebrated these ways: Stanley Diamond (Diamond 1974), and Pierre Clastres (Clastres 1977).

6 Capital and the domination of nature

1 In *Capital*, Marx (1967) makes clear how technology and the industrial mode of organization are necessities for maximizing surplus-value extraction, the *sine qua non* of the production of capital. At this point we need also to anticipate the commonly made point in support of the thesis that industrialization is to blame, namely, that it was during the regime of the USSR, hell-bent on industrialization presumably in opposition to capitalism, that an immense amount of ecological havoc was wrought. I deal with this question in Chapter 9, below.

2 This is not to assert the doctrine of European exceptionalism, which has been thoroughly debunked by scholars such as James Blaut (1993) and Andre Gunder Frank (1998), who have decisively shown that there was no innate European genius that gave command over the capitalist world. However, there were cultural differences between Europe and other, more advanced nations, like China and India, at the dawn of the modern era; and it is a fair question to ask whether those differences, which prominently included Christianity, played a role, not in the superior virtue of the West, but in the development of its pathology, and with it, the pathology of capital.

3 DeLumeau (1990) documents bodily estrangement in compelling detail. For a view of Christianity that parallels many of the arguments taken here, see Ruether 1992.

4 Joseph Needham (1954) summarizes this in his titanic study of Chinese science. As for Calvinism and capitalism, we cannot take up this famous debate here. See, of course, Weber 1976; and Tawney 1998; as well as Leiss 1972; Glacken 1973.

5 The most compelling exposition of this theme so far as I know, and the one to which this account is the most indebted, is Mies 1998. See also Salleh 1997; and O'Brien 1981.

6 My best guide to this mode of being was Stanley Diamond (1974).

7 At present, roughly two-thirds of actual social production is carried out by females. This figure is also the best estimate for the actual productive efforts of women in archaic hunter-gatherer societies (Mies 1998).

8 As Mies (1998) emphasizes, this account is within the frame of classical Marxism, with its central role given to the exploitation of productive labor. At the same time it challenges Engels' understanding of the primacy of cause. In Engels' canonical view, social production develops, so-to-speak, in a gender-neutral way until a surplus is gathered, which then becomes expropriated through violence, leading to class and gender domination. However, it is more cogent to invoke the violent control of female productive labor as the original lesion. For Engels (1972), the seizure of property appears the result of innate aggression instead of an event that became historically generalized into domination through the development of systems of force. The implication is important, for if innate aggression is the motor behind the seizure of surplus, then the entire Marxist project is brought down, and one might as well adhere to Freud's account in *Civilization and Its Discontents* (1931).

9 The account given here condenses a wealth of psychoanalytic knowledge deriving from a core contradiction in male-dominated societies, viz: that the female dominated by the grown male was

once represented by his mother at an infantile moment in the life-cycle when he was utterly dependent and lacked all of those powers that came to be his stock in trade. It may be presumed in what follows that this nexus reverberates throughout the history of humankind, inscribed in the dialectics of desire. See Chodorow 1978; Kovel 1981; Benjamin 1988. Cf also the quatrain from Blake's "The Mental Traveller": "And if the Babe is born a Boy / He's given to a Woman Old / Who nails him down upon a rock / Catches his Shrieks in Cups of gold."

10 Notably, Islam stands outside this pattern. The Prophet Muhammad is unique in history for developing a universalizing religion and a state formation more or less simultaneously out of a tribal, pre-state configuration. The larger significance of this remains to be drawn for the current world conflict between the West and Islam. See Rodinson 1971.

11 For a discussion, see Kovel 1984.

12 Braudel 1997: 64.

13 For a good discussion of Marx's development of these ideas, see Rosdolsky 1977: 109–66.

14 From *pecus*, the Latin word for cattle, comes "pecuniary."

15 That is, I may value air because I need it to live, or I may not. Where air is concerned the brain stem disregards what the "I", or self, demands, and goes on breathing. However, there are innumerable instances wherein we live in refusal. Kierkegaard, Nietzsche, and Dostoevsky were much preoccupied with this conjuncture, which represents a breakdown of Hegelian rationalism as the nineteenth century increasingly exposed a civilization in crisis.

16 Simmel 1978: 60.

17 Daydreams have utility, which can be private or shared, as between friends. But they cannot join the economy until embedded in a material object. Even as such, they need not have exchange-value – as, for instance, in a gift economy, or where they are bartered for another concrete item, or where they are dreamt for personal satisfaction.

18 Simmel 1978: 259.

19 Murray 1978. Islamic society, by contrast (along with China, India and others), was well acquainted with the use of money, and was not overtaken by Europe in this respect until the Crusades. This striking backwardness of that area of the world which would come to dominate capitalism centuries later is a remarkable fact. One would speculate that money represented a kind of taboo, or forbidden desire, and that the overcoming of this inhibition released the powerful energies that have made Western capitalism specially malignant.

20 Arrighi 1994; Frank 1998.

21 Marx 1964: 67.

22 See Polanyi 1957. The theme was classically drawn by Rosa Luxemburg, *The Accumula-*

tion of Capital (1968), one of whose chief theses was that accumulation always required the destruction of precapitalist economies.

23 A restoration of the commons gained as a result of the revolution, 1911–20, and under savage attack under NAFTA.

24 Marx 1978b; Sheasby 1997.

25 Thompson 1967.

26 The witch craze was an assault on the female gender unmatched in the history of any other civilization. It was part of the suppression of "pagan," i.e. earth and female-centered religions that stood in the way of Christian patriarchy; and specifically to the driving out of female and naturopathic healers on behalf of an embryonic male-dominated medical establishment. See Ehrenreich and English 1974. As for Bacon, his rendering of science as an exercise of the phallus – indeed, as a kind of rape of mother-nature – is explored in Carolyn Merchant's pathbreaking *The Death of Nature* (1980). It is equally necessary to point out Bacon's paramount role in defining scientific progress as integral to capitalism – and also, because the two developments are but sides of the same coin, that he was, in Merchant's words, the "inspiration behind the Royal Society" of 1660, the first state-sponsored research institute (160). It was the state, then, that organized the scientific revolutions that gave birth to industrial capitalism, and did so profoundly within the terms of the gendered bifurcation of nature. Federici (2004) provides the definitive account of how gender domination and the rise of capitalism accompanied each other.

27 Slavery being an infamous feature of early capitalist development, continuing today, and in fact on the rise. But slavery fails to provide flexible labor markets and restricts the moment of consumption. Thus it cannot be generalized within capitalism, as is the case for wage labor.

28 Gare 1996.

29 For a discussion of the relations between spiritual/philosophical systems and historical structures that takes up the question of Nazism and Heidegger, see Kovel 1998b.

30 Heidegger 1977. All quotes in this section are from this text. See also, Zimmerman 1994.

31 Farias 1989.

32 As of 2007, the average American family spends 108 percent of its income each month.

33 Kovel 1998a.

34 Of modern Marxists, Raya Dunayevskaya was most faithful to the need for a philosophical moment in order to unify theory and praxis. Her great achievement was to reconnect Marx to Hegel's *Science of Logic* (1969). See Dunayevskaya 1973, 2000.

35 Derived from the famous work of Engels; see Engels 1940.

36 See, for example, Wilbur (2001), who assembles mystical writings of major twentieth-

century physicists; and Punter (1982), who details the remarkable dialectical prescience of William Blake.

37 The term, of course, has many psychological implications, most famously Freud's tripartite version of the psyche, in which the Ego's non-recognition of the "id," or the "it-ness" of the world, i.e. nature, was given the status of normalcy instead of being seen as a psychological reflex of capital. Here we see the Ego ontologically, from the standpoint of being and not the psyche. For discussion see Kovel 1981; 1998b; also Lichtman 1982; and Wolfenstein 1993.

38 O'Connor 1998: 183.

39 For example, in 1999, a fine year for capital, the amount of the 644 toxic chemicals tracked by the US EPA rose 5 percent over 1998, to 7.8 billion pounds.

40 This line of thought was developed by the Romanian-American economist Nicholas Georgescu-Roegen, who had the insight that *our whole economic life feeds on low entropy*." Georgescu-Roegen 1971: 277; italics in text. It therefore follows, though Georgescu-Roegen does not emphasize the point, that an out-of-control, expanding economy will hasten entropic decay.

8 *A critique of actually existing ecopolitics*

1 Gore 2000, Gore 2006.

2 It is doubtlessly relevant that Gore's family was heavily involved with Occidental Petroleum through a gift of Armand Hammer, and that for a while he had a zinc mine on one of his properties. But we can set this aside here, since if Gore really understood the import of his ecological vision, he could have overriden these influences while still maintaining a reasonably comfortable life.

3 Cockburn and St Clair 2000. Wolfe's remarks were made at a public lecture in 2000.

4 As this is being written, we learn that "Gore was speaking alongside Virgin Atlantic chief Richard Branson at the launch of the Virgin Earth Challenge, a 25-million-dollar science and techology prize to encourage a viable technology to remove greenhouse gases from the atmosphere" (AFP 2007).

5 A word about solid waste. There is no doubt that the crisis would be worse if we did nothing about garbage, just as it would be worse if lead were still in gasoline. But the crisis already factors in these palliations, which set certain rates of ecosystem decay, slowing it to the extent we now see without altering the dynamics an iota. In the case of waste management, the large corporations who run the show provide another source of accumulation, exploitation of labor, criminality, and concentration – and another kind of industrial setting, the recycling plant. "[M]ost of the recycling plants [that do New York City's work] are owned by big waste companies, and the few

that are not will probably wind up being absorbed," writes the *New York Times* in a recent report (Stewart 2000: B1). The workers are "a legion of low-paid workers, including a high percentage of immigrants," who do work that is "sometimes boring and sometimes dangerous," as a man from Senegal, who works endless hours so he can send money back to his family, put it. In fact, the plant seems a regular satanic mill, as the fantastic detritus of consumer society is moved on conveyer belts past the workers, who have to concentrate intently, and "all day ... grab and flip. The stuff is thrown into holes, where it falls into heaps," to be collected and resold on a very volatile market. But what good does it really do, besides making more money from exploited labor? "The dirty secret of recycling is the waste. A third of the trash dumped at the plant is not salvageable, and is hauled to private landfills" – where the environment is subjected to the unsavory mix. New York is, as can be imagined, the worst case, where only 2,400 tonnes of the 13,000 generated each and every day is recycled, 800 tonnes of which ends up in landfills anyway. But even the more ecologically sane cities only approach 50 percent recyclability, scarcely reassuring when one looks at the Wal-Marts, etc., springing up all over the landscape, spewing forth garbage-to-be. For a comprehensive recent study, see Rogers 2005.

6 Manning 1996 offers a paean to the New Energy movement. I would not want to rule out all of the energy fixes discussed with breathless enthusiasm by Manning, but I would not bet the future of civilization on them, either. One matter persistently begged by this kind of reasoning is the economics of gathering, storing, and distributing the energy. Yes, there may be "space energy," but how is one to collect it? No doubt, the energy of even a small black hole would suffice to keep us going to eternity, but that and a dollar will buy a copy of the *New York Times*.

7 A recent, horrific finding: the Associated Press reported on July 10, 2000, that the US Fish and Wildlife Service estimated that 40 million birds a year are killed by crashing into the 77,000 microwave transmission towers that dotted the American landscape at that time, with relentless pressure for more. So much for this "ecologically benign" technology (not to mention the effects of electromagnetic fields from transformers, cell phones, etc., recently suggested as possible causes of the alarming disappearance of honeybees).

8 For an excellent discussion of the environmental load of the information economy, see Huws 1999.

9 The same may be said for wind power, another form of solar energy and perhaps the most benign of the renewables, given the extensive chemical inputs for solar panels. But here, too, there is

a pronounced limit to the amount of the landscape that windmills take up in relation to the electricity they generate.

10 See Sarkar 1999: 93–139, for a thorough discussion of the material limits to growth. Sarkar may be overly pessimistic, but his reasoning remains fundamentally sound.

11 Lovins 1977. Lovins is perhaps the premier techno-enthusiast of our time.

12 Though they often have secure and desirable jobs, as in academia. But, then, so does the author of this work.

13 Costanza et al. 1997: 5. Of the work's five authors, Robert Costanza and John Cumberland are associated with the University of Maryland; Herman Daly (see below) and Robert Goodland have been connected with the World Bank; while the fifth, Richard Norgaard, is at UC Berkeley, and the author of *Development Betrayed* (1994), a work that approaches the crisis from the standpoint of a "coevolutionary" paradigm. A related approach with considerable historical depth, and closer to the perspective offered here, may be found in Martinez-Alier 1987.

14 Breyer 1979. This was published under the title of "Analyzing regulatory failure, mismatches, less restrictive alternatives and reform," in the *Harvard Law Review*. For a discussion, see Tokar 1997: 35–45.

15 In one of the earliest studies of the folly of carbon trading, Brian

Tokar hit the nail on the head, writing that Kyoto gave the "largest 'players' ... substantial control over the whole 'game'" (1997: 41). The marketing of pollution will drive down the cost of the credits and give incentive to cheating rather than reducing emissions. "There is little doubt," Tokar continues, "that an international market in 'pollution rights' would widen existing inequalities among nations and increase the dominance of those best able to shift their assets from country to country based on the daily fluctuation of financial markets ... the potential for unaccountable manipulation of industrial policy would easily compound the disruptions already caused by often reckless international traders in stocks, bonds and currencies" (42). The best and most comprehensive recent study, which takes up a number of sequestration schemes, is Lohmann 2006.

16 Korten 1996: 187. Another neo-Smithian is Paul Hawken, author of *The Ecology of Commerce* (1993). For my thoughts about Hawken, see Kovel 1999.

17 Korten 2000.

18 Schumacher's Buddhist view of labor includes that it must "give a man a chance to utilise and develop his faculties"; also that work not be separated from leisure, as the two are both sides of the living process. The emphasis is on work as an expression of life and the purification of character – actually rather close to Marx's

views, especially in the early philosophical writings and the theory of alienation. However, Schumacher gives no concrete understanding of class struggle, nor of agency in general, nor does he have a theory of capital as such, nor, it follows, of what it would take to get beyond capital. Schumacher 1973: 50–9.

19 Proudhon 1969; Kropotkin 1975.

20 Morrison 1995: 151. Italics in original.

21 Karl Marx, "Inaugural Address of the Working Men's International Association" (Marx 1978d: 1864). It is worth noting that Marx wrote in a letter to Engels at the time that the speech was difficult to "frame ... so that our view should appear in a form acceptable from the present standpoint of the workers' movement" (512), an acknowledgment that revolutionary hopes had waned from 1848, when the more militant *Communist Manifesto* was written.

22 HMOs, or Health Maintenance Organizations, refer to a great variety of prepaid health plans that originated early in the twentieth century in the USA as an alternative to private insurance, on the one hand, and state-sponsored health care, on the other. These have become increasingly bloated and powerful as the American health crisis has developed, though ostensibly they can be organized cooperatively.

23 Marx 1967b: 440. The closest exception is the Mondragon system of cooperatives of northern Spain, perhaps the greatest success of the movement – though it is fair to say that, given the system constraints to which it is exposed, Mondragon has probably reached its limits, without in any way threatening the overall capitalist regime (Morrison 1991).

24 Mintz 1995.

25 "Smith's solution could not survive the changed circumstances of the transition to industrial capitalism" (McNally 1993: 46).

26 Costanza et al. 1997: 177, 180. The authors also mangle their representation of Marx, limiting his contribution to the ownership and allocation of physical resources, and blaming the "labor theory of value that neglected nature's contributions" for the ecological devastation wrought by communist societies. It is hard to imagine a grosser distortion.

27 In Daly and Cobb 1994, the following appears, after a statement of respect for academic standards: "But at a deeper level of our being we find it hard to suppress the cry of anguish, the scream of horror – the wild words required to express wild realities. We human beings are being led to a *dead* end – all too literally. We are living by an ideology of death and accordingly we are destroying our own humanity and killing the planet" (21).

28 Daly 1991.

29 Daly 1996: 39.

30 Daly and Cobb 1994: 299, 370. Italics added.

31 Elementary reflection will tell us that as humans are born radically undeveloped, they need to be cared for in order to survive. And for this the affect of love is biologically necessary. Who would care for her or his children if they were not loved? And being loved, children learn to love: it is very much consonant with "nature."

32 Stille 2000. See also Cronon 1996; Hecht and Cockburn 1990: 269–76 has a discussion of the expulsions from Yosemite.

33 Naess 1989: 157.

34 One exception is David Orton, a Canadian who has developed a tendency within deep ecology called "left biocentrism." This contains many of the features of the present argument, explicitly calling for treating all humans as inherently worthy (while sensibly calling for population limitation), radically calling into question the capitalist economy and empire, and so forth. Like many deep greens, however, Orton hates socialism and considers it doomed to remain in its twentieth-century form. He also shares the common misunderstanding of Marx's labor theory of value, regarding it as a prescription for labor over nature, and not seeing it as Marx's pinpointing of the heart of capital's pathological treatment of nature (Orton 2003, Orton 2005).

35 For a comprehensive survey, see Zimmerman 1994, a work uncontaminated by the actual world.

36 Devall and Sessions 1985: 145.

37 Sale 1996: 477.

38 As in Mies 1998; Shiva 1989; Salleh 1997.

39 Cf. for example, the arguments of Eisler 1987, which make an effort to bring historical understanding to bear, but end by substituting New Age slogans and postulating the existence of a "Goddess," a notion that replaces male domination with a female-centered hierarchy.

40 For a history, see Woodcock 1962.

41 Yuen et al. 2001.

42 Humans cannot be free unless they affirm the self-determination of all creatures. This essentially Buddhist insight is the ground of the animal-rights movement, which must be integral to any fully thought-through ecopolitics and philosophy. Needless to say, the problem is greatly complicated by the fact that one creature's "nature" will often consist of eating another creature.

43 Bookchin 1970. Bookchin's *chef d'oeuvre* is *The Ecology of Freedom* (1982). I have discussed this complicated figure in some detail in Kovel 1997c. See also Light 1998 (in which my essay is reprinted); as well as Watson 1996. An inkling of the problems with Bookchin's approach, which, aside from being rigidly anti-Marxist, is also rigidly anti-spiritual and highly Eurocentric, may be sensed by the fact that the only political path he can envision is that of "libertarian municipalism," a confederation of social-ecologic small cities

which is somehow supposed to revolutionize society from below. Individuals greatly influenced by Bookchin, yet who have proven capable of moving social ecology along a more open road, include John Clark and Brian Tokar. See Clark 1984, 1997; see also the Symposium on Clark, with comments by myself, Kate Soper, Mary Mellor, and Clark's reply in Kovel et al. 1998; Tokar 1992.

44 The first volume of Marx's *Capital* appeared in 1867, before the appearance of large corporations and the 14th Amendment; what, then, could he have been worried about?

45 Sheasby 2000a. We should not forget that the origins of the Ku Klux Klan lay similarly in rural discontent.

46 For a summary of Coughlin and further references, see Kovel 1997a.

47 Bramwell 1989 offers an overview of Nazi–green connections.

48 Himmler, addressing *Einsatzgruppen*, or mobile killing teams, in Poland, 1943: "We Germans, who are the only people in the world who have a decent attitude to animals, will also adopt a decent attitude to these human animals, but it is a crime against our own blood to worry about them and to bring them ideals" (quoted in Fest 1970: 115).

49 Biehl and Staudenmaier 1995. See also the useful website: www.savanne.ch/right-left.html.

50 Rampton and Stauber 1997.

9 *Prefiguration*

1 Zablocki 1971. A great deal of information is also available through Plough publications.

2 All youths are required to live away for two years following graduation from high school, either at college or in supervised settings doing good works. Following this, the individual must decide him- or herself whether to return and re-enter the community as an adult. From what I have been told, about three-quarters decide to do so.

3 The phrase is from his "Critique of the Gotha Program" (Marx 1978e: 531). The literature on this subject is vast. See Cort 1988. For Marx himself, see Miranda 1974.

4 Bruderhof are very strongly homophobic; for example, they went out of their way to try to close gay bars in their vicinity, and they refused to join coalitions against the death penalty in which gay rights groups participated. Within the commune, though women have a definite voice, there is also distinct inequality, for example, in dress code, where the men can wear what they please while the women must wear traditional calico. Furthermore, divorce is forbidden. Moreover, the moral authority of the community devolves from the paternal voice of the Arnold family. There are signs that the generation coming up may see things differently; it will be interesting to follow this development. But in general, it remains harder for radical religions to give up patriarchal than class domination.

5 Could this be the hidden meaning of the Fall? One should not be too hasty, for a pre-economic life of pure utilization is not free of aggression or ambivalence, though it does lack expansive and cancerous implications.

6 "The Sick Rose," from *Songs of Experience*, in Blake 1977: 123.

7 The values are grassroots democracy, social justice, ecological wisdom, non-violence, decentralization, community-based economics and economic justice, feminism, respect for diversity, personal and global responsibility, and future-focus and sustainability. The closest candidate, economic justice, goes no further than the call for protecting workers' rights and a mixture of economic forms, including "independently owned companies" – in short, stays within the perspective criticized in the previous chapter.

8 Well into the last century, American socialists used the term, "cooperative commonwealth." No doubt, that's a good way of putting socialism; but then, does one call what we have in mind an "eco-cooperative commonwealth"? Whatever the short-term tactical gains of such circumlocutions, it is clear that they gain nothing overall. If the word "socialism" is in that much disfavor, then the fact had better be confronted and not evaded.

9 Marx and Engels 1978: 491.

10 For Marx, see Draper 1977, *et. seq.*; for a magisterial account of the failings of the Soviet bloc, see Mészáros 1996; for a general survey of the whole socialist tradition in this light, see Bronner 1990.

11 Figes 1997.

12 Hinton 1967; Meisner 1996.

13 I tried to put some of this in writing. See Kovel 1988.

14 Rosset and Benjamin 1994, Levins 2005a.

15 Of course, what they got after socialism's breakdown was a special version of capitalism, overseen by the IMF and the US Treasury, where the rapid sell-off of state assets was used to finance accumulation in its most ruthless and uncontrolled form. Russia's domestic output fell by about half in the first decade after the collapse of the USSR; and while this kept planetary growth artificially down and limited the effects of pollution, there was virtually no effort to improve the dismal record of the Soviet years with respect to the environment. In May, 2000, Russian President Vladimir Putin, in his effort to reinstate the iron hand while pleasing transnational capital, dissolved Russia's State Committee on Ecology as well as the Forest Service, whereupon the World Bank approved another billion dollars in loans. From this point forward, Putin redirected the economy toward extraction of the immense petroleum and natural gas reserves of Russia, sparking a great accumulation of wealth, along with phenomenal gangsterism. Now Russia is once again approaching "great power" status, worse luck for the ecosphere.

16 Arran Gare 1996: 266, 211–28. At its height early in the revolution, *Proletkul't* had 400,000 members, published twenty journals, and drew in great numbers of artists and intellectuals. Material on Bogdanov can be found in Martinez-Alier 1987, as well as Gare. Martinez-Alier also writes extensively about Sergey Podolinsky, a nineteenth-century engineer who pioneered the integration of thermodynamic and Marxist theory, and can be seen as the progenitor of ecological economics. Gare's treatment of the Soviets is very extensive (see pp. 233–80, *passim*). A shorter and more accessible version of the argument may be found in Gare's "Soviet Environmentalism: The Path not Taken," in Benton 1996. Similar considerations pertained to communist China. Although the manifest ideology was highly productivist in accordance with first-epoch socialist values and in contrast to the ecocentric philosophy of traditional China, still, "until recently it has had a far better record than traditional China in relation to environmental problems. The Communists, at least when Mao Ze Dong ruled, did much to reforest the country, to conserve resources and to improve the environment in other ways" (36). In support of this, Gare cites an article by Leo A. Orleans and Richard P. Suttmeier (1970), along with Geping and Lee (1984).

17 Nothing if not complex, Lenin veered away from this in his later philosophical writings, notably his reading of Hegel's *Logic* (1969). It is safe to say, however, that it was the cruder and more mechanistic side of Lenin's ambivalence that sedimented into Soviet practice.

18 Classically depicted in Goncharov's novel, *Oblomov*, about a man who could not get out of bed. Lenin would frequently inveigh to his followers against the dangers of succumbing to "oblomovism."

19 "Man, who will learn how to move rivers and mountains, how to build people's palaces on the peaks of Mont Blanc and at the bottom of the Atlantic, will not only be able to add to his own life richness, brilliance and intensity, but also a dynamic quality of the highest degree. The shell of life will hardly have time to form before it will be burst open again under the pressure of new technical and cultural inventions and achievements ... Emancipated man will want to attain a greater equilibrium in the work of his organs and a more proportional development and wearing out of his tissues, in order to reduce the fear of death ... [he will] raise himself to a new plane, to create a higher social biologic type, or if you please, a superman" (Trotsky 1960: 253).

20 Gare 1996: 267–9.

21 McNally 1993: 206–8. Italics added.

22 The great British socialist thought in terms of a production that incorporated craft and the

aesthetic dimension, thereby envisioning an emancipation of use-value. See especially the utopian novel, *News from Nowhere* (Morris 1993).

23 Bronner 1981: 75. Italics in original.

24 The list of plaintiffs in the case ranges from members of the socialist and Marxist traditions, like Ted Benton and Rainer Grundmann (who is for the Promethean attitude), to anarchist/ social ecologists like John Clark, to ecocentric philosophers like Robyn Eckersley. See Benton 1996 for a survey from the Marxist side; also Clark 1984; Eckersley 1992. There is an associated question, of Marx's relation to Engels, and of Engels himself on these matters. This is an important issue, which cannot, however, be taken up here. The cover of the paperback edition of Bertell Ollman's *Alienation* (1971) shows an illustration from 1842, when Marx was all of twenty-four, directly depicting him as Prometheus. Marx's later physical afflictions, notably his boils, reinforced this association. See Wheen 2000.

25 See Burkett 1999; Foster 2000. For my assessment of Foster's book, see Kovel 2001a.

26 Parsons 1977 provides a good anthology of relevant passages. For an earlier contribution of mine on this theme, see Kovel 1995.

27 From a youthful letter to Arnold Ruge (Marx 1978a).

28 Marx's most important statement about use-value appears in the little-read *Theories of Surplus Value* (Marx 1971: 296–7), where we learn that the terms of value "originally express nothing but the use-value of things for people, those qualities which make them useful or agreeable etc. to people. It is in the nature of things that 'value', 'valeur', 'Wert' can have no other etymological origin. Use-value expresses the natural relationship between things and men, in fact the existence of things for men. *Exchange-value*, as the result of the social development which created it, was later superimposed on the word value, which was synonymous with use-value. It [exchange=value] is the *social existence* of things. [There follows an etymological passage, viz: 'Sanskrit – Wer means cover, protect, consequently respect honour and love, cherish ...' etc., and then] The value of a thing is, in fact, its own *virtus* [virtue], while its exchange-value is quite independent of its material properties." Italics in original. I am indebted to Walt Sheasby for pointing out this passage, which clearly reveals that, for Marx, use-value is embedded in natural ecologies, but at the same time, that he sees no need to differentiate use-value from any notion of intrinsic value to nature. In other words, a term belonging to economic discourse suffices to embrace the entirety of what nature means. See also, however, Sheasby's important studies, inter-

rupted by his untimely death, in which a case is made for a much deeper appreciation of nature by Marx (Sheasby 2004a; Sheasby 2004b).

29 Enrique Leff has made an important contribution to this concept in his *Green Production* (1995). However, the subjective elements developed here are not incorporated in his approach, nor does he set the goal of overcoming capital.

30 The linkage between use- and exchange-values needs to be kept in mind, as many cases of enhanced use-value exist whose outcome need not be inherently ecocentric. Thus, fine and en-hanced use-values occur regularly within a regime of exchange, as in the production of luxury goods; while at the other end, we find collapsing states of production, in which both forms of value deteriorate. A recent example is the former USSR, especially in the 1990s, where demoralized workmanship abounded, creating "accidents waiting to happen" (viz, the submarine *Kursk*), while at the same time exchange-functions broke down for great blocs of the population, many of whom had to resort to barter and other circuitous means in order to survive. Even so, life expectancy sank to levels of very poor Third World countries, especially for males – nor has this improved substantially.

31 See Leff 1995.

32 Two recent works that do

this theme justice are Kidner 2000; Fisher 2001.

33 Even a garden slug, though here I must confess a certain bar-rier of recognition.

34 Mellor 1997.

10 Ecosocialism

1 Marx 1963: 107. I became acquainted with this passage through Mészáros 1996.

2 This was the general conclusion of Karl Polanyi's *The Great Transformation* (1957). We should add that not all ways of production would be retained under ecosocialism. For example, serfdom or slavery are ruled out by deeply established values – though these coexist quite readily in vari-ous niches within capitalism, like sweatshops and the sex industries. See also Mies and Bennholdt-Thomsen 2000.

3 See Chapter 1, Introduction, note 4.

4 Hardin 1968, one of the most reprinted works of the entire neo-liberal era. This stemmed from his error, because by mistaking mem-bers of the Commons for bourgeois self-maximizers, he cleared a way for authoritarian enclosures. For a thorough discussion, see Ross 1998; and Naess 2004.

5 Marx 1967a; Luxemburg 1968; Harvey 2003.

6 The Commune was the actual launching point for violent anti-communist campaigns in the United States and elsewhere (Kovel 1997b). See Marx 1978d for a famous treatment.

7 As Marx, Lenin, and others pointed out, this is really what was intended by the phrase, the "dictatorship of the proletariat," a readily misunderstood term, since in the nineteenth century "dictatorship" simply meant emergency rule, and had none of the connotations given by the grim developments of twentieth-century socialism.

8 For a discussion of the corruptions of this process, see Bond 2006.

9 See Abahlali 2006. The Wikipedia entry for the Paris Commune provides this link to *Abahlali baseMjondolo* as an example of the contemporary version of 1871.

10 Marcos 2001 provides a good introduction to the EZLN.

11 Weisman 1998.

12 Ibid.: 10.

13 There were twenty-eight indymedia centers in 2000, and roughly 170 in 2006. One of their number, Brad Will, was killed in the streets of Oaxaca in the fall of 2006 while documenting street protests. Another, Josh Wolf, was recently released from US Federal prison where he spent six months for refusing to turn over his sources.

14 For the many aspects of the alternative media movement, see Halleck 2002. See also Stimson and Sholette 2007.

15 In May 2007 the first conference on global warming and the trade union movement was held in New York, a major step forward. See Brecher 2006 for an appraisal of the present state of organized labor *vis à vis* the ecological crisis. The chief barrier to progress, unsurprisingly, comes from the upper echelons of organized labor. Thus the task is to organize from below.

16 GreenLeft-Australia 2007: "According to *Prensa Latina* on March 24, Venezuela has replaced some 45 million incandescent light bulbs with white light thrifty bulbs, benefiting more than 4 million households. The move is part of an energy saving program, the Energy Revolution Mission. More than 3000 activists have been involved in carrying out the bulb changes, and are aiming to replace about 54 million in total. The mission is also expanding renewable energy sources such as solar and wind, and beginning to replace petrol with gas to supply cars. *Prensa Latina* points out that while Venezuela is the fifth-largest exporter of hydrocarbons, it is encouraging the use of less contaminating energy sources."

17 It being impossible to say more of the Chávez government at this point, given its emergence from a major oil economy, its dependence on the military, etc.

18 And nitrogen, sulfur, etc. We set the added details aside to draw the main point so far as the struggle for ecosocialism is concerned. The other greenhouse gases, including methane, add new dimensions but do not affect the logic of the struggle itself.

19 To return to the title of Al Gore's video of 2006 which did much to catalyze the new level of awareness. See video by Cambiz Khosravi and Joel Kovel, *A Really Inconvenient Truth* (Khosravi 2007) for a critique.

20 And some not so worthy measures, for example, substituting nuclear energy for carbon-driven energy, and using lots of biofuels for the latter. Both are unacceptable, the former for well-known reasons of toxicity, the latter because it portends mass starvation, brutally exploits agricultural workers, and destroys such swathes of old-growth forests as to end up spewing more carbon than before into the atmosphere.

21 A number of countries, South Africa, for example, but also Brazil, India, and even China, contain major zones of both types. In Canada and the United States, as well as other large Northern countries like Russia and Scandinavia, there are far-North enclaves of indigenous folk like Inuit who bear this burden as well.

22 See Lohmann 2006: 329–55. A portion of the factual basis of this section has been drawn from this source, adding, however, the implication of ecosocialist prefiguration.

23 Turner and Brownhill 2004. I am indebted to these scholar-activists for much of the information in this section. For the Nigerian struggle, see also Rowell et al. 2005. Thanks to David Miller for providing this source.

24 The final IPCC report (see above) itself dismisses the Kyoto regime as likely to have little effect on the actual reduction of atmospheric carbon in the critical period ahead. Its only virtue is in setting the price of carbon and enabling other projects to go forward. Somehow the world's peoples are supposed to applaud this.

25 The IPCC reports, for instance, leave out the effects of positive feedback, whether from innate or politically induced conservatism.

26 One such is the green-left faction of the British Green Party, which is consciously ecosocialist.

27 Faber 1998.

28 Or, to repeat, this could happen focally in the context of widespread chaos and collapse, the various focal alternatives coming together.

29 Marx 1967b: 776.

30 Marx 1967a: 71–83.

31 István Mészáros writes: "the socialist undertaking cannot even begin to realize its fundamental objectives without successfully accomplishing at the same time the shift from the exchange of products ... to the exchange of genuinely *planned* and *self-managed* (as opposed to bureaucratically *planned from above*) productive activities" (Mészáros 1996: 761, italics in text). These can be translated into ecosystemic terms.

Bibliography

Abahlali (2006) available at:<www.abahlali.org/node/237>

AFP (2007) "Gore Rules out 2008 Presidential Run," Agence France Presse, February 9.

Altvater, E. (1993) *The Future of the Market*, trans. Patrick Camiller, London: Verso.

Aristotle (1947) *Introduction to Aristotle*, ed. R. McKeon, New York: Modern Library.

Arrighi, G. (1994) *The Long Twentieth Century*, London: Verso.

Athanasiou, T. (1996) *Divided Planet*, Boston, MA: Little, Brown.

Bachram, H. (2004) "Climate Fraud and Carbon Colonialism: The New Trade in Greenhouse Gases," *Capitalism, Nature, Socialism*, 15 (4): 5–20.

Bader, S. (1997) *Global Spin*, Foxhole, Devon: Green Books.

Barlow, M. (2000) "The World Bank Must Realize Water is a Basic Human Right," *Toronto Globe and Mail*, May 9.

Bass, C. (2000) "A Smile in Conflict with Itself," *Sacramento Bee*, February 28: D1.

Bateson, G. (1972) *Notes Toward an Ecology of Mind*, New York: Ballantine Books.

Beder, S. (1997) *Global Spin*, Foxhole, Devon: Green Books.

Benjamin, J. (1988) *The Bonds of Love*, New York: Pantheon.

Benton, T. (ed.) (1996) *The Greening of Marxism*, New York: Guilford.

Bergman, L. (2000) "US Companies Tangled in Web of Drug Dollars," *New York Times*, October 10: A1.

Biehl, J. and P. Staudenmaier (1995) *Ecofascism: Lessons from the German Experience*, Edinburgh and San Francisco, CA: AK Press.

Blake, W. (1977) *The Complete Poems*, ed. Alicia Ostriker, London: Penguin Books.

Blaut, J. (1993) *The Colonizer's View of the World*, New York: Guilford.

Bond, P. (2004) "The World Bank: Should It be Fixed or Nixed?", *Capitalism, Nature, Socialism*, 15 (2).

— (2006) *Talk Left, Walk Right*, 2nd edn, Pietermaritzburg: University of Kwazulu-Natal Press.

Bookchin, M. (1970) *Post-Scarcity Anarchism*, Palo Alto, CA: Ramparts Press.

— (1982) *The Ecology of Freedom*, Palo Alto, CA: Cheshire Books.

Botkin, D. (1990) *Discordant Harmonies*, New York: Oxford University Press.

Bowden, C. (1996) "While You were Sleeping," *Harpers*, December: 44–52.

Bramwell, A. (1989) *Ecology in the Twentieth Century: A History*, New Haven, CT: Yale University Press.

Braudel, F. (1977) *Afterthoughts on Material Civilization and Capitalism*, Baltimore, MD: Johns Hopkins Press.

Breyer, S. (1979) "Analyzing Regulatory Failure, Mismatches, Less Restrictive Alternatives and Reform," *Harvard Law Review*, 92 (3): 597.

Bronner, S. (1981) *A Revolutionary for Our Times: Rosa Luxemburg*, London: Pluto Press.

— (1990) *Socialism Unbound*, London: Routledge.

Brown, P. (1999) "More Refugees Flee from Environment than Warfare," *Manchester Guardian Weekly*, July 1–7: 5.

Burkett, P. (1999) *Marx and Nature*, New York: St Martin's Press.

Call, W. (2001) "Accelerating the Decomposition of Capitalism," *ACERCA Notes*, 8.

Chodorow, N. (1978) *The Reproduction of Mothering*, Berkeley: University of California Press.

Clark, J. (1984) *The Anarchist Moment*, Montreal: Black Rose.

— (1997) "A Social Ecology," *Capitalism, Nature, Socialism*, 8 (3): 3–34.

Clastres P. (1977) *Society Against the State*, trans. Robert Hurley, New York: Urizen.

Cockburn, A. and J. St Clair (2000) *Al Gore: A User's Manual*, New York: Verso.

Colburn, T. et al. (1996) *Our Stolen Future*, New York: Dutton-Penguin.

Cort, J. (1988) *Christian Socialism*, Maryknoll, NY: Orbis.

Costanza, R., J. Cumberland, H. Daly, R. Goodland and R. Norgaard (1997) *An Introduction to Ecological Economics*, Boca Raton, FL: St Lucie Press.

Cronon, W. (ed.) (1996) *Contested Ground*, New York: W. W. Norton.

Crossette, B. (2000a) "In Numbers, the Heavy Now Match the Starved," *New York Times*, January 17: A1.

— (2000b) "Unicef Issues Report on Worldwide Violence Facing Women," *New York Times*, June 1: A15.

Daly, H. (1991) *Steady-State Economics*, Washington, DC: Island Press.

— (1996) *Beyond Growth*, Boston, MA: Beacon Press.

Daly, H. and J. Cobb (1994) *For the Common Good*, Boston, MA: Beacon Press.

Davies, P. (1983) *God and the New Physics*, London: Penguin Books.

Davis, M. (2006) *Planet of Slums*, London: Verso.

DeBord, G. (1992) *Society of the Spectacle*, New York: Zone Books.

de Brie, C. (2000) "Crime, the World's Biggest Free Enterprise," *Le Monde Diplomatique*, April.

de Duve, C. (1995) *Vital Dust*, New York: Basic Books.

DeLumeau, J. (1990) *Sin and Fear: Emergence of a Western Guilt Culture 13th–18th Centuries*, trans. Eric Nicholson, New York: St Martin's Press.

Deogun, N. (1997) "A Coke and a Perm? Soda Giant is Pushing into Unusual Locales," *Wall Street Journal*, May 5: A1.

Devall, B. and G. Sessions (1985) *Deep Ecology*, Salt Lake City, UH: Peregrine Smith Books.

Diamond, S. (1974) *In Search of the Primitive*, New Brunswick, NJ: Transaction Books.

Dobrzynski, J. (1997) "Big Payoffs for Executives Who Fail Big," *New York Times*, July 21: D1.

Draper, H. (1977, 1978, 1985, 1990) *Karl Marx's Theory of Revolution*, 4 vols, New York: Monthly Review Press.

Drexler, K. (1986) *Engines of Creation*, New York: Doubleday, 1986.

Dunayevskaya, R. (1973) *Philosophy and Revolution*, New York: Dell.

— (2000) *Marxism and Freedom*, Amherst, NY: Humanity Books.

Eckersley, R. (1992) *Environmentalism and Political Theory*, Albany, NY: SUNY Press.

Ecologist, The (1993) *Whose Common Future? Reclaiming the Commons*, Philadelphia, PA: New Society Publishers.

Ehrenreich, B. and D. English (1974) *Witches, Midwives and Nurses*, London: Compendium.

Eisler, R. (1987) *The Chalice and the Blade*, San Francisco, CA: Harper and Row.

Engels, F. (1940) *Dialectics of Nature*, New York: International Publishers.

— (1972 [1884]) *Origins of the Family, Private Property, and the State*, ed. Eleanor Leacock, New York: International Publishers.

— (1987 [1845]) *The Conditions of the Working Class in England*, ed. Victor Kiernan, London: Penguin Books.

Faber, D. (ed.) (1998) *The Struggle for Ecological Democracy*, New York: Guilford.

Fagin, D. and M. Lavelle (1996) *Toxic Deception*, Secaucus, NJ: Birch Lane Press.

Farias, V. (1989) *Heidegger and Nazism*, ed. Joseph Margolis and Tom Rockmore, Philadelphia, PA: Temple University Press.

Federici, S. (2004) *Caliban and the Witch: Women, the Body, and Primitive Accumulation*, New York: Autonomedia.

Fest, J. (1970) *The Face of the Third Reich*, New York: Pantheon.

Fiddes, N. (1991) *Meat – a Natural Symbol*, London: Routledge.

Figes, O. (1997) *A People's Tragedy*, London: Pimlico.

Fisher, A. (2002) *Radical Ecopsychology: Psychology in the Service of Life*, Albany, NY: State University of New York Press.

Fortey, R. (1997) *Life: An Unauthorized Biography*, London: HarperCollins.

Foster, J. (2000) *Marx's Ecology*,

New York: Monthly Review Press.

Frank, A. (1998) *ReORIENT: Global Economy in the Asian Age*, Berkeley: University of California Press.

Freud, S. (1931) *Civilization and Its Discontents*, in J. Strachey (ed.), *The Standard Edition of the Complete Psychological Works of Sigmund Freud*, London: Hogarth Press, 21: 59–148.

Freund, P. and G. Martin (1993) *The Ecology of the Automobile*, Montreal: Black Rose Books.

Gardner, G. and B. Halweil (2000) "Underfed and Overfed," Washington, DC: Worldwatch Institute, March.

Gare, A. (1996a) *Nihilism Inc.*, Sydney: Eco-Logical Press.

— (1996b) "Soviet Environmentalism: The Path Not Taken," in T. Benton (ed.), *The Greening of Marxism*, New York: Guilford: 111–28.

— (2000) "Creating an Ecological Socialist Future," *Capitalism, Nature, Socialism*, 11 (2): 23–40.

Gelbspan, R. (1998) *The Heat is On*, Reading, MA: Perseus Books.

George, S. (1992) *The Debt Boomerang*, London: Pluto Press.

Georgescu-Roegen, N. (1971) *The Entropy Law and the Economic Process*, Cambridge, MA: Harvard University Press.

Geping, Q. and W. Lee (eds) (1984) *Managing the Environment in China*, Dublin: Tycooley.

Gibbs, L. (1995) *Dying from Dioxin*, Boston, MA: South End Press.

Glacken, C. (1973) *Traces on the Rhodian Shore*, Berkeley: University of California Press.

Glieck, J. (1987) *Chaos*, New York: Penguin Books.

Gore, A. (2000) *Earth in the Balance*, Boston, MA: Houghton-Mifflin.

— (2006) *An Inconvenient Truth*, Emmaus, PA: Rodale.

Goudie, A. (1991) *The Human Impact on the Natural Environment*, Cambridge, MA: MIT Press.

GreenLeft Australia (2007) available at: <www.greenleft.org.au/2007/705/36638>

Gunn, C. and H. Gunn (1991) *Reclaiming Capital*, Ithaca, NY: Cornell University Press.

Halleck, D. (2002) *Hand-Held Visions*, New York: Fordham University Press.

Hanna, B., W. Morehouse and S. Sarangi (eds) (2006) *The Bhopal Reader*, New York: Apex Press.

Hardin, G. (1968) "The Tragedy of the Commons," *Science*, 162: 1243–8.

Harvey, D. (1993) *The Condition of Postmodernity*, Oxford: Blackwell.

— (2003) *The New Imperialism*, Oxford: Oxford University Press.

Hawken, P. (1993) *The Ecology of Commerce*, New York: HarperCollins.

Hecht, S. and A. Cockburn (1990) *The Fate of the Forest*, New York: HarperCollins.

Hegel, G. (1969) *Hegel's Science of*

Logic, trans. A. Miller, London: George Allen and Unwin.

Heidegger, M. (1977) "The Question Regarding Technology," in *Basic Writings*, ed. David Farrell Krell, New York: Harper and Row: 283–317.

Herbert, B. (2007) Column, *New York Times*, January 15.

Herrnstein R. and C. Murray (1996) *The Bell Curve*, New York: Free Press.

Hinton, W. (1967) *Fanshen*, New York: Monthly Review Press.

Ho, M. (1998) *Genetic Engineering: Dream or Nightmare?* Bath: Gateway Books.

Hussey, E. (1972) *The Presocratics*, New York: Charles Scribner's Sons.

Huws, U. (1999) "Material World: The Myth of the Weightless Economy," in L. Panitch and C. Leys (eds), *Socialist Register 1999*, Suffolk: Merlin Press: 29–55.

Isla, A. (2007) "The Kyoto Protocol: A War on Subsistence," *Women and Environments International Magazine*, 74/75: 31–3.

Jenkins, Jr, H. (1997) "Who Needs R&D When You Understand Fat?," *Wall Street Journal*, March 25: A19.

Kanter, R. (1997) "Show Humanity When You Show Employees the Door," *Wall Street Journal*, July 21: A22.

Karliner, J. (1997) *The Corporate Planet*, San Francisco, CA: Sierra Club.

Kempf, H. (2000) "Every Catastrophe Has a Silver Lining," *Manchester Guardian Weekly*, January 20–26: 30.

Khosravi, C. (2007) *A Really Inconvenient Truth*, DVD-Video, with Joel Kovel.

Kidner, D. (2000) *Nature and Psyche*, Albany, NY: State University of New York Press.

Korten, D. (1996) "The Mythic Victory of Market Capitalism", in J. Mander and E. Goldsmith (eds), *The Case Against the Global Economy*, San Francisco, CA: Sierra Club Books: 183–91.

— (2000) The FEASTA annual lecture, Dublin, Ireland, July 4.

Kovel, J. (1981) *The Age of Desire*, New York: Random House.

— (1984) *White Racism*, 2nd edn, New York: Columbia University Press.

— (1988) *In Nicaragua*, London: Free Association Books.

— (1995) "Ecological Marxism and Dialectic," *Capitalism, Nature, Socialism*, 6 (4): 31–50.

— (1997a) "Bad News for Fast Food," *Z*, September: 26–31.

— (1997b) *Red Hunting in the Promised Land*, 2nd edn, London: Cassell.

— (1997c) "Negating Bookchin," *Capitalism, Nature, Socialism*, 8 (1): 3–36.

— (1998a) "Dialectic as Praxis", *Science and Society*, 62 (3): 474–82.

— (1998b) *History and Spirit*, 2nd edn, Warner, NH: Essential Books.

— (1999) "The Justifiers," *Capitalism, Nature, Socialism*, 10 (3): 3–36.

— (2001a) "A Materialism Worthy of Nature," *Capitalism, Nature Socialism*, 12 (2): 73–84.

— (2001b) "The Fossils Seize Power," *Against the Current*, XVI, September–October: 14–16.

— (2005) "The Ecological Implications of the Iraq War," *Capitalism, Nature Socialism*, 16 (4): 7–17.

— (2007) *Overcoming Zionism*, London: Pluto Press.

Kovel, J., K. Soper, M. Mellor and J. Clark (1998) "John Clark's 'A Social Ecology': Comments/ Reply", *Capitalism, Nature, Socialism*, 9 (1): 25–46.

Kropotkin, P. (1902) *Mutual Aid*, London: Heinemann.

— (1975) *The Essential Kropotkin*, ed. E. Capouya and K. Tompkins, New York: Liveright.

Kurzman, D. (1987) *A Killing Wind: Inside Union Carbide and the Bhopal Catastrophe*, New York: McGraw-Hill.

Lappé, F., J. Collins and P. Rosset (1998) *World Hunger: Twelve Myths*, 2nd edn, New York: Grove Press.

Leff, E. (1995) *Green Production*, New York: Guilford.

Leiss, W. (1972) *The Domination of Nature*, Boston, MA: Beacon Press.

Lepkowski, W. (1994) "Ten Years Later: Bhopal," *Chemical & Engineering News*, December 19: 8–18.

Levins, R. (2005a) "How Cuba is Going Ecological," *Capitalism, Nature, Socialism*, 16 (3): 7–26.

— (2005b) "Cuba's Example," *Capitalism, Nature, Socialism*, 16 (4): 5–6.

Levins, R. and R. Lewontin (1985) *The Dialectical Biologist*, Cambridge, MA: Harvard University Press.

Lichtman, R. (1982) *The Production of Desire*, New York: Free Press.

Light, A. (ed.) (1998) *Social Ecology After Bookchin*, New York: Guilford.

Lohmann, L. (2006) *Carbon Trading: A Critical Conversation on Climate Change, Privatisation and Power*, Uppsala, Sweden: Dag Hammerskjöld Foundation: <www.dhf.uu.se>.

Lovelock, J. (1979) *Gaia: A New Look at Life on Earth*, Oxford: Oxford University Press.

Lovins, A. (1977) *Soft Energy Paths*, San Francisco, CA: Friends of the Earth International.

Luxemburg, R. (1968 [1913]), *The Accumulation of Capital*, New York: Monthly Review Press.

McNally, D. (1993) *Against the Market*, London: Verso.

Manning, J. (1996) *The Coming of the Energy Revolution*, Garden City Park, NY: Avery Publishing Group.

Marcos, Subcommandante (2001) *Our Word is Our Weapon*, ed. Juana Ponce de León, New York: Seven Stories Press.

Margulis, L. (1998) *Symbiotic Planet*, New York: Basic Books.

Martinez-Alier, J. (1987) *Ecological Economics*, Oxford: Blackwell.

Marx, K. (1963 [1847]) *The Poverty*

of Philosophy, New York: International Publishers.

— (1964 [1858]) *Pre-Capitalist Economic Formations*, trans. Jack Cohen, ed. E. J. Hobsbawm, New York: International Publishers.

— (1967a [1867]) *Capital, Vol. I*, ed. Frederick Engels, New York: International Publishers.

— (1967b [1894]) *Capital, Vol. 3*, ed. Frederick Engels, New York: International Publishers.

— (1971 [1863]) *Theories of Surplus Value, Vol. III*, Moscow: Progress Publishers.

— (1973 [1858]) *Grundrisse*, trans. and ed. Martin Nicolaus, London: Penguin Books.

— (1978a [1843]) "Letter to Arnold Ruge, of September, 1843," in Tucker (ed.): 13.

— (1978b [1844]) *Economic and Philosophic Manuscripts of 1844*, in Tucker (ed.): 66–125.

— (1978c [1864]) "Inaugural Address of the Working Men's International Association", in Tucker (ed.): 517–18.

— (1978d [1871]) *The Civil War in France*, in Tucker (ed.): 618–52.

— (1978e [1875]) "Critique of the Gotha Program," in Tucker (ed.): 525–41.

Marx, K. and F. Engels (1978 [1848]) *The Communist Manifesto*, in Tucker (ed.): 469–500.

Meadows, D., D. Meadows and J. Randers (1992) *Beyond the Limits*, London: Earthscan.

Meadows, D., D. Meadows, J. Randers and W. Behrens

(1972) *The Limits to Growth*, London: Earth Island.

Meeker-Lowry, S. (1988) *Economics as if the Earth Really Mattered*, Philadelphia, PA: New Society Publishers.

Meisner, M. (1996) *The Deng Xiaoping Era*, New York: Hill and Wang.

Mellor, M. (1997) *Feminism and Ecological Polity*, Cambridge and New York: New York University Press.

Merchant, C. (1980) *The Death of Nature*, San Francisco, CA: Harper and Row.

Mészáros, I. (1996) *Beyond Capital*, New York: Monthly Review Press.

Mies, M. (1998) *Patriarchy and Accumulation on a World Scale*, 2nd edn, London: Zed.

Mies, M. and V. Bennholdt-Thomsen (2000) *The Subsistence Perspective*, London: Zed.

Mihill, C. (1996) "Health Plight of Poor Worsening," *Manchester Guardian Weekly*, May 5: 5.

Millennium Ecosystem Assessment (2005) *Report*, Washington, DC: Island Press: <www.maweb.org/en/Index.aspx>

Mintz, S. (1995) *Sweetness and Power*, New York: Viking.

Miranda, J. (1974) *Marx and the Bible*, Maryknoll, NY: Orbis.

Mollison, B. (1988) *Permaculture: A Designer's Manual*, Tygalum, Australia: Tagari Publications.

Montague, P. (1996) "Things to Come," *Rachel's Environment and Health Weekly*, 523, December 5.

Moody, K. (1997) *Workers in a Lean World*, London and New York: Verso.

— (2000) "Global Labor Stands up to Global Capital," *Labor Notes*, July: 8.

Morehouse, W. (1993) "The Ethics of Industrial Disasters in a Transnational World: The Elusive Quest for Justice and Accountability in Bhopal," *Alternatives*, 18: 487.

Morris, W. (1993) *News from Nowhere*, London: Penguin Books.

Morrison, R. (1991) *We Build the Road as We Travel*, Philadelphia, PA: New Society.

— (1995) *Ecological Democracy*, Boston, MA: South End Press.

Murphy, D. (2000) "Africa: Lenders Set Program Rules," *Los Angeles Times*, January 27: A1.

Murray, A. (1978) *Reason and Society in the Middle Ages*, Oxford: Clarendon Press.

Naess, A. (1989) *Ecology, Community and Lifestyle*, trans. and ed. David Rothenberg, Cambridge: Cambridge University Press.

Naess, P. (2004) "Live and Let Die: The Tragedy of Hardin's Social Darwinism," *Journal of Environmental Policy and Planning*, 6 (1): 19–34.

Nahm, M. (ed.) (1947) *Selections from Early Greek Philosophy*, New York: Appleton Century Crofts.

— (1997) "Death Comes to the *Maquilas*: A Border Story," *The Nation*, 264 (2), January 13–20: 18–22.

Needham, J. (1954) *Science and Civilization in China, Vol. 1, Introduction and Orientations*, Cambridge: Cambridge University Press.

Norgaard, R. (1994) *Development Betrayed*, London: Routledge.

O'Brien, M. (1981) *The Politics of Reproduction*, London: Routledge and Kegan Paul.

O'Connor, J. (1998) *Natural Causes*, New York: Guilford.

— (2001) "House Organ," *Capitalism, Nature, Socialism*, 13 (1): 1.

Ollman, B. (1971) *Alienation*, Cambridge: Cambridge University Press.

Ordonez, J. (2000) "An Efficiency Drive: Fast Food Lanes are Getting Even Faster," *Wall Street Journal*, May 18: 1.

Orleans, L. and R. Suttmeier (1970) "The Mao Ethic and Environmental Quality," *Science* 170: 1173–6.

Orton, D. (2003) "Deep Ecology Perspectives," *Synthesis/Regeneration*, 32.

— (2005) "Economic Philosophy and Green Electoralism," *Synthesis/Regeneration*, 37.

Parayil, G. (ed.) (2000) *Kerala: The Development Experience*, London: Zed.

Parsons, H. (1977) *Marx and Engels on Ecology*, Westport, CT: Greenwood Press.

Peet, R. (2003) *Unholy Trinity*, London: Zed.

Penrose, R. (1990) *The Emperor's New Mind*, London: Vintage.

Platt, A. (1996) *Infecting Ourselves*,

Worldwatch Paper 129, Washington, DC: Worldwatch Institute.

Polanyi, K. (1957) *The Great Transformation*, Boston, MA: Beacon Press.

Ponting, C. (1991) *A Green History of the World*, London: Penguin Books.

Pooley, E. (2000) "Doctor Death," *Time*, April 24.

Pring, G. and P. Canan (1996) *SLAPPs: Getting Sued for Speaking Out*, Philadelphia, PA: Temple University Press.

Proudhon, P. (1969) *Selected Writings*, ed. S. Edwards, trans. E. Fraser, Garden City, NY: Anchor Books.

Public Citizen (1996) *NAFTA's Broken Promises: The Border Betrayed*, Washington, DC: Public Citizen.

Punter, D. (1982) *Blake, Hegel and Dialectic*, Amsterdam: Rodopi.

Purdom, T. (2000) "A Game of Nerves, with No Real Winners," *New York Times*, May 17: H1.

Quammen, D. (1996) *The Song of the Dodo*, New York: Scribner.

Quigly, B. (2007) *Democracy Now!* January 31.

Rampton, S. and J. Stauber (1997) *Mad Cow U.S.A.*, Monroe, ME: Common Courage Press.

Rodinson, M. (1971) *Mohammed*, trans. Anne Carter, New York: Pantheon.

Rogers, H. (2005) *Gone Tomorrow: The Hidden Life of Garbage*, New York: New Press.

Romero, S. (2000) "Rich Brazilians Rise Above Rush-Hour Jams," *New York Times*, February 15: A1.

Rosdolsky, R. (1977) *The Making of Marx's Capital*, trans. Pete Burgess, London: Verso.

Ross, E. (1998) *The Malthus Factor*, London: Zed.

Rosset, P. and M. Benjamin (1994) *The Greening of the Revolution: Cuba's Experiment with Organic Farming*, Melbourne: Ocean.

Rowell, A. with J. Marriott and L. Stockman (2005) *The Next Gulf*, London: Constable.

Ruether, R. (1992) *Gaia and God*, San Francisco, CA: HarperSanFrancisco.

Sale, K. (1996) "Principles of Bioregionalism," in J. Mander and E. Goldsmith (eds), *The Case Against the Global Economy*, San Francisco, CA: Sierra Club Books: 471–84.

Salleh, A. (1997) *Ecofeminism as Politics*, London: Zed.

Sample, I. (2007) "Scientists Offered Cash to Dispute Climate Study," *Guardian*, February 2.

Sarkar, S. (1999) *Eco-socialism or Eco-capitalism*, London: Zed.

Schrödinger, E. (1967) *What is Life?*, Cambridge: Cambridge University Press.

Schumacher, E. F. (1973) *Small is Beautiful*, New York: Harper and Row.

Sheasby, W. (1997) "Inverted World: Karl Marx on Estrangement of Nature and Society," *Capitalism, Nature, Socialism*, 8 (4): 31–46.

— (2000a) Unpublished ms.

— (2000b) "Ralph Nader and the Legacy of Revolt," *Against the Current*, 88 (4): 17–21; 88 (5): 29–36; 88 (6): 39–42.

— (2004a) "Karl Marx and the Victorians' *Nature*: The Evolution of a Deeper View. Part One: Oceanus," *Capitalism, Nature, Socialism*, 15 (2): 47–64.

— (2004b) "Karl Marx and the Victorians' *Nature*: The Evolution of a Deeper View. Part Two: The Age of Aquaria," *Capitalism, Nature, Socialism*, 15 (3): 59–78.

Shiva, V. (1991) *The Violence of the Green Revolution*, Penang: Third World Network.

— (1989), *Staying Alive*, New Delhi: Kali for Women.

Simmel, G. (1978) *The Philosophy of Money*, trans. Tom Bottomore and David Frisby, London: Routledge and Kegan Paul.

Slatella, M. (2000) "Boxed In: Exploring a Big-Box Store Online," *New York Times*, January 27: D4.

Slater, J. (2007) "World's Assets Hit Record Value of $140 Trillion," *Wall Street Journal*, January 10: C8.

Steingraber, S. (1997) *Living Downstream*, New York: Addison Wesley.

Stewart, B. (2000) "Retrieving the Recyclables," *New York Times*, June 27: B1.

Stiglitz, A. (2000) "What I Learned at the World Economic Crisis," *New Republic*, April 17.

Stille, A. (2000) "In the 'Greened' World, It isn't Easy to be Human," *New York Times*, July 15: A17.

Stimson, B. and G. Sholette (eds) (2007) *Collectivism after Modernism*, Minneapolis: University of Minnesota Press.

Summers, L., J. Wolfensohn and J. Skilling (1997) *Multinational Monitor*, June: 6.

Taub, E. (2000) "Radios Watch Weather So You Don't Have To," *New York Times*, March 30: D10.

Tawney, R. H. (1998 [1926]) *Religion and the Rise of Capitalism*, New Brunswick, NJ: Transaction.

Thernstrom, A. and S. Thernstrom (1997) *America in Black and White*, New York: Simon and Schuster.

Thompson, E. P. (1967) "Time, Work Discipline, and Industrial Capitalism," *Past and Present*, 38: 56–97.

Thornton, J. (2000) *Pandora's Poison*, Cambridge, MA: MIT Press.

Tokar, B. (1992) *The Green Alternative*, San Pedro, CA: R. & E. Miles.

— (1997) *Earth for Sale*, Boston, MA: South End Press.

Trotsky, L. (1960) *Literature and Revolution*, Ann Arbor: University of Michigan Press.

Tucker, R. (ed.) (1978) *The Marx–Engels Reader*, 2nd edn, New York: W. W. Norton.

Turner, A. (2000) "Tempers in Overdrive," *Houston Chronicle*, April 8: 1A.

Turner, T. and L. Brownhill (2004)

"We Want Our Land Back: Gendered Class Analysis, the Second Contradiction of Capitalism, and Social Movement Theory," *Capitalism, Nature, Socialism*, 54 (4): 21–40.

Wald, M. (1997) "Temper Cited as Cause of 28,000 Road Deaths a Year," *New York Times*, July 18: A14.

Watson, D. (1996) *Beyond Bookchin*, Brooklyn, NY: Autonomedia.

Watson, J. (ed.) (1997) *Golden Arches East: McDonald's in East Asia*, Stanford, CA : Stanford University Press.

Weber, M. (1976) *The Protestant Ethic and the Spirit of Capitalism*, trans. Talcott Parsons, London: Allen and Unwin.

Weisman, A. (1998) *Gaviotas*, White River Junction, VT: Chelsea Green.

Wheen, F. (2000) *Karl Marx: A Life*, New York: W. W. Norton.

White, L. (1967) "The Historical Roots of our Ecological Crisis," *Science*, 155, March 10: 1203–7.

— (1978) *Medieval Religion and Technology: Collected Essays*, Berkeley: University of California Press.

Whitefield, P. (2004) *The Earth Care Manual*, East Meon, Hants [GU32 1HR], UK.

Wilber, K. (ed.) (2001) *Quantum Questions: Mystical Writings of the World's Great Physicists*, Boston, MA: Shambhala.

Williams, A. (2000) "Washed Up at 35," *New York Times*, April 17: 28ff.

Wisner, B., P. Blaikie, T. Cannon and I. Davis (2005) *At Risk*, 2nd edn, London and New York: Routledge.

Wolfenstein, E. (1993) *Psychoanalytic Marxism*, London: Free Association Books.

Woodcock, G. (1962) *Anarchism*, New York: New American Library.

Worster, D. (1994) *Nature's Economy*, 2nd edn, Cambridge: Cambridge University Press.

WWF Living Planet Report (2006): <assets.panda.org/downloads/living_planet_report.pdf>

Yuen, E., G. Katsiaficas and D. Rose (eds) (2002) *The Battle of Seattle*, New York: Soft Skull Press.

Zablocki, B. (1971) *The Joyful Community*, Baltimore, MD: Penguin Books.

Zachary, G. Pascal (1997) "The Right Mix: Global Growth Attains a New, Higher Level that Could be Lasting," *Wall Street Journal*, March 13: A1.

Zimmerman, M. (1994) *Contesting Earth's Future*, Berkeley: University of California Press.

Index

foundational for Christianity, 209–10

Communist Manifesto, 218

communities of resistance, 256, 273

conditions of production, 15

conservation projects, displacement of populations, 189

consumption, 233; alteration of patterns of, 122; light, 209

cooperatives, 178–80, 211, 255, 273; short-comings of, 181

corporate culture, 80–1

corruption, 21

Costa Rica, action against oil industry, 261

costs, lowering of, under capitalism, 34–5, 40

Coughlin, Father, 203

criminality, 80–1

Cuba, 221, 222, 258

Daly, Herman, 186–7

Darwin, Charles, 119, 232

debt, 75, 76–7; of Third World, 2; personal, 65

deep ecology, 188–91, 195

deforestation, 2, 13, 24

democracy, 167, 185, 199–206, 264, 275; radical, 244; victim of globalization, 81

democratic pluralism, 177

Deng Xiao Peng, 221

dialectical processes, 150; of nature, 151

differentiation, 114–15, 149, 151–2

dioxin, 56; emissions of, 171

disease, 14, 15

disintegration of ecosystems, 113–20, 137, 141

disposability of commodities, 215

division of labor, 126, 256

Dow Chemical corporation, 37–8

dream-time, 126

drive-through culture, 60–1

drought, xi, xv, 18

Earth Day, 1

earthquakes, 13

eating, industrialization of, 55, 60–3

ecocentric values, 10, 97, 184, 195, 211, 228, 230, 244, 250, 257, 265; in Chiapas, 253

ecocentric mode of production, 241, 243

ecocentric production, 234–41; zones of, 255–8

ecofascism, 205–6

ecofeminism, 8, 194–5, 240

ecological crisis, xi, xii, 3, 6, 13–25, 36, 41, 47, 69, 76, 81, 83, 87, 89, 107, 116, 121, 159, 170, 277

ecological politics, 90

ecological thinking, 14, 97–8

Ecologist magazine, 178

ecology, 95–120; concept of, history of, 96; four-fold meaning of, 96–7; human, xii *see also* deep ecology *and* social ecology

economics: Buddhist, 178; community-based, 178–82; ecological, 174–8

ecophilosophies, 7, 187–99

ecopolitics, 7–8; critique of, 164–206

ecosocialism, 7, 8, 163, 164, 206, 215, 216–17, 234, 240, 241, 242–75

ecosocialist mobilization, principles of, 248–58

ecosocialist party, 263–8

ecosphere, 96

ecosystems, 15, 53, 54, 96, 101,

relationships, 172; as element of ecological crisis, 123; as precondition of growth, 170; belief in, 229; critique of, 144, 149; fetish of, 86; in ecocentric production, 237; is not the answer, 169–73

temporality specific to societies, 112–13

Teresa of Avila, Saint, 124

terrorism, 16–18

thermodynamics, laws of, 99–103, 155

Tomney, Ryan, 60–1

torture, systems of, 17

trade unions, 33, 221, 248, 251

trading of emissions, , 47–50, 89, 163, 174–6, 262

trans-statal formations, 75

tribal way of life, 54

Trotsky, Leon, 221, 224–5; worship of technology, 224

Union Carbide corporation, 78; Bhopal disaster, 28–35 (damages claim against, 29); rise in company's stocks, 36

Union of Soviet Socialist Republics (USSR), xiv, 219, 223–6; collapse of, 198, 218; ecocatastrophe in, 226

United States of America (USA), 76; as global gendarme, 75

universality, 146

University of KwaZulu Natal, Centre for Civil Society, 251

use-value, 8, 39–40, 53, 112, 135, 136, 186, 212–13, 216, 232, 235, 237, 243, 268; as site of contestation, 215, 269

usufruct, 268, 271, 278

value, 134, 180–1

vanguardism, 263–4

Venezuela, 258

Vietnam, 221; war, xii

violence, male, development of, 126–8

virtue, 236, 239

voluntarism, 167–9, 173, 250

wage, maximum, 186

wage-relation, 141

Wal-Mart, in China, 52

Wall Street, as control center, 37

Wall Street Journal, 5

war, permanence of, 16–18

waste: management of, 168; production of, 64, 69; toxic dumps, 85, 86 (in South Africa, 251–2)

water, privatization of, in Bolivia, 78–9

Wendy's Old-Fashioned Hamburgers, 60–1

Whole, notion of, 114, 115, 141

wilderness, 231; as constructed category, 239; preservation of, 189

Wolfe, Sidney, 166

Wolfensohn, James, 79, 82, 84

women, 9, 266; exploitation of, 56–7, 131; role of, 239–40; seizure of, 127; work of, 240, 253

World Bank, 77–8, 82, 189

World Trade Organization (WTO), 76, 166; Qatar meeting, xiv

World Wildlife Fund, "Living Planet" report, 4

"wrong turn" of civilization, 142

youth, as commodity, 65

Zachary, G. Pascal, 46

Zapatismo, 252–3